A. Pitcher

R.F.A.

lottery
tickets

!! 6-3-81 !!

International Safety Guide for Oil Tankers & Terminals

International Chamber of Shipping
Oil Companies International Marine Forum

First Published in 1978 by
Witherby & Co. Ltd., 32/36 Aylesbury Street,
London, EC1R 0ET. England.

ISBN 0 900886 36 6

Printed in England by
Witherby & Co. Ltd., London, EC1.

Contents

iii

APPENDICES

Purpose and Scope

This safety guide makes recommendations for practices to be adopted by tanker and terminal personnel to ensure safety in operations relating to the carriage by sea and the handling on tankers and at terminals of crude oil and petroleum products. It has been prepared by combining the contents of the 'Tanker Safety Guide (Petroleum)' published by the International Chamber of Shipping and the 'International Oil Tanker and Terminal Safety Guide' published on behalf of the Oil Companies International Marine Forum, and supersedes both those publications. All the information has been reviewed to ensure that it is in accordance with present practices, and additional aspects have been covered.

The contents of the guide are arranged in two parts. Part I covers operational procedures and is designed to provide guidance to personnel in the safe practices to be followed. The basic approach has been to arrange the material so that each chapter is concerned with a particular type of operation. However some chapters deal with precautions that are generally applicable, and these should be followed as well as those for the operation concerned. Each chapter has a small introductory paragraph describing the scope of its contents, and, where appropriate, drawing attention to other related chapters.

Part II contains additional information about the subjects under consideration, and gives the reasons for many of the precautions described in Part I.

Certain subjects are dealt with in greater detail in other publications of the International Chamber of Shipping and the Oil Companies International Marine Forum. Where this is the case an appropriate reference is made, and a list of all these publications is given below.

It should be borne in mind that in all cases the guidance given is subject to any terminal, local or national regulations that may be applicable, and those concerned should ensure that they are aware of any such requirements.

It is not the purpose of the guide to make recommendations as to design or construction. Information on these matters may be obtained from national authorities and from authorized bodies such as classification societies. The guide does not deal with matters concerning navigation, helicopter operations or pollution prevention, although some of these questions are inevitably touched upon. It should also be noted that this guide does not relate to cargoes other than crude oil and petroleum products which may be carried in tankers and combination carriers. It is not concerned with the carriage of chemicals or liquefied gases.

Publications of the International Chamber of Shipping and the Oil Companies International Marine Forum to which reference is made in the guide:

OCIMF	Buoy Mooring Forum Hose Guide — 'Guide for the Handling, Storage, Inspection and Testing of Hoses in Field'.
OCIMF	Buoy Mooring Forum Hose Standards — 'Specification for Rubber, Wire-reinforced Oil Suction and Discharge Hoses for Offshore Moorings'.
ICS & OCIMF	'Guidelines for Tankwashing with Crude Oil.'
ICS & OCIMF	'Inert Flue Gas Safety Guide.'
ICS & OCIMF	'Prevention of Oil Spillage through Cargo Pumproom Sea Valves.'
ICS & OCIMF	'Ship-to-Ship Transfer Guide (Petroleum).'
OCIMF	'Standards for Tanker Manifolds and Associated Equipment.'
ICS	'Tanker Safety Guide (Chemicals).'

Definitions

For the purpose of this safety guide the following interpretations apply:

Antistatic additive

A substance added to a petroleum product to raise its electrical conductivity above 100 picoSiemens/metre (pS/m) to prevent accumulation of static electricity.

Approved equipment

Equipment of a design that has been tested and approved by an appropriate authority such as a government department or classification society. The authority should have certified the equipment as safe for use in a specified hazardous atmosphere.

Auto ignition

The ignition of a combustible material, without initiation by a spark or flame, when the material has been raised to a temperature at which self-sustaining combustion occurs.

Bonding

The connecting together of metal parts to ensure electrical continuity.

Cathodic protection

The prevention of corrosion by electrochemical techniques. On tankers it may be applied either externally to the hull or internally to the surfaces of tanks.

Combination carrier

A ship which is designed to carry either petroleum cargoes or dry bulk cargoes.

Combustible (also referred to as 'Flammable')

Capable of being ignited and of burning. For the purposes of this guide the terms 'combustible' and 'flammable' are synonymous.

Combustible gas indicator

An instrument for measuring the composition of hydrocarbon gas/air mixtures, usually giving the result as a percentage of the lower flammable limit.

Dangerous area

An area on a tanker which for the purposes of the installation and use of electrical equipment is regarded as dangerous.

Dry chemical powder

A flame inhibiting powder used in fire fighting.

Earthing (also referred to as 'Grounding')

The electrical connecting of equipment to the main body of the earth to ensure that it is at earth potential. On board ship the connection is made to the main metallic structure of the ship which is at earth potential because of the conductivity of the sea.

Explosion Proof (also referred to as 'Flame Proof')

Electrical equipment is defined and certified as explosion proof or flame proof when it is enclosed in a case which is capable of withstanding the explosion within it of a hydrocarbon gas/air mixture or other specified flammable gas mixture. It must also prevent the ignition of such a mixture outside the case either by spark or flame from the internal explosion or as a result of the temperature rise of the case following the internal explosion. The equipment must operate at such an external temperature that a surrounding flammable atmosphere will not be ignited thereby.

Flammable (also referred to as 'Combustible')

Capable of being ignited and of burning. For the purposes of this guide the terms 'flammable' and 'combustible' are synonymous.

Flammable range (also referred to as 'Explosive range')

The range of hydrocarbon gas concentrations in air between the lower and upper flammable (explosive) limits. Mixtures within this range are capable of being ignited and of burning.

Flashlight (also referred to as 'Torch')

A battery operated hand lamp.

Flash point

The lowest temperature at which a liquid gives off sufficient gas to form a flammable gas mixture near the surface of the liquid. It is measured in the laboratory in standard apparatus using a prescribed procedure.

Foam (also referred to as 'Froth')

The aerated solution which is used for fire prevention and fire fighting.

Foam concentrate (also referred to as 'Foam compound')

The full strength liquid received from the supplier which is diluted and processed to produce foam.

Foam solution

The mixture produced by diluting foam concentrate with water before processing to make foam.

Free fall

The uninhibited fall of liquid in a tank.

Gas free

A tank, compartment or container is gas free when sufficient fresh air has been introduced into it to lower the levels of any flammable, toxic or inert gases to those required for a specified purpose, e.g. hot work, entry etc.

Gas free certificate

A certificate issued by an authorized person confirming that at the time of testing a tank, compartment or container it was gas free for a specific purpose.

Gauze screen (also referred to as 'Flame screen')

A portable or fitted device incorporating one or more corrosion resistant wire woven fabrics of very small mesh used for preventing sparks from entering a tank or vent opening or, for a short time, preventing the passage of flame.

Grounding (also referred to as 'Earthing')

The electrical connecting of equipment to the main body of the earth to ensure that it is at earth potential. On board ship the connection is made to the main metallic structure of the ship which is at earth potential because of the conductivity of the sea.

Halon

A halogenated hydrocarbon used in fire fighting which inhibits flame propagation.

Hazardous area

An area on shore which, for the purposes of the installation and use of electrical equipment, is regarded as dangerous. Such hazardous areas are graded into hazardous zones depending upon the probability of the presence of a flammable gas mixture.

Hazardous zone

See 'Hazardous area'.

Hot work

Work involving sources of ignition or temperatures sufficiently high to cause the ignition of a flammable gas mixture. This includes any work requiring the use of welding, burning or soldering equipment, blow torches, some power driven tools, portable electrical equipment which is not intrinsically safe or contained within an approved explosion proof housing, sand blasting, or internal combustion engines.

Hot work permit

A document issued by an authorized person permitting specific hot work to be done during a specific time interval in a defined area.

Hydrocarbon gas

A gas composed entirely of hydrocarbons.

Incendive spark

A spark with sufficient temperature and energy to ignite a flammable gas mixture.

Inert condition

A tank is in an inert condition when the oxygen content of the atmosphere throughout the tank has been reduced to 8% by volume by the addition of inert gas.

Inert gas

A gas, such as nitrogen or carbon dioxide, or a mixture of gases, such as flue gas, containing insufficient oxygen to support the combustion of hydrocarbons.

Insulating flange

A flanged joint incorporating an insulating gasket and washers to prevent electrical continuity between pipelines, hose strings or loading arms.

Intrinsically safe

An electrical circuit or part of a circuit is intrinsically safe if any spark or thermal effect produced normally (that is, by breaking or closing the circuit) or accidentally (for example, by short circuit or earth fault) is incapable, under prescribed test conditions, of igniting a prescribed gas mixture.

Loading overall

The loading of cargo or ballast 'over the top' through an open ended pipe or by means of an open ended hose entering a tank through a hatch or other deck opening, resulting in the free fall of liquid.

Lower flammable limit (LFL)

The concentration of a hydrocarbon gas in air below which there is insufficient hydrocarbon to support and propagate combustion. Sometimes referred to as lower explosive limit (LEL).

Naked lights

Open flames or fires, exposed incandescent material or any other unconfined source of ignition.

Non-volatile petroleum

Petroleum having a flash point of 60°C (140°F) or above as determined by the closed cup method of test.

Packaged cargo

Petroleum or other cargo in drums, packages or other containers.

Petroleum

Crude oil and liquid hydrocarbon products derived from it.

Petroleum gas

A gas evolved by or derived from petroleum. The main constituents of petroleum gases are hydrocarbons, but they may also contain other substances, such as hydrogen sulphide or lead alkyls, as minor constituents.

Pressure surge

A sudden increase in the pressure of the liquid in a pipeline brought about by an abrupt change in flow velocity.

Pressure/vacuum relief valve (P/V valve)

A dual purpose valve frequently incorporated in the cargo venting system of tankers which, except during cargo and ballast handling, automatically prevents excessive pressure or vacuum in the tank or tanks which it serves.

Reid vapour pressure (RVP)

The vapour pressure of a liquid determined in a standard manner in the Reid apparatus at a temperature of 100°F (37·8°C) and with a ratio of gas to liquid volumes of 4 : 1.

Responsible officer

The master or any officer to whom the master may delegate responsibility for any operation or duty on the ship.

Resuscitator

Equipment to assist or restore the breathing of a man overcome by gas or a lack of oxygen.

Self stowing mooring winch

A mooring winch fitted with a drum on which a wire or rope is made fast and permanently stowed.

Sour crude oil

A crude oil containing appreciable amounts of hydrogen sulphide and/or mercaptans.

Spontaneous combustion

The ignition of material brought about by a heat producing (exothermic) chemical reaction within the material itself without exposure to an external source of ignition.

Static accumulator oil

An oil with an electrical conductivity less than 100 picoSiemens/metre (pS/m), so that it is capable of retaining a significant electrostatic charge.

Static electricity

The electricity produced on dissimilar materials through physical contact and separation.

Static non-accumulator oil

An oil with an electrical conductivity greater than 100 picoSiemens/metre (pS/m), which renders it incapable of retaining a significant electrostatic charge.

Stripping

The final operation in pumping bulk liquid from a tank or pipeline.

Tanker

A ship designed to carry liquid petroleum cargo in bulk, including a combination carrier when being used for this purpose.

Tension winch

A self stowing mooring winch fitted with a device which may be set to adjust automatically the tension on a mooring line.

Terminal

A place where tankers are berthed or moored for the purpose of loading or discharging petroleum cargo.

Terminal representative

The person designated by the terminal to take responsibility for an operation or duty.

Threshold limit value (TLV)

The highest concentration of a harmful substance in air to which it is believed a person may be exposed for eight hours per day for an indefinite period without danger to health.

Topping off

The operation of completing the loading of a tank to a required ullage.

Torch (also referred to as 'Flashlight')

A battery operated hand lamp.

True vapour pressure (TVP)

The true vapour pressure of a liquid is the absolute pressure exerted by the gas produced by evaporation from a liquid when gas and liquid are in equilibrium at the prevailing temperature and the gas/liquid ratio is effectively zero.

Ullage

The depth of the space above the liquid in a tank.

Upper flammable limit (UFL)

The concentration of a hydrocarbon gas in air above which there is insufficient air to support and propagate combustion. Sometimes referred to as upper explosive limit (UEL).

Volatility

The tendency of a liquid to produce gas by evaporation.

Volatile petroleum

Petroleum having a flash point below 60°C (140°F) as determined by the closed cup method of test.

Water fog

A suspension in the atmosphere of very fine droplets of water usually delivered at a high pressure through a fog nozzle for use in fire fighting.

Water spray

A suspension in the atmosphere of water divided into coarse drops by delivery through a special nozzle for use in fire fighting.

Work permit

A document issued by an authorized person permitting specific work to be done during a specified period in a defined area.

Part I

Operations

Chapter 1

Hazards of Petroleum

In order to appreciate the reasons for the practices adopted to ensure safety in tanker and terminal operations, all personnel should be familiar with the flammable properties of petroleum, the effects of the density of petroleum gases and their toxic properties. This Chapter contains a brief summary, and fuller information is given in Chapters 14 and 15.

1.1 FLAMMABILITY

When a petroleum is ignited it is the gas progressively given off by the liquid which burns as a visible flame. The quantity of gas available to be given off by a petroleum liquid depends on its volatility which is frequently expressed for purposes of comparison in terms of Reid Vapour Pressure (RVP). A more informative measure of volatility is the True Vapour Pressure (TVP) but unfortunately this is not easily measured. It is referred to in this guide only in connection with venting problems with very volatile cargoes, such as some crude oils and natural gasolines.

Petroleum gases can be ignited and will burn only when mixed with air in certain proportions. If there is too little or too much petroleum gas the mixture cannot burn. The limiting proportions, expressed as percentage by volume of petroleum gas in air, are known as the lower and upper flammable limits. They vary amongst the different possible components of petroleum gases. For the gas mixtures from the petroleum liquids encountered in normal tanker practice the overall range is from a minimum lower flammable limit of about 1% gas by volume in air to a maximum upper flammable limit of about 10% gas by volume in air.

As a petroleum liquid is heated the concentration of gas in air above it increases. The temperature of the liquid at which this concentration, using a specified measuring technique, reaches the lower flammable limit is known as the flash point of the liquid.

1.2 FLAMMABILITY CLASSIFICATION

There are many classification systems for defining the flammability characteristics of petroleum liquids, most of which are based on flash point and Reid Vapour Pressure data. For the purpose of this guide, which deals only with the particular conditions in petroleum tanker cargo handling, the division of such liquids into the two broad categories of non-volatile and volatile, as defined below, is in general sufficient to ensure that proper precautions can be specified.

NON-VOLATILE

Flash point of 60°C (140°F) or above as determined by the closed cup method of testing.

VOLATILE

Flash point below 60°C (140°F) as determined by the closed cup method of testing.

If there is any doubt as to the characteristics of a cargo, or if a non-volatile cargo is being handled at a temperature above its flash point, it should be treated as volatile petroleum.

1.3 GAS DENSITY

The gases from the normal petroleum liquids are heavier than air and the possibility of layering of gases is very important in cargo handling operations. The density of the undiluted gas from a high vapour pressure distillate, such as motor gasoline, is likely to be about twice that of air and that from a typical crude oil about 1·5 times. These density differences diminish as the gases are diluted with air. Flammable mixtures, which contain at least 90% by volume of air, have densities almost indistinguishable from that of air.

Fuller information on the density of petroleum gases is given in Chapter 14.

1.4   **TOXICITY**

Comparatively small quantities of petroleum gas when inhaled can cause symptoms of diminished responsibility and dizziness similar to drunkenness, with headache and irritation of the eyes. The inhalation of a sufficient quantity can be fatal.

These symptoms can occur at concentrations well below the lower flammable limit. However, petroleum gases vary in their physiological effects and human tolerance to these effects also varies widely. It should not be assumed that because conditions can be tolerated the gas concentration is not harmful or in the flammable range.

The smell of petroleum gas mixtures is very variable, and in some cases the gases may dull the sense of smell. The impairment of smell is especially likely and particularly serious if the mixture contains hydrogen sulphide.

THE ABSENCE OF SMELL SHOULD NEVER BE TAKEN TO INDICATE THE ABSENCE OF GAS

Fuller information on the toxicity properties of petroleum, and of substances associated with the carriage of petroleum, is given in Chapter 15.

Chapter 2

General Precautions on Tankers

This Chapter deals primarily with the precautions to be taken on board a tanker at all times, at sea and in port. Reference should be made to Chapter 4 for additional precautions to be taken in port, and to the appropriate Chapters for precautions relating to specific operations such as cargo handling, ballasting or tank cleaning, or entry into enclosed spaces.

2.1　GENERAL PRINCIPLES

In order to reduce the risk of a fire and explosion on a tanker it is necessary to avoid both a source of ignition and a flammable atmosphere being present in the same place at the same time. It is not always possible to ensure the absence of both these factors, and precautions on a tanker are therefore generally intended rigorously to exclude one of them.

In the case of cargo compartments, pumprooms, and at times the tank deck, flammable gases are to be expected and the strict elimination of all possible sources of ignition in these locations is essential. Living accommodation, galley and engine room are spaces within which sources of ignition are inevitably present because of electrical equipment and boiler fires, etc. Here, while it is good practice to minimize and control the various sources of ignition, it is essential to avoid the presence of flammable gas. In certain areas, such as in deck workshops, store rooms, forecastle and centrecastle, dry cargo holds etc, it may be possible, by good design and operational practice, for both flammable gases and sources of ignition to be excluded.

2.2　SMOKING AND NAKED LIGHTS

2.2.1　SMOKING AT SEA

While a tanker is at sea, smoking should be permitted only at times and in places specified by the master. Paragraph 4.6.2 lists criteria which should be taken into account in determining the location of smoking places. Smoking should not be permitted on the tank deck or any other place where petroleum gas may be encountered. Additional restrictions on smoking in port are contained in Section 4.6.

2.2.2　MATCHES AND LIGHTERS

The use of matches and lighters outside accommodation spaces should be prohibited, except in places where smoking is permitted. In general matches and lighters should not be taken by personnel outside these places, nor should they be carried on the tank deck or in any other place where petroleum gas may be encountered.

The risk involved in carrying matches, and more particularly lighters, should be impressed on all personnel. Matches used on board should be of the 'safety' type.

2.2.3　NAKED LIGHTS

Naked lights should be prohibited on the tank deck and in any other place where there is a risk that petroleum gas may be present.

2.2.4　NOTICES

Permanent notices should be displayed in conspicuous places on board indicating where smoking and the use of naked lights are prohibited.

2.3 GALLEY

Galley personnel should be instructed in the safe operation of the cooking equipment. Galley burners should be adjusted to ensure efficient combustion in order to prevent galley funnel fires and sparks from incandescent soot. Flues and filters should be cleaned at regular intervals.

When bottled gas equipment is used, the gas should contain an additive which gives it a distinctive odour to permit detection in case of leakage.

Appropriate fire extinguishers should always be provided near the galley.

Oily rags and fat should not be allowed to accumulate and the trunkings of extractor fans should be kept clean.

Additional restrictions on the use of galleys while in port are contained in Section 4.7.

2.4 PORTABLE LAMPS AND ELECTRICAL EQUIPMENT

2.4.1 GENERAL

All portable electrical equipment including lamps should be carefully examined for possible defects before being used. Special care should be taken to ensure that the insulation is undamaged and that cables are securely attached and remain so while the equipment is in use. Special care should also be taken to prevent mechanical damage to flexible cables (wandering leads).

2.4.2 LAMPS AND OTHER ELECTRICAL EQUIPMENT ON FLEXIBLE CABLES (WANDERING LEADS)

The use of portable electrical equipment on wandering leads should be prohibited within cargo tanks and adjacent spaces, or over the tank deck unless throughout the period the equipment is in use:

(i) (a) the compartment within which or over which the equipment and the lead is to be used is gas free for hot work (see paragraph 10.5.7), and

(b) the adjacent compartments are also gas free for hot work or have been rendered safe by inerting or completely filling with water, and

(c) all tank openings to other compartments if not gas free for hot work or treated as in (b) are closed and remain so; or

(ii) the equipment including all wandering leads is intrinsically safe; or

(iii) the equipment is contained within an approved explosion proof housing. Any flexible cables should be of a type approved for extra hard usage, have an earth conductor, and should be permanently attached to the explosion proof housing in an approved manner.

In addition there are certain types of equipment which are approved for use over the tank deck only.

The foregoing does not apply to the proper use of signal or navigation lights or of approved types of telephones.

2.4.3 AIR DRIVEN LAMPS

Air driven lamps of an approved type may be used in non-gas free atmospheres, although to avoid the accumulation of static electricity on the lamp it should either be earthed or the hose should have a resistance low enough to allow static dissipation.

2.4.4 TORCHES (FLASHLIGHTS), LAMPS AND PORTABLE BATTERY EQUIPMENT

Only approved self-contained torches or lamps should be used on board a tanker. Portable UHF/VHF transceivers (walkie-talkies) should be intrinsically safe.

Small personal battery powered items such as watches, miniaturized hearing aids, and heart pacemakers are not significant ignition sources when correctly used.

Portable domestic radios, photographic flash equipment, portable electronic calculators and recorders and other battery powered equipment of non-approved type should not be used on the tank deck or in any other place where petroleum gas may be encountered.

2.5 SYNTHETIC CLOTHING

Experience has shown that clothing made from man made fibres does not give rise to any significant electrostatic hazard on tankers.

However, clothing made from man made fibres should not be worn when carrying out hot work due to the added risk of burns.

2.6 TANKER TRANSMITTING AERIALS

Main radio transmitters should not be used if the aerial is located over the tank deck and there is a risk of petroleum gas being present, because:

Energy may be induced into conducting objects in the field of the radio waves which can be sufficient to create an arc if discontinuity occurs.

Heavy sparking can occur at the insulators, particularly in humid weather.

Further restrictions upon the use of radio and communications equipment when at a petroleum berth are given in Section 4.9.

2.7 USE OF TOOLS

2.7.1 POWER TOOLS AND HAMMERING

Before any hammering, chipping or sandblasting is undertaken, or any power tool is used outside the boiler or engine rooms on board a tanker at sea, the responsible officer should satisfy himself that the area is gas free throughout the period that the tools are being used.

2.7.2 HAND TOOLS

Hand tools should be used only for the purpose for which they are designed. The risk of ignition of petroleum gas by frictional sparks produced by metal to metal impact in correct and normal use is slight, but care must be taken to prevent improper use.

Non-ferrous so called non-sparking tools are only marginally less likely to give rise to an incendive spark, and, because of their comparative softness, are not as efficient as their ferrous equivalents. Particles of concrete, sand or other hard, rock-like substances are likely to become embedded in the working face or edge of non-ferrous tools and can then cause incendive sparks on impact with ferrous or other hard metals.

The use of so called non-sparking tools is therefore not recommended.

2.7.3 APPROVAL FOR HOT WORK

Before approval for hot work is given the officer responsible should test and examine the area to ensure that:

No flammable or toxic gas is present in the vicinity.

No oil impregnated scale or other material likely to give off gas is present in any compartment where work is to be done.

Adjacent compartments are gas free for hot work, or in an inert condition, or water filled, and no gas from other compartments can be introduced by way of common lines.

No flammable material is present which might catch fire.

No material is present in an adjacent space which might ignite by the transmission of heat through the bulkhead.

No release of petroleum gas or liquid can occur while hot work is in progress.

Adequate fire extinguishing equipment is ready for immediate use.

Pipelines and heating coils may contain flammable material even though the tanker may have been declared gas free.

Consideration should be given to introducing a system for issuing permits for hot work on tankers. Such permits should authorize the work to be done, specifying the area involved and the time permitted, and may specify the tools and equipment to be used, and any special precautions or conditions to be observed.

Additional restrictions upon hot work while in port are given in paragraph 4.10.3, and upon hot work in enclosed spaces in paragraph 10.5.7.

2.8 ALUMINIUM

Aluminium equipment should not be dragged or rubbed across steel since it may leave a smear, which, if it is on rusty steel and is subsequently struck, can cause an incendive spark.

2.9 CATHODIC PROTECTION ANODES IN CARGO TANKS

Magnesium anodes are very likely to produce incendive sparks on impact with rusty steel, and such anodes should never be fitted inside cargo tanks.

Aluminium anodes can also give rise to similar sparking but only when the impact is comparatively violent. They should therefore be installed only at approved locations within cargo tanks, and should never be moved to another location without proper supervision and expert advice.

Zinc anodes are not subject to the hazard described above.

In addition to the varying degrees of hazard associated with different anode materials, if the anode mounting rod or base becomes detached from the ship's structure, it could in some circumstances create a hazard. All anodes fitted in cargo tanks should therefore be inspected as frequently as possible for security of mounting. The type, location and method of attachment of anodes is subject to approval by authorities. When anodes are replaced only approved means of attachment should be used.

2.10 SPONTANEOUS COMBUSTION

Some materials when damp or soaked with oil, especially oil of vegetable origin, are liable to ignite without the external application of heat due to gradual heating up within the material produced by oxidation. The risk of spontaneous combustion is less with petroleum oils than with vegetable oils, but it can still occur, particularly if the material is kept warm, for example by proximity to a hot pipe.

Cotton waste, rags, canvas, bedding, jute sacking or any similar absorbant material should therefore not be stowed in close proximity to oil, paint, etc and should not be left lying on the jetty, on decks, on equipment, on or around pipelines, etc. If such materials become damp, they should be dried before being stowed away. If soaked with oil, they should be cleaned or destroyed.

2.11 AUTO-IGNITION

If petroleum liquids fall or are sprayed onto hot surfaces, they may ignite even though there is no other source of ignition present. Care must therefore be taken to prevent oils coming into contact with hot surfaces. Lagging should not be allowed to become saturated with oil.

2.12 ENGINE AND BOILER ROOMS

2.12.1 COMBUSTION EQUIPMENT

As a precaution against funnel fires and sparks, the burners, tubes, uptakes, exhaust manifolds and spark arresters should be maintained in good working condition. If there is a funnel fire or sparks are emitted from the funnel, the tanker should, as soon as possible, alter course to avoid sparks falling on the tank deck. Any cargo, ballasting or tank cleaning operations that are taking place should be stopped and all tank openings closed.

2.12.2   BLOWING BOILER TUBES

Funnel uptakes and boiler tubes should not be blown in port. At sea they should be blown only when soot will not fall on the tank deck.

2.12.3   CLEANING LIQUIDS

It is preferable that cleaning liquids should be non-toxic and non-flammable. If flammable liquids are used, they should have a high flash point. Highly volatile liquids such as gasoline or naphtha should never be used.

Cleaning liquids which are flammable should be kept in closed, unbreakable, correctly labelled containers in a suitable compartment when not in use.

Direct skin contact with cleaning liquids should be avoided.

2.12.4   OIL SPILLAGE AND LEAKAGE

Oil spillage and leakage in the engine room should be avoided. Floor plates should be kept clean and bilges should be kept free of oil and waste.

2.13   COLD WEATHER PRECAUTIONS

During cold weather, the functioning of pressure/vacuum relief valves (P/V valves) should be checked. On inerted vessels, precautions are necessary to prevent freezing of deck water seals or any water filled P/V breakers.

2.14   ENTRY INTO ENCLOSED SPACES

Due to the possible presence of gas and/or oxygen deficiency no one should enter a cargo tank, cofferdam, double bottom tank or any similar enclosed space unless he has the permission of a responsible officer and then only after all appropriate measures have been taken to ensure that it is safe to enter (see Chapter 10).

2.15   PUMPROOM PRECAUTIONS

Pumprooms, by virtue of their location, design, and operation, constitute a particular hazard and therefore necessitate special precautions.

2.15.1   VENTILATION

Before anyone enters a pumproom, it should be thoroughly ventilated and the atmosphere checked for petroleum gas. Ventilation should be maintained until access to the pumproom is no longer required.

Special attention should be paid to levels below the lower platform where petroleum gas is liable to accumulate.

2.15.2   DESCENT INTO PUMPROOM

No one should descend into a pumproom at any time without first advising a responsible officer of his intention. The officer should ensure that appropriate safety measures are taken, including adequate means of communication so that immediate help will be available if necessary.

2.15.3   AVAILABILITY OF SAFETY EQUIPMENT

The pumproom life lines and harness should be rigged ready for immediate use, and an approved breathing apparatus should be available in an accessible position.

2.15.4   OPENING OF PUMPS, VALVES OR EQUIPMENT

Any operation or repair involving the opening up of pumps, valves or other equipment should be conducted with the immediate knowledge of the responsible officer. There is a risk that unsuspected pockets of petroleum liquid or gas or inert gas may be released when such equipment is opened up, even after a tanker or a tank has been cleaned and pronounced gas free. Precautions should therefore be taken to avoid any hazards which may arise.

| 2.15.5 | ACCUMULATION OF OIL, WASTE, ETC. |

To minimize fire and gas hazards, pumproom bilges should be kept free of waste, and rubbish and oil should not be allowed to accumulate.

| 2.15.6 | PUMPROOM LIGHTING |

Care should be taken to ensure that the integrity of the approved lighting system is maintained. If additional lighting is required, only approved equipment should be used.

| 2.15.7 | PUMPROOM NOTICES |

There should be a notice at the pumproom entrance forbidding access without prior authorization from a responsible ship's officer.

Chapter 3

Arrival in Port

This Chapter deals with the preparations and procedures for the arrival of a tanker in port, with particular reference to mooring and unmooring arrangements. Precautions to be taken when entering or leaving port are also given.

3.1   PREPARATIONS FOR ARRIVAL

3.1.1   EXCHANGE OF INFORMATION

Before the tanker arrives at the terminal there should be an exchange of information on the following matters as necessary:

Tanker to terminal

Ship's draft and trim on arrival.

Maximum draft and trim expected during and upon completion of cargo handling.

Advice from the master on tug assistance required.

Whether the ship's tanks are in an inert condition and whether the inert gas system is operational.

Whether the ship has any requirement for tank cleaning.

Any hull, bulkhead, valve or pipeline leaks which could affect cargo handling or cause pollution.

Any repairs which could delay commencement of cargo handling.

Whether crude oil washing is to be employed.

Ship's manifold details.

Whether the ship has external impressed cathodic protection.

Terminal to tanker

The depth of water at the berth at low water.

The availability of tugs and mooring craft, when necessary to assist in manoeuvring and mooring.

Whether the ship's or the tugs' lines are to be used.

The mooring lines and accessories which the ship is required to have available for initial mooring operations.

Any particular feature of a jetty berth or buoy mooring which it is considered essential to bring to the prior notice of the master.

The maximum allowable speed and angle of impact at the jetty.

Any code of visual or audible signals for use during mooring.

For jetty berths, arrangement of gangway landing space or availability of terminal access equipment.

In addition to the above information exchange the opportunity may be taken to give appropriate advance information about the proposed cargo handling operations (see Sections 5.1 and 5.2).

The terminal should ensure that the tanker is provided with general port information as soon as practicable.

Before berthing the terminal should provide the master, through the pilot or berthing master, with details of the mooring plan. The procedure for mooring the vessel should be specified and this should be reviewed and agreed between the master and the pilot or berthing master.

Additional information should include:

For jetty berths, the minimum number of the tanker's moorings and a diagram showing the relative positions of bollards or quick release hooks and the cargo handling manifold.

For buoy moorings, the minimum number of shackles of cable that may be required during the course of mooring and the number and position of mooring lines, shackles and other mooring equipment likely to be needed.

3.1.2   TANKER'S MOORING EQUIPMENT

Before arrival at the berth, all necessary mooring equipment should be ready for use and the terminal should be informed of any deficiencies or incompatibilities in the equipment which might affect the safety of the mooring. Anchors should be ready to let go if required, unless this is prohibited. There should also be an adequate number of personnel available to handle the moorings.

3.2   ENTERING OR LEAVING PORT

3.2.1   SECURITY OF BUOYANCY

When entering or leaving port in a loaded condition it is important that the tanker's buoyancy is secured against ingress of water due to damage. Forepeak and foredeep covers and ventilators should be securely closed, and cargo, bunker, cofferdam and pumproom openings also secured. Ullage ports should be securely closed.

3.2.2   TUGS ALONGSIDE

Before tugs come alongside to assist a tanker, all cargo and ballast tank lids and ullage ports should be closed, no matter what grade of oil is being or has been carried, unless all the cargo tanks are gas free.

Tugs should have adequate fendering to avoid causing damage, and should push at appropriate positions on the tanker. Tankers may have markings to indicate these positions.

3.3   JETTY BERTHS

3.3.1   CAPACITY OF FENDERING

The capacity of the fendering system to absorb energy is limited. Masters, berthing masters and pilots should be made aware by the terminal of the limitations of the fendering system and of the maximum displacement, impact velocity and angle of impact for which the berth and fendering system has been designed.

3.3.2   ADEQUACY OF MOORINGS

Any excessive movement or breakaway of the tanker due to inadequate moorings could cause severe damage to the jetty installations. Although adequate mooring of the tanker is the master's responsibility it is also in the interest of the terminal to ensure that tankers are safely moored. Cargo hoses or metal arms should not be connected until the terminal representative is satisfied that the ship is adequately moored.

3.3.3   TYPE AND QUALITY OF MOORING LINES

Preferably the mooring lines used to secure the tanker should all be of the same materials and construction. Wire ropes are recommended especially for larger tankers as they limit the tanker's movement at the berth. Moorings composed entirely of fibres, especially synthetics, are not recommended as their high elasticity can allow excessive movement due to strong wind or current forces or passing ships. Wire ropes and fibre ropes should never be used together in the same direction (i.e. breasts, springs, head or stern) because of the difference in their elastic properties.

Where dynamic (shock) loading on moorings can occur due to swell conditions or closely passing ships, fibre tails on the ends of mooring wires can provide sufficient elasticity to prevent failure of wires and other components of the mooring system. Such tails may be provided by the tanker or the terminal. Because fibre tails deteriorate more rapidly than wires, they should be at least 25% stronger than the wires to which they are attached. They should be inspected frequently and replaced at regular intervals.

3.3.4   TENSION WINCHES

Self tensioning winches used for automatic rendering and hauling should not be used in the automatic mode when cargo hoses or metal arms are connected because they may not always satisfactorily hold a tanker in position at a berth.

3.3.5   SELF STOWING MOORING WINCHES

After the tanker has been secured alongside, the winch power should never be used instead of the brake. In an emergency it may be necessary to apply power in addition to the brake, but this must be done with caution as the winch may be damaged or the breaking load of the mooring line may be exceeded.

The holding power of the brake depends on several factors:

(a) *Brake design*

Many self stowing mooring winch brakes are designed to render with loads which are less than 60% of the minimum breaking load of the new mooring line. This holding power can be further decreased by brake lining wear.

Winch brakes should be tested during scheduled shipyard periods.

Kits are available for testing brake holding power aboard ship in the intervals between scheduled shipyard periods.

(b) *Number of layers of wire on drum*

The holding power of the brake varies with the number of layers of wire on the drum. The nominal holding power of the brake usually refers to the first layer, and the following table shows the typical reduction of brake holding power for each layer:

         1st   layer 100% nominal brake holding power
         2nd   "   88%
         3rd   "   80%
         4th   "   73%
         5th   "   67%
         6th   "   61%

Except on split drum winches, little can be done to influence the number of layers of wire on the drum.

Correct layering of the wire on an undivided drum winch is important if the wire, when under load, is not to be forced down into lower layers and damaged or prevented from running freely when the brake is released.

However, on most split drum self stowing winches the brakes have a designed holding power based on the lever arm represented by one layer of mooring wire or rope on the working half of the split drum only. Excessive layers remaining on the working half when the load is being held by the brake reduce its holding power. The proper operation of split

13

drums requires pre-planning of the moorings at a given terminal or the adjustment of the moorings after berthing to ensure that the manufacturer's instructions are followed with regard to the minimum number of turns on the working drum.

(c) *Direction of reeling on winch drums*

On both undivided and split drum winches, the holding power of the brake is decreased substantially if the mooring line is reeled on the winch drum in the wrong direction. Before arrival at the berth, it is important that the mooring line is reeled so that its pull will be against the fixed end of the brake strap rather than the pinned end. The correct direction of reeling should be marked on winch housings.

(d) *Wet brake linings*

The brake holding power can be decreased by up to 25% by wet brake linings. Wet linings should be dried off by running the winch with the brake lightly engaged before the wire is run off the drum.

(e) *Winch brake application*

Brakes must be adequately tightened to manufacturers' recommended values to achieve design holding capacity. The use of automatic brake applicators or a torque wrench for this purpose is desirable.

3.3.6 MANAGEMENT OF MOORINGS WHILST ALONGSIDE

The tanker is responsible for frequent monitoring and careful tending of her moorings, but suitably qualified shore personnel should check the moorings periodically to satisfy themselves that they are being properly tended.

When tending moorings which have become slack or too taut, an overall view of the mooring system should be taken so that the tightening or slackening of individual moorings does not allow the tanker to move or place undue loading on to other moorings. The tanker should maintain contact with the fenders, and moorings should not be slackened if the tanker is lying off the fenders. A joint review of the tanker's mooring system and planned cargo operations should be made by tanker and terminal personnel and the possible use of tugs to maintain position should be considered whenever the following conditions exist or are expected:

Significant increase in wind speed or change in wind direction, particularly if the tanker is light laden.

Swell conditions.

Periods of maximum tidal flow.

Low underkeel clearance.

The close passing of other ships.

3.3.7 SHORE MOORINGS

At some terminals, shore moorings are used to supplement the tanker's moorings. If the adjustable ends are on board the tanker these moorings should be tended by the tanker's personnel in conjunction with its own moorings. If shore based wires with winches are provided, agreement should be reached over the responsibility for tending. If shore based quick release pulleys are provided, the tanker should tend the mooring since both ends of the line are on board.

3.4 BUOY MOORINGS

3.4.1 GENERAL

All normal precautions taken during berthing and cargo handling operations alongside a jetty also apply when a tanker is at a buoy mooring.

At terminals with buoy moorings for ocean going tankers it may be desirable to have professional advice on aspects of safety related to the marine operations. This may be by the assignment of a berthing master (mooring master) to the terminal, or by consultation with a port or pilotage authority, if available. It is essential that good communications between the tanker and the terminal are maintained. If the buoy mooring is in an exposed location the berthing master should remain on board the tanker during cargo handling operations. At some buoy moorings, there may be a quick release device for mooring lines and hoses for use in an emergency.

3.4.2 MANAGEMENT OF MOORINGS

While the tanker is at a multi-buoy mooring, frequent and regular inspection is essential to ensure that mooring lines are kept taut and that movement of the tanker is kept to a minimum. Excessive movement may cause rupture of the cargo connections.

At single point moorings a watchman should be stationed on the forecastle head to report any failure or imminent failure of moorings or leakage of oil. He should also report immediately if the tanker 'rides up' to the buoy. He should be equipped with appropriate means to communicate with the officer of the watch.

3.4.3 BALLAST AT BUOY BERTHS

To avoid excessive freeboard, especially in adverse weather conditions, tankers at buoy moorings may need to handle cargo and ballast simultaneously.

3.4.4 MAINTENANCE

Routine inspections of buoys, mooring lines and hoses should be carried out at each berthing and during the operations.

3.5 EMERGENCY TOWING OFF WIRES

Except at terminals where no tugs are available, towing off wires of adequate strength and condition should be made fast to bollards on the tanker, forward and aft, and their eyes run out and maintained at or about the waterline. For tankers alongside a jetty the wires should be over the offshore side, and for tankers at a buoy mooring they should be placed on the side opposite to the hose strings.

In order that sufficient wire can pay out to enable the tugs to tow effectively, enough slack should be retained between bollard and chock and prevented from running out by a ropeyarn or other easily broken means.

The arrangement will vary from port to port and the officer responsible should be advised of local requirements.

3.6 PERSONNEL SAFETY

Mooring and unmooring operations including tug line handling have a very high personnel accident rate both on tankers and at jetties. It is important that everybody concerned realizes this and is on his guard.

Chapter 4

General Precautions while a Tanker is at a Petroleum Berth

This Chapter deals with the precautions to be taken both on a tanker and ashore while the tanker is at a petroleum berth. These are additional to the general precautions described in Chapter 2 but do not include precautions that are related to specific operations, such as cargo handling, ballasting, bunkering or tank cleaning for which reference to the appropriate Chapter should be made.

4.1 SAFETY PRECAUTIONS AND EMERGENCY PROCEDURES

4.1.1 COMPLIANCE WITH TERMINAL AND LOCAL REGULATIONS

Any terminal or local regulations relating to safety should be complied with by tanker and terminal personnel, and the provisions of this guide should be interpreted subject to such regulations.

4.1.2 TANKER AND TERMINAL LIAISON ON SAFETY PROCEDURES

After the tanker has berthed the terminal representative should contact the officer responsible to:

Agree designated smoking places.

Agree galley fire and cooking appliance limitations.

Advise on 'Work Permit' and 'Hot Work Permit' procedures.

Provide information about other terminal or local safety regulations.

Discuss means for summoning assistance from terminal, fire, medical, police and other emergency services.

Advise each other upon the availability of fire fighting equipment on the terminal and the tanker.

Discuss action to be taken in case of fire or other emergency (see Section 13.5 and Appendix B).

The other safety precautions to be observed before cargo handling begins, including implementation of the Ship/Shore Safety Check List, are given in Chapter 5.

4.2 STATE OF READINESS

4.2.1 FIRE FIGHTING EQUIPMENT

On the tanker, immediately before or on arrival at the terminal to load or discharge cargo, the ship's fire hoses should be connected to the fire main, one forward and one aft of the ship's manifold. If practicable a pump should maintain pressure on the ship's fire main while cargo or ballast is being handled. If this is not possible the fire pump should be in a standby condition and ready for immediate operation. In cold weather, freezing of fire mains and hydrants should be avoided by continuously bleeding water overboard from hydrants at the extreme end of each fire main. Alternatively, all low points of the fire main may be kept drained.

17

Monitors should be ready for use. Portable fire extinguishers, preferably of the dry chemical type, should be conveniently placed near the ship's manifold.

A check should be made to confirm that both ship and shore have an International Shore Fire Connection for the transfer of water for fire fighting (see Appendix E).

On the terminal fire fighting appliances should all be ready for immediate use.

4.2.2 READINESS TO MOVE UNDER OWN POWER

While a tanker is berthed at a terminal its boilers, main engines, steering machinery and other equipment essential for manoeuvring should normally be maintained so as to permit the ship to move away from the berth at short notice.

Repairs and other work which may immobilize the tanker should not be undertaken at a berth without prior written agreement with the terminal. It may also be necessary to obtain permission from the local port authority before carrying out such repairs or work.

4.3 COMMUNICATIONS

The provision of adequate means of communication between ship and shore is the responsibility of the terminal.

Where practicable, terminals should provide a reliable safe telephone system or UHF/VHF radio transceivers for communication between the terminal control centre, the jetty or berth and the tanker. Telephone equipment and flexible interconnecting cable should be of safe design suitable for the location in which it is to be used. Portable UHF/VHF transceivers (walkie-talkies) should be intrinsically safe.

When there may be language difficulties between ship and shore personnel, agreement should be reached on verbal expressions and language to be used, especially regarding the terms used to describe the more important aspects of cargo handling operations as given in this safety guide. Where there are difficulties in verbal communication it may be necessary for a member of the terminal staff with a knowledge of tanker practices to be put on board.

4.4 ACCESS BETWEEN SHIP AND SHORE

4.4.1 MEANS OF ACCESS

Personnel should use only the designated access.

Gangways or other means of access should be provided with a safety net where appropriate, and lifebuoys with lifelines should be available in the vicinity of the gangway.

4.4.2 GANGWAY LANDING

When terminal access facilities are not available and a tanker's gangway is used, the berth should have a landing sufficient to provide the gangway with an adequate clear run of space so as to maintain safe convenient access to the tanker at all states of tide and changes in the ship's freeboard.

Particular attention to safe access should be given where the difference in level of tanker's and jetty deck becomes large. There should be special facilities where the level of a tanker's deck can fall considerably below that of the jetty.

4.4.3 LIGHTING

During darkness, the means of access to the tanker should be well and safely lit.

4.4.4 UNAUTHORIZED PERSONS

Persons who have no legitimate business on board, or who do not have the master's permission, should be refused access to a tanker. The terminal should restrict access to the jetty or berth.

4.4.5 PERSONS SMOKING OR INTOXICATED

Personnel on duty on a jetty or on watch on a tanker should ensure that no one approaches the jetty or boards a tanker when smoking.

Persons apparently intoxicated should not be allowed to board a tanker unless special preparations for their reception have been made.

4.5 NOTICES

4.5.1 NOTICES ON THE TANKER

On arrival at a terminal, a tanker should display notices at the gangway in appropriate languages stating:

> WARNING
>
> NO NAKED LIGHTS
>
> NO SMOKING
>
> NO UNAUTHORIZED PERSONS

Alternative wording containing the same prohibitions may also be used.

In addition, notices are to be found on board tankers which are primarily for the information of the crew. Shore personnel should observe their requirements when on board the tanker.

4.5.2 NOTICES ON THE TERMINAL

Permanent notices and signs should be conspicuously displayed on a jetty indicating that smoking and naked lights are prohibited. Similar permanent notices and signs should be displayed at the entrance to the terminal area or the shore approaches to a jetty.

In buildings and other shore locations where smoking is allowed, appropriate notices should be conspicuously displayed.

4.6 SMOKING

4.6.1 CONTROLLED SMOKING

Smoking should be permitted under controlled conditions. This is because a total prohibition of smoking at terminals and on a tanker at a berth is in general unrealistic and unenforceable, and may give rise to surreptitious smoking. There may however be occasions when due to the nature of the cargo being transferred or other factors, a total prohibition of smoking may be necessary.

Smoking should be strictly prohibited within the restricted area enclosing all tanker berths and on board any tanker whilst at a berth, except in designated smoking places.

4.6.2 LOCATION OF DESIGNATED SMOKING PLACES

The designated smoking places on a tanker or on shore should be agreed in writing between the master and the terminal representative before operations start. The master is responsible for ensuring that all on board the tanker are informed of the selected places for smoking and for posting suitable notices in addition to the tanker's permanent notices.

Certain criteria should be followed in the selection of smoking places whenever petroleum cargoes are being handled or when ballasting, inert gas, gas freeing and tank cleaning operations are taking place.

The criteria are:

> The agreed smoking places should be confined to locations abaft the cargo tanks, except when the entry of petroleum gas into the tanker's amidships accommodation is highly improbable.

> The agreed smoking places should not have doors or ports which open directly on to or over the cargo deck or on to decks overlooking cargo spaces or shore connections.

> Account should be taken of conditions that may suggest danger, any indication of unusually high petroleum gas concentrations, particularly in the absence of wind, and when there are operations on adjacent tankers or on the jetty or berth.

In the designated smoking places all ports should be kept closed, and doors into passageways should be kept closed except when in use.

When none of the above operations is in progress, smoking may be permitted by the master in any closed accommodation while the tanker is in port.

4.7 GALLEY STOVES AND COOKING APPLIANCES

4.7.1 USE OF GALLEY STOVES AND COOKING APPLIANCES

While the tanker is at a berth, in addition to the precautions given in Section 2.3 the use of galley stoves and cooking appliances with non-immersed elements, such as electric hot-plates and toasters, may be permitted in galleys, pantries and accommodation provided that the master and terminal representative jointly agree that no hazard exists. Any doors or ports opening directly on to or overlooking the tank deck must be kept shut.

Galley stoves and cooking appliances with non-immersed elements in the galley should not be used when the stern discharge line is in use for cargo operations.

4..2 STEAM COOKERS AND WATER BOILERS

Cookers and other equipment heated by steam may be used at all times.

4.8 PORTABLE LAMPS AND ELECTRICAL EQUIPMENT

4.8.1 AREA CLASSIFICATIONS

Different criteria are employed for classifying areas on board a tanker and ashore in relation to the use of electrical equipment. Fuller details of the classifications are given in Chapter 18.

When a tanker is at a petroleum berth it may come within a shore hazardous zone. The precautions relating to the use of electrical equipment within that zone should then be observed on board the ship, in addition to the precautions contained in Section 2.4.

4.8.2 LAMPS AND OTHER ELECTRICAL EQUIPMENT ON FLEXIBLE CABLES (WANDERING LEADS) IN TERMINALS

Portable electric lamps and portable electrical equipment for use in hazardous zones should be of approved type. Special care should be taken to prevent mechanical damage to the flexible cables (wandering leads).

4.8.3 TORCHES (FLASHLIGHTS), LAMPS AND PORTABLE BATTERY EQUIPMENT IN TERMINALS

Only approved self-contained torches or lamps should be used within hazardous zones at a terminal.

4.9 COMMUNICATIONS EQUIPMENT

4.9.1 GENERAL

Unless certified intrinsically safe or of other approved design, the normal communications equipment on board ships such as telephones, talk-back systems, signalling lamps, search lights, loud hailers, and electrical controls for ship's whistles should neither be used, nor should they be connected or disconnected, when the areas in which they are positioned come within the classification of a hazardous zone ashore.

4.9.2 RADIO EQUIPMENT

The use of a tanker's radio equipment during cargo or ballast handling operations is potentially dangerous (see Section 2.6). This does not apply to the use of permanently and correctly installed VHF equipment, provided the power output is reduced to one watt or less.

When a tanker is at a berth, its main transmitting aerials should be earthed.

If it is necessary to operate the ship's radio in port for servicing purposes, arrangements for ensuring safety should be agreed between tanker and terminal and these may require the issue of a work permit. Amongst the precautions that might be agreed are operating at low power, use of a dummy aerial load or confining the transmission to times when no cargo handling operations are in progress.

4.9.3 RADAR SCANNERS

The radiation of radar waves from a properly sited radar scanner presents no ignition hazard. However the operation of tanker radar will involve running non-approved electrical equipment. Consultation is therefore advisable between the tanker and the terminal before using or repairing this equipment.

4.9.4 SATELLITE COMMUNICATIONS TERMINALS

These terminals normally radiate at $1 \cdot 6$ GigaHertz and at the power levels contemplated are not considered to present an ignition hazard. However the pointing of the antennae may involve the running of non-approved electrical equipment, and consultation between the tanker and the terminal is advised before the satellite terminal is operated.

4.9.5 CLOSED CIRCUIT TELEVISION

If fitted on a tanker or on a jetty, cameras and associated equipment should be of approved design for the areas or zones in which they are positioned, in which event there is no restriction upon their use.

When a tanker is at a berth, the servicing of this equipment should be agreed between the ship and the shore.

4.10 WORK ON A JETTY OR BERTH, OR ON A TANKER AT A BERTH

4.10.1 USE OF TOOLS

No hammering, chipping or sand blasting should take place or any power tool be used outside the boiler or engine rooms on a tanker or on a jetty at which a tanker is berthed without joint agreement being reached between the terminal representative and the officer responsible.

In all cases the terminal representative and the responsible officer should jointly satisfy themselves that the area is gas free, and remains so while the tools are in use.

4.10.2 APPROVAL FOR WORK

Before repairs, renewals or maintenance work, including hot work, are undertaken on a jetty or berth the approval of the terminal representative should be obtained. If a tanker is berthed at the jetty, the agreement of the master should be obtained by the terminal representative before the work commences.

Where such work is to be done outside the boiler or engine rooms on a tanker at a berth, the officer responsible should discuss the position with the terminal representative. Agreement should be reached upon the details of the work to be done and the safety precautions to be taken.

A work permit should be issued and, depending upon the circumstances, it may also be necessary for a gas free certificate to be obtained before commencing such work either on a jetty or berth or on a tanker.

4.10.3 APPROVAL FOR HOT WORK

Approval for hot work on a jetty or berth or outside the boiler or engine rooms on a tanker should only be given when the terminal representative and the officer responsible have satisfied themselves that the area is safe, taking particular account of the matters listed in paragraph 2.7.3.

4.10.4 ISSUE OF WORK PERMIT

When the terminal representative and the responsible officer have satisfied themselves that work can be safely undertaken, a work permit should be issued to the person in charge of the work as follows:

For work on the jetty or berth by the terminal representative, countersigned by the officer responsible.

For work on the ship by the officer responsible, countersigned by the terminal representative.

A hot work permit should authorize the specific work to be done in a defined area together with a specified time limit.

The permit may specify the type of tools and equipment which may be used for hot work and any other special conditions or precautions to be observed, such as the isolation of a pipeline.

In all cases adequate fire fighting equipment should be ready for immediate use.

Chapter 5

Liaison between Tanker and Terminal before Cargo Handling

Exchange of information between the tanker and the terminal concerning mooring arrangements is dealt with in Chapter 3. Certain additional information relating to cargo, ballast and bunker handling should be exchanged before these operations begin. This Chapter sets out the subjects about which additional information should be available, and the aspects upon which agreement should be reached.

5.1　　　　**TERMINAL ADVICE TO THE TANKER**

The following information should be made available to the responsible officer:

(a)　*Information in preparation for loading and bunkering*

Cargo specifications.

Whether the cargo includes sour crude oil.

Any other characteristics of the cargo requiring special attention, e.g. aromatic, benzene or lead contents or True Vapour Pressure (where applicable).

Flash points (where applicable) of products and their estimated loading temperatures, particularly when the cargo is non-volatile.

Bunker specifications.

Nominated quantity or quantities of cargo to be loaded.

Preferred order of loading of cargo.

Maximum shore loading rates.

Maximum pressure available at the ship/shore cargo connection.

Number and sizes of hoses or loading arms available for each product or grade of the cargo and whether these loading arms are common with each other.

Limitations on the movement of hoses or loading arms.

Proposed bunker loading rate.

Communication system for loading control, including the signal for emergency stop.

(b)　*Information in preparation for discharge*

Order of discharge of cargo acceptable to terminal.

Maximum acceptable discharge rates.

Maximum pressure acceptable at ship/shore cargo connection.

Any booster pumps that may be on stream.

23

Any other limitations at the terminal.

Communication system for discharge control including the signal for emergency stop.

5.2 TANKER ADVICE TO THE TERMINAL

Before cargo handling commences the officer responsible should inform the terminal of the general arrangement of the cargo, ballast and bunker tanks and should have available the information listed below:

(a) *Information in preparation for loading and bunkering*

Details of last cargo carried, method of tank cleaning (if any) and state of the cargo tanks and lines.

Maximum acceptable loading rates and topping off rates.

Maximum acceptable pressure at the ship/shore cargo connection during loading.

Cargo quantities acceptable from terminal nominations.

Proposed disposition of nominated cargo and preferred order of loading.

Maximum acceptable cargo temperature (where applicable).

Maximum acceptable true vapour pressure (where applicable).

Proposed method of venting.

Quantities of bunkers required.

Disposition, composition and quantities of ballast and time required for discharge.

Quantity and disposition of slops.

(b) *Information in preparation for discharge*

Cargo specifications.

Whether the cargo includes sour crude oil.

Any other characteristics of the cargo requiring special attention, e.g. aromatic, benzene or lead contents, or true vapour pressure (where applicable).

Flash points (where applicable) of products and their temperatures upon arrival particularly when the cargo is non-volatile.

Cargo quantity or quantities loaded and disposition in ship's tanks.

Quantity and disposition of slops.

Any unaccountable changes of ullages in ship's tanks since loading.

Water dips in cargo tanks (where applicable).

Preferred order of discharge from ship's tanks.

Maximum attainable discharge rates and pressures.

Whether crude oil washing is to be employed.

Approximate time of commencement and duration of ballasting into permanent ballast tanks and cargo tanks.

24

5.3   **AGREED LOADING PLAN**

On the basis of the information exchanged a loading plan should be agreed between the responsible ship's officer and the terminal representative covering the following:

(a) *The sequence in which ship's tanks are to be loaded, taking into account:*

Ship and shore tank change over.

Avoidance of contamination of cargo.

Pipeline clearing for loading.

Other movements or operations which may affect flow rates.

Limiting stresses and trim of the tanker.

(b) *The initial and maximum loading rates, topping off rates and normal stopping times, having regard to:*

The nature of the cargo to be loaded.

The arrangement and capacity of the ship's cargo lines and gas venting system.

The maximum allowable pressure and flow rate in the ship/shore hoses or loading arms.

Precautions to avoid accumulation of static electricity.

Any other flow control limitations.

(c) *The method of tank venting to avoid or reduce gas emissions at deck level. Account should be taken of:*

The true vapour pressure of the cargo to be loaded.

The loading rates.

Atmospheric conditions.

(d) *Emergency stop procedure*

5.4   **INSPECTION OF SHIP'S CARGO TANKS BEFORE LOADING**

Any inspection of ship's tanks should, if possible, be done from the tank hatch using a mirror or an approved torch. If a more rigorous inspection is necessary than is possible from the tank hatch, the tank may be entered but in that case all precautions for tank entry should be observed (see Chapter 10). In the case of ships having inert gas systems reference should also be made to Chapter 9.

5.5   **AGREED DISCHARGE PLAN**

On the basis of the information exchanged a discharge plan should be agreed between the responsible ship's officer and the terminal representative covering the following:

(a) *The sequence in which the ship's tanks are to be discharged, taking account of:*

Ship and shore tank change over.

Avoidance of contamination.

Pipeline clearing for discharge.

Crude oil washing, if employed.

Other movements or operations which may change flow rates.

Limiting stresses and trim of the tanker.

(b) *The initial and maximum discharge rates, having regard to:*

The nature of the cargo to be discharged.

The arrangements and capacity of the ship's cargo lines, shore pipelines and tanks.

The maximum allowable pressure and flow rate in the ship/shore hoses or loading arms.

Precautions to avoid accumulation of static electricity.

Any other limitations.

(c) *Emergency stop procedure*

5.6 COMMUNICATIONS

Before loading or discharging commences, a reliable communications system should be established and tested for control of the operation. A secondary stand-by system should also be established and agreed. Allowance should be made for the time required for action in response to signals.

These systems should include signals for:

'Stand By'.

'Start Loading' or 'Start Discharging'.

'Slow Down'.

'Stop Loading' or 'Stop Discharging'.

'Emergency Stop'.

Any other necessary signals should be agreed and understood.

When different products or grades are to be handled, their names and descriptions should be clearly understood by the ship and shore personnel on watch and on duty during cargo handling operations.

5.7 SHIP/SHORE SAFETY CHECK LIST

A recommended Ship/Shore Safety Check List is given in Appendix A.

The Ship/Shore Safety Check List is for the safety of both ship and terminal and of all personnel, and it should be completed jointly by the responsible officer and the terminal representative. Each item should be positively verified before it is ticked. In many cases this will entail a physical check by the two officials concerned; it is of little value if it is regarded as a paper exercise only.

The Check List should be accompanied by an explanatory letter, for which a suggested text is given in Appendix A, inviting the co-operation and understanding of the tanker's personnel. The letter should be given to the master or officer responsible by the terminal representative. The master should acknowledge receipt of the letter on a copy, which should then be retained by the terminal representative.

Chapter 6

Precautions Before and During Cargo Handling and Other Cargo Tank Operations

This Chapter sets out the precautions to be taken before and during cargo handling, ballasting, bunkering, tank cleaning, gas freeing and inert gas purging operations. These precautions are additional to those given in Chapters 2 and 4, but do not include precautions and procedures related to specific operations which are dealt with in Chapters 7, 8 and 9.

6.1   OPENINGS IN SUPERSTRUCTURES

6.1.1   GENERAL

A tanker's accommodation usually abounds in equipment involving ignition sources and it is therefore imperative for safety to keep out petroleum gas.

Closure of openings is required and other precautions should therefore be taken during any of the following operations:

Handling of volatile petroleum or of non-volatile petroleum above its flash point.

Loading of non-volatile petroleum into non-gas free tanks.

Crude oil washing.

Ballasting, inert gas purging, gas freeing or tank washing after discharge of volatile petroleum.

Although discomfort may be caused to personnel in accommodation that is completely closed down during conditions of high temperature and humidity, this discomfort must be accepted in the interests of safety.

6.1.2   DOORS, PORTS AND WINDOWS

All external doors, ports and windows in the amidships accommodation should be kept closed.

In the after accommodation all external doors, ports and similar openings which lead directly from the tank deck to the accommodation or machinery spaces (other than the pumproom) or which overlook the tank deck at any level should be kept closed.

Additional doors and ports may have to be closed in special circumstances, e.g. during stern loading, or due to constructional features of the tanker.

If doors have to be opened for access they should be closed immediately.

Doors that are required to be kept closed should be clearly so marked but in no case should doors be locked.

6.1.3   VENTILATORS

Ventilators should be kept trimmed to prevent the entry of petroleum gas, particularly on tankers which depend on natural ventilation. If ventilators are located so that petroleum gas can enter regardless of the direction in which they are trimmed, they should be covered or closed.

6.1.4   CENTRAL AIR CONDITIONING AND MECHANICAL VENTILATING SYSTEMS

Intakes of central air conditioning or mechanical ventilating systems should be adjusted to prevent the entry of petroleum gas, if possible by recirculation of air within the enclosed spaces.

If at any time it is suspected that gas is being drawn into the accommodation, central air conditioning and mechanical systems should be stopped and the intakes covered or closed.

6.1.5   WINDOW TYPE AIR CONDITIONING UNITS

Window type air conditioning units should be electrically disconnected.

Most window type air conditioning units contain electric motors, switches and other spark producing devices which are capable of igniting flammable gas drawn through them. Although some window type units are manufactured with special equipment to make them safe in the presence of flammable gas, it is not possible without internal inspection to determine if changes made since manufacture have rendered the unit unsafe, so that all window type air conditioning units are considered to be hazardous when flammable gas is present.

Window type air conditioning units which are located completely inside the amidships or after accommodation can remain in operation, provided no external connection draws air from the outside.

6.2   OPENINGS IN CARGO TANKS

6.2.1   CARGO TANK LIDS

During the handling of volatile petroleum and loading of non-volatile petroleum into non-gas free tanks, and while ballasting after the discharge of volatile cargo, all cargo tank lids should be closed and secured.

Tank lids of cargo tanks not gas free should normally be kept closed unless gas freeing alongside by agreement.

6.2.2   SIGHTING AND ULLAGE PORTS

During any of the cargo and ballast handling operations referred to in paragraph 6.2.1 sighting and ullage ports should be kept closed wherever possible. When open for operational purposes, the openings should be protected by gauze screens.

These screens must be kept clean and in good condition. Portable screens should be a good fit.

6.2.3   CARGO TANK VENT OUTLETS

The cargo tank ventilation system should be set for the operation concerned and the outlets should be protected by gauze screens to reduce the possibility of flame propagation from an external ignition source.

Pressure/vacuum relief valves (P/V Valves) should be either opened or bypassed during loading or ballasting. High velocity vent valves should be set in the operational position to ensure the high exit velocity of vented gas.

When volatile cargo is being loaded into tanks served by a vent system which also serves tanks into which non-volatile cargo is to be loaded, particular attention should be paid to the setting of P/V valves and the associated vent system in order to avoid flammable gas entering the tanks to be loaded with non-volatile cargo.

6.2.4   TANK WASHING OPENINGS

During tank cleaning or gas freeing operations tank washing covers should be removed only from the tanks where these operations are taking place. Other tank washing covers may be loosened in preparation, but they should be left in their fully closed position.

6.2.5   SEGREGATED BALLAST TANK LIDS

Segregated ballast tank lids should be kept closed when cargo or ballast is being handled as petroleum gas could be drawn into these tanks. If adequate tank venting is not otherwise provided, however, these tank lids may have to be opened during ballast handling. Segregated ballast tank lids should be clearly marked.

6.3 PUMPROOM PRECAUTIONS

6.3.1 GENERAL

The pumproom precautions set out in Section 2.15 should be observed before and during all cargo handling operations.

Loading through or pressurizing the pumproom piping system should be avoided if possible.

6.3.2 INSPECTION OF GLANDS, BEARINGS ETC

Before starting cargo operations, an inspection should be made to ensure that strainer covers, inspection plates and drain plugs in the pumproom cargo system are in position and secure.

During pumping operations, all pump glands should be inspected for tightness at regular intervals, and glands and bearings checked for overheating. In the event of excessive leakage or overheating, the pump should be stopped. No attempt should be made to tighten pump glands while the pump is running.

6.4 TESTING OF CARGO SYSTEM ALARMS AND TRIPS

Pump alarms and trips, level alarms etc., where fitted, should be tested to ensure that they are functioning correctly.

6.5 SHIP AND SHORE CARGO CONNECTIONS

6.5.1 FLANGES

Flanges for ship to shore cargo connections, at the end of the terminal pipelines and on the ship's manifold, should be in accordance with OCIMF publication 'Standards for Tanker Manifolds and Associated Equipment'.

All bolt holes should be used and care taken in tightening bolts, as uneven or over tightening of bolts could result in leakage or fracture. Boiler clamps should not be used for flange connections.

Each tanker manifold flange should have a removable steel blank flange fitted with handles.

6.5.2 REDUCERS

Reducers should be made of steel and fitted with flanges conforming with B.S.1560, ANSI B16.5 or equivalent; cast iron should not be used.

When reducers are made of other materials, particular attention is necessary in their manufacture to achieve the equivalent strength of steel and to avoid the possibility of fracture.

6.5.3 LIGHTING

During darkness, adequate safe lighting should be arranged for the ship to shore cargo connection and for any hose handling equipment, so that the need for any adjustment can be seen in good time, as well as to detect any leakage or spillage of oil.

6.5.4 EMERGENCY RELEASE

Some form of emergency release device for disconnecting the ship to shore cargo manifold connection may be used for emergency disconnection of cargo hoses or metal loading arms.

Before either routine or emergency disconnection of these couplings the hoses or arms should always be drained, purged or isolated, as appropriate, so that oil spillage is avoided.

Periodic checks should be made to ensure that all safety features are operational.

6.6 CARGO HOSES

6.6.1 EXAMINATION BEFORE USE

It is the responsibility of the terminal to provide hoses which are in good condition but the master of a tanker may reject any which appears to be defective.

Before they are connected up, hose strings should be examined for any possible defect which may be visible in the bore or outer covers such as blistering, abrasion, flattening of the hose or evidence of leakage.

Hoses in which the rated pressure has been exceeded should be removed and retested before further use.

Hoses should be tested annually to manufacturer's specifications and/or as detailed in the OCIMF Buoy Mooring Forum Hose Guide 'Guide for the Handling, Storage, Inspection and Testing of Hoses in Field'. The date of such testing should be indicated on the hose.

6.6.2 HANDLING, LIFTING AND SUSPENDING

Hoses should always be handled with care and should not be dragged over a surface or rolled in a manner which would twist the body of the hose. Hoses should not be allowed to come into contact with a hot surface, such as a steam pipe. Protection should be provided at any point where chafing or rubbing can occur.

Lifting bridles and saddles should be provided and the use of steel wires in direct contact with the hose cover should not be permitted. Hoses should not be lifted at a single place with ends hanging down, but should be supported at a number of places so that they are not bent to a radius less than that recommended by the manufacturer.

Excessive weight on the ship's manifold should be avoided. If there is an excessive overhang or the ship's valve is outside the stool support, additional support should be given to the manifold. A horizontal curved plate or pipe section should be fitted at the ship's side to protect the hose from sharp edges and obstructions. Adequate support for the hoses, when connected to the manifold, should be provided. Where this is a single lifting point, such as a derrick, then the hose string should be supported by bridles or saddles.

6.6.3 SUBMARINE AND FLOATING HOSE STRINGS

Hoses in service at offshore mooring installations should be inspected periodically by divers. Particular attention should be paid to kinked or damaged sections, oil seepage from the hose flange areas, heavy marine growth, and scuffing on the sea bed.

Where hose strings are lowered and raised repeatedly from the sea bed care should be taken to avoid damage from chains and lifting plates.

Particular attention should be paid when lowering hose strings to avoid coiling down. Dragging hoses over the sea bed should be minimized.

Before attempting to lift a hose string on board, the officer responsible should check that the total weight involved does not exceed the safe working load of the ship's derrick or crane which he proposes to use. The terminal should advise the total weight of the hose string to be lifted related to the height of lift, which could be as much as 8 metres (25 feet) above deck level for a tanker's manifold connection 4·5 metres (15 feet) inboard. In wave and/or swell conditions above 1 metre (3 feet) significant height, dynamic loads may be imposed by the movement of the hose. In these circumstances the load to be lifted may be as much as 1·5 times the static weight of the hose and its contents.

Appendix C lists representative weights of hose strings when full of oil for submarine pipeline connections at multi-buoy moorings, and for floating hose strings at single buoy moorings. These tables are for general guidance only and a check should be made with the terminal.

During the lifting of hose strings, contact with the ship's side and any sharp edges should be avoided.

When the hose string has been lifted to the required height for connection to the manifold, and while it remains connected, the vertical section of the hose string should be supported by hang off chains or wires made fast to a strong point on the ship's deck.

Visual inspection should be made of each floating hose string before connecting to the tanker manifold to find out if damage has been caused by contact with other vessels, crossed lines, possible kinking, oil seepage etc.

If any damage to the hose is found which is considered to be critical to the intended operation, the hose should be withdrawn from use to allow further inspection and repair.

6.6.4   ADJUSTMENT DURING CARGO HANDLING OPERATIONS

As the tanker rises or falls due to tide or cargo operations, the hose strings should be adjusted to avoid strain on the hoses, connections, and ship's manifold and to ensure that the curvature of the hoses remains within the limits recommended by the manufacturer.

6.7   CARGO METAL ARMS

6.7.1   OPERATING ENVELOPE

Each installation of metal arms has a designed operating envelope which takes into account the elevation changes due to tide and freeboard of the largest and smallest tankers for which the berth was intended, minimum and maximum manifold setbacks, limited changes in horizontal position due to drift off and ranging, and maximum and minimum spacing when operating with other arms in the bank. The extent of this envelope should be thoroughly understood by operators, because operating outside it can cause overstress. Metal arm installations should have alarms for excessive range and drift.

The person in charge of operations on a berth should ensure that the tanker's manifolds are maintained within the operating envelope during all stages of loading and discharge operations.

6.7.2   FORCES ON MANIFOLDS

Most metal arms are counterbalanced so that no weight other than that of the liquid contents of the arms is placed on the manifold. As the weight of oil in the arms, particularly the larger diameter arms, can be considerable, it may be advisable for this weight to be relieved by a support or jack. Some arms have integral jacks which are also used to avoid overstressing of the tanker's manifold by the weight of the loading arm or other external forces such as the wind.

Some counterbalanced arms are made slightly 'tail heavy' to allow for clingage of oil in the arms and so that arms will normally return to the parked position if released, not under power, from the ship's manifold. Additionally, in some aspects of the operating envelope of the arms there can be an uplift on the manifold. For both these reasons manifolds should also be secured against upward forces.

6.7.3   TANKER'S MANIFOLD RESTRICTIONS

The construction material, support of a manifold, cantilever length and the distances apart of adjacent outlets must be checked for compatibility with the metal arms. Manifold flanges should be vertical and parallel to the ship's side. The spacing of the manifold outlets sometimes dictates the number of arms which can be connected if interference between adjacent arms is to be avoided. In most cases overstress will occur in cast iron manifolds unless jacks are used.

6.7.4   INADVERTENT FILLING OF ARMS WHILST PARKED

The parking lock on an arm should not be removed before checking that the arm is empty. If this precaution is not taken, the arm could crash on to the ship's deck on removal of the parking lock.

6.7.5   ICE FORMATION

Ice formation affects the balance of the arms, and any ice should be cleared off before removing the locks.

6.7.6   MECHANICAL COUPLERS

For most mechanical couplers the ship's flange face must be smooth and free of rust if a tight seal is to be achieved.

Care should be taken when connecting to ensure that the coupler is centrally placed on the manifold flange and that all claws or wedges are pulling up on the flange.

6.7.7   WIND FORCES

Wind loading of metal arms may place an excessive strain on the tanker's manifolds as well as on the arms. At those terminals where wind loading is critical a close watch should be kept on wind speed and direction, and operations should be suspended, and arms drained and disconnected, if wind limits are approached.

6.7.8 PRECAUTIONS WHILST ARMS ARE CONNECTED

The following precautions should be taken during the period that arms are connected:

The ship's moorings should be frequently monitored by ship and shore personnel, and tended as necessary to restrict any movement of the ship to that acceptable by the metal arm operating envelope.

If drift off or range alarms are actuated all transfer operations should be stopped and remedial measures taken.

Arms should be free to move with the motion of the ship. Care should be taken to ensure that hydraulic or mechanical locks cannot be engaged.

Arms should not foul each other.

Excessive vibration should not be permitted.

6.8 CLIMATIC CONDITIONS

6.8.1 TERMINAL ADVICE OF ADVERSE WEATHER CONDITIONS

The terminal representative should warn the tanker of the possibility of adverse weather conditions which may require the cessation of operations or a reduction of loading or discharge rates.

6.8.2 WIND CONDITIONS

If there is little air movement petroleum gas may persist on deck in heavy concentrations. If there is a wind, eddies can be created on the lee side of a tanker's house or deck structure, so carrying vented gas towards the house or structure.

Either of these effects may result in heavy local petroleum gas concentrations and it may then be necessary to extend the precautions set out in paragraph 6.1, or to stop loading, ballasting, inert gas purging, tank cleaning or gas freeing whilst these wind conditions persist. These operations should also be stopped if wind conditions cause funnel sparks to fall on deck.

6.8.3 ELECTRICAL STORMS

During electrical storms in the vicinity of the tanker, the handling of volatile petroleum, loading non-volatile petroleum into non-gas free tanks, ballasting, inert gas purging, tank cleaning or gas freeing after the discharge of such cargoes should be stopped and all tank openings and vent-line valves closed, including the bypass valve on the tank venting system, if fitted.

6.9 ACCIDENTAL OIL SPILLAGE AND LEAKAGE

6.9.1 GENERAL

Both ship and shore personnel should maintain a close check against the escape of oil when starting and during loading or discharging. In particular, care should be taken to ensure that pipeline valves, including drop valves, are closed if not in use.

Cargo tanks that have been topped up should be checked frequently during the remainder of loading operations to avoid an overflow.

If leakage occurs from a pipeline, valve, hose or metal arm, operations through that connection should be stopped until the cause has been ascertained and the defect remedied. If a pipeline, hose or metal arm bursts, or if there is an overflow, all cargo and bunker operations should be stopped immediately and should not be restarted until the fault has been rectified and all hazard from the released oil eliminated. If there is any possibility of any of the released oil or of petroleum gas entering an engine room intake, appropriate steps must be taken quickly to prevent this occurring.

Harbour authorities and any adjacent ship or shore installation should be warned of any hazard.

6.9.2   SEA AND OVERBOARD DISCHARGE VALVES

At the start of and at regular intervals throughout loading, discharging, ballasting and tank washing, watch should be kept to ensure that oil is not escaping through sea valves.

When not in use, sea and overboard discharge valves connected to the cargo or ballast system should be closed and lashed. When lashing is not practical, as with hydraulic valves, some suitable means of marking should be used to indicate clearly that the valves are to remain closed.

For further information on this subject reference should be made to the ICS/OCIMF publication 'Prevention of Oil Spillage through Cargo Pumproom Sea Valves'.

6.9.3   SCUPPER PLUGS

Before cargo handling commences, all deck scuppers should be effectively plugged to prevent spilled oil escaping overboard. Accumulations of water should be drained off periodically and scupper plugs replaced immediately after the water has been run off.

6.9.4   DRIP PANS

Unless there are permanent means for the retention of any slight leakage at ship and shore connections, it is essential that drip pans should be used to catch any such leakage.

6.9.5   SHIP AND SHORE CARGO AND BUNKER PIPELINES NOT IN USE

The tightness of valves should not be relied upon to prevent the escape or seepage of oil and all shore pipelines not in use at a berth should be securely blanked.

On a tanker all cargo and bunker pipelines not in use should be securely blanked at the manifold. The stern cargo pipelines should be isolated from the tanker's main pipeline system forward of the aft accommodation by blanking, or by removal of a spool piece.

6.10   EARTHING, BONDING AND CATHODIC PROTECTION

6.10.1   SHIP/SHORE EARTHING AND BONDING

Cargo hose strings and cargo metal arms should be fitted with an insulating flange or a single length of non-conducting hose to ensure electrical discontinuity between the ship and shore. When handling static accumulator oils all metal on the shore side of the insulating flange or the non-conducting hose should be electrically continuous to the jetty earthing system and all metal on the seaward side should be electrically continuous to the ship.

When an insulating flange or a single length of non-conducting hose is installed, it must not be short-circuited by contact with external metal; for example, an exposed metallic flange on the seaward side of the insulating flange or hose length should not make contact with the jetty structure either directly or through hose handling equipment.

As explained in Chapter 19, a ship/shore bonding cable has been shown to be quite ineffective as a safety precaution. The use of a ship/shore bonding cable is therefore not recommended. If nevertheless a bonding cable is insisted upon, it should first be visually checked to see that it is mechanically and electrically sound. The connection point for the cable should be well clear of the manifold area. There should always be a switch on the jetty in series with the bonding cable, of a type suitable for use in a Zone 1 hazardous area. It is important to ensure that the switch is always in the 'off' position before connecting or disconnecting the cable. Only when the cable is properly fixed and in good contact with the ship should the switch be closed. The cable should be attached before the cargo hoses are connected and removed only after the hoses have been disconnected.

It should be noted that switching off a cathodic protection system is not a substitute for the installation of an insulating flange or a length of non-conducting hose.

Insulating flanges should be visually inspected periodically to ensure that the insulation is clean and in good condition.

The resistance should be measured between the metal pipe on the shore side of the flange and the end of the hose or metal arm when freely suspended. A resistance as low as a few ohms is sufficient to reduce the current to a safe level but the measured value should be substantially higher, say 1000 ohms. A very low resistance may indicate damage to, or deterioration of, the insulation. See Appendix D for a typical insulating flange joint.

Cargo hoses with internal bonding between the end flanges should be checked for electrical continuity before they are taken into service and periodically thereafter.

6.10.2   APPLICATION TO OFFSHORE FACILITIES

Offshore facilities which are used for tanker cargo handling operations should be treated in the same way as shore terminals for the purpose of earthing and bonding.

6.11   PROXIMITY TO OTHER VESSELS

6.11.1   TANKERS AT ADJACENT BERTHS

Flammable concentrations of petroleum gas may occur if cargo or ballast handling, crude oil washing, inert gas purging, tank cleaning or gas freeing operations are being carried out by another tanker at an adjacent berth. In such circumstances appropriate precautions should be taken as described in Section 6.1.

6.11.2   GENERAL CARGO SHIPS AT ADJACENT BERTHS

It is unlikely that general cargo ships could comply with safety requirements relating to possible sources of ignition such as smoking, naked lights, cooking and electrical equipment; or that personnel, cranes and other equipment on a wharf or jetty used by such ships would normally be required to comply with safety requirements of that kind.

Accordingly when a tanker is at a wharf or jetty used for general cargo ships, or to which the public have access, it may be necessary when loading or discharging volatile petroleum, loading non-volatile petroleum into non-gas free tanks, or ballasting, inert gas purging or gas freeing after the discharge of volatile petroleum to take precautions additional to those set out in this Chapter.

6.11.3   TUGS AND OTHER CRAFT ALONGSIDE

The number of craft which come alongside and the duration of their stay should be kept to a minimum.

Only authorized craft having the permission of the officer responsible and the terminal representative should be permitted to come alongside or remain alongside a tanker while it is handling volatile petroleum or is ballasting when not gas free. The responsible officer should instruct craft personnel that smoking, naked light and cooking appliance regulations must be observed on the craft. In the event of a breach of the regulations, it may be necessary to cease operations.

Terminals should issue appropriate instructions to the operators of authorized craft on the use of engines, apparatus and equipment to avoid sources of ignition when going alongside a tanker or a jetty, including spark arresters on engine exhausts where applicable and proper fendering. Terminals should also ask for suitable notices to be prominently posted on the craft informing personnel and passengers of the safety precautions to be observed.

If unauthorized craft come alongside, or secure at an adjacent jetty, this should be reported to the local authorities, and if necessary operations should cease.

Chapter 7

Handling of Cargo and Ballast

The contents of this Chapter relate to the precautions to be taken and the procedures that should be observed on all occasions when handling of cargo or of ballast takes place, whether at terminals, during transfers between vessels or for jettison of cargo. These precautions are additional to those given in Chapters 2, 4 and 6.

7.1   **SUPERVISION AND CONTROL**

7.1.1   JOINT AGREEMENT ON READINESS TO LOAD OR DISCHARGE

Before starting to load or discharge cargo the responsible officer and the terminal representative should formally agree that from the safety aspect both the tanker and the terminal are ready.

7.1.2   SUPERVISION

The following safeguards should be maintained throughout loading or discharging:

A responsible officer should be on watch and sufficient crew should remain on board to deal with the operation and security of the tanker. A member of the tanker's crew should be continuously on watch on the tank deck unless adequate supervision can be maintained from the tanker's control room.

A senior terminal representative should be on duty and his location and telephone number should be provided to the responsible officer on watch. A member of the terminal organization should be on continuous duty at the shore end of the ship to shore connnections, or arrangements made for continuous supervision e.g. by television.

The agreed ship to shore communications system should be maintained in good working order.

At the commencement of loading or discharging, and at each change of watch or shift, the responsible officer and the terminal representative should confirm with each other that the communication system for loading and discharging control is understood by them and by personnel on watch and on duty.

The stand-by requirements for normal stopping of shore pumps on completion of loading and the emergency stop system of both tanker and terminal should be fully understood by all concerned.

7.1.3   CHECKS DURING CARGO HANDLING

At the start of and during cargo handling frequent checks should be made by the responsible officer to see that cargo is entering or leaving the designated cargo tanks only, and that there is no escape of oil into pumprooms and cofferdams, or through sea and overboard discharge valves.

Tanker and terminal personnel should regularly check the pipeline and hose or metal arm pressures, and the estimated quantity of oil loaded or discharged. Any drop in pressures or any marked discrepancy between tanker and terminal estimates of quantities could indicate pipeline or hose leakage, particularly in submarine pipelines, and require interruption of cargo operations until investigated.

7.2   **ULLAGING AND SAMPLING**

7.2.1   GENERAL

When ullaging or sampling care should be taken to avoid inhaling gas. Personnel should therefore keep their heads well away from the issuing gas and stand at right angles to the direction of the wind. Standing immediately up wind of the ullage port might create a back eddy of gas towards the operator.

When manual ullaging or sampling of volatile petroleum is carried out, the openings should be uncovered only long enough to complete the operation.

7.2.2   CARGOES CONTAINING HYDROGEN SULPHIDE OR BENZENE

Special precautions should be taken if the cargo to be loaded contains hydrogen sulphide or benzene in concentrations sufficient to cause the gases vented during loading or when ballasting after discharge to be hazardous if inhaled.

In particular ullage plugs should be opened only for the shortest time possible. In extreme cases such as when there are still air conditions and the issuing gas has a low efflux velocity, consideration should be given to using breathing apparatus.

See Chapter 15 for a description of the effects of exposure to hydrogen sulphide and benzene.

7.2.3   USE OF ROPES MADE FROM MAN MADE FIBRES

Ropes made from man made fibres should not be used for lowering sounding rods or sample cans into cargo tanks.

7.2.4   STATIC ACCUMULATOR OILS

The precautions to be taken against static electricity when ullaging or sampling static accumulator oils are given in paragraph 7.4.3(b), although the exceptions in paragraph 7.4.2 should be noted.

7.3   **OPERATION OF PUMPS AND VALVES**

7.3.1   PRESSURE SURGES

It is possible to produce pressure surges in a pipeline system by the incorrect operation of pumps and valves. These surges may be sufficiently high to damage the pipeline, hoses or metal arms. The most vulnerable part of the system is the ship to shore connection. Pressure surges are produced upstream of a closing valve and may become excessive if the valve is closed too quickly. They are more likely to be severe with long shore pipelines and high flow rates.

In order to minimize the risk of pressure surges, information should be exchanged between the tanker and the terminal about control of flow rates, rate of valve closure and pump speed. This should include the closure periods of remote control and automatic shut down valves.

7.3.2   VALVE OPERATION

To avoid pressure surges, valves at the downstream end of a pipeline system should, as a general rule, not be closed against the flow of liquid, except in an emergency. This should be stressed to all personnel responsible for cargo handling operations on the tanker and at the terminal.

In general where pumps are used for cargo transfer, all valves in the transfer system (both ship and shore) should be open before pumping begins, although the discharge valve next to the pump may be kept closed until the pump is up to speed, and the valve then opened slowly. For discharge of cargo this procedure may be changed (see paragraph 7.6.1). In the case of transfers by gravity, the final valve to be opened should be that at the upstream end of the system.

If the flow is to be diverted from one tank to another, either the valve on the second tank must be opened before the valve on the first tank is closed, or pumping should stop while the change is being made.

Valves which control liquid flow should be closed slowly. The time for power operated valves to move from open to shut and from shut to open should be checked regularly at their operating temperatures.

7.3.3   CONTROL OF PUMPING

Throughout pumping operations there should be no abrupt changes in the rate of flow.

Where a reciprocating pump is used, it is important that pump pulses should not be in resonance with the pipeline or ship to shore connection. Speed should be adjusted accordingly.

To avoid damage to pumps and excessive strain on tanker and terminal equipment, cavitation of pumps for extended periods should be avoided as much as possible.

7.3.4   BUTTERFLY AND NON-RETURN (CHECK) VALVES

Butterfly and pinned back non-return valves in ship and shore cargo systems have been known to slam shut when cargo is flowing through them at high rates during loading, thereby setting up very large surge pressures which can cause line or hose or metal arm failures or even structural damage to jetties. These failures are usually due in the first place to the valve disc not being completely parallel to, or fully withdrawn from, the flow when in the open position. This can create a closing force which, if it becomes great enough, shears the valve spindle in the case of butterfly valves or the hold open pin in the case of pinned back non-return valves. It is therefore important to check that all such valves are fully open when they are passing cargo or ballast.

7.4   HANDLING STATIC ACCUMULATOR OILS

Precautions against static electricity are necessary when the oil being handled is an accumulator of static electricity and the tank atmosphere may be flammable. See Table 7-1 on page 43 for a summary indicating whether or not precautions are necessary.

7.4.1   STATIC ACCUMULATION

The first consideration is whether the oil is an accumulator of static electricity. As explained in Chapter 19, black oils have sufficient conductivity to prevent accumulation of static electricity. These oils may be loaded without static precautions regardless of tank flammability. Such oils include:

> Crude oils
> Residual fuel oils
> Black diesel oils
> Asphalts (bitumens)

Clean oils (distillates) are, in general, accumulators of static electricity due to their low conductivity and may require static precautions. These oils include:

> Natural gasolines
> Kerosenes
> White spirits
> Motor and aviation gasolines
> Jet fuels
> Naphthas
> Heating oils
> Heavy gas oils
> Clean diesel oils
> Lubricating oils

However a clean oil containing an antistatic additive may be handled as a non-accumulator provided its conductivity is known to be greater than 100 picoSiemens/metre.

7.4.2   FLAMMABLE TANK ATMOSPHERE

The second consideration is the flammability of the tank atmosphere. No precautions are necessary if the tank is maintained in an inert condition. A non-volatile static accumulator oil requires the precautions against static electricity given in paragraph 7.4.3 only if the tank is not gas free or if the oil temperature is near or above its flash point. A volatile static accumulator oil requires these precautions although two exceptions are permissible:

(a)   If the oil temperature is significantly below the flash point, as is normally the case for kerosene and heating oils, and the tank is gas free, the precautions of paragraph 7.4.3 need not be observed.

(b) If the oil has a high vapour pressure, as with gasolines, the region immediately above the liquid surface will be over rich and the precautions of paragraph 7.4.3 need not be observed, except that metallic dipping, ullaging, and sampling equipment should be earthed to prevent sparks at the deck opening where the atmosphere may be flammable.

7.4.3   PRECAUTIONS WHEN LOADING STATIC ACCUMULATOR OILS

(a) During loading the flow rate in the branch line into each individual tank should not exceed a linear velocity of 1 metre/second (3 feet/second) until all splashing and surface turbulence has ceased.

After all splashing and surface turbulence has ceased and pipelines are free of air and water, the flow rate can be increased to the maximum permitted by the design of the ship and shore pipeline and pumping systems and consistent with proper control of the operation.

To assist in calculating the volumetric loading rate which corresponds to a linear velocity in a branch line of 1 metre/second (3 feet/second), the following table can be used to relate the volumetric flow rate to the line diameter:

Flow rates corresponding to 1 metre/second

Nominal Diameter Inches	Approximate Flow Rate Cubic metres/hour
3	16
4	29
6	65
8	116
10	182
12	262
14	320
16	424
18	542
20	676
24	986
28	1350
32	1780

Note that the diameters given are nominal diameters which are not necessarily the same as the actual internal diameters.

(b) During and for 30 minutes after the completion of loading, no metallic dipping, ullaging or sampling equipment should be introduced into or remain in the tank; examples are manual steel ullage tapes, metal sampling apparatus and metal sounding rods. Non-conducting equipment with no metal parts may, in general, be used at any time. However, ropes used for lowering equipment into tanks should always be made of natural fibres and not synthetic polymers.

At the end of the 30 minutes delay period, metallic dipping, ullaging and sampling equipment may also be used but it is essential that it should be bonded and firmly earthed to the structure of the ship before its introduction into the tank and should remain earthed until after its removal.

Operations within sounding pipes are permissible at any time.

A permanently fitted metal float level gauge does not present a static electricity hazard provided the metal float has electrical continuity through the tape to the structure of the ship, and the metal guide wires are intact.

(c) If there is a micropore filter in the shore pipeline system the loading rate should be adjusted so that at least 30 seconds elapse between the time the cargo leaves the filter and the time that it enters any cargo tank.

7.4.4	DISCHARGE OF STATIC ACCUMULATOR OILS

The initial flow rate of static accumulator oils into shore tanks may need to be restricted to 1 metre/second (3 feet/second) at the inlet to the tank until shore personnel are satisfied that it can be increased. This restriction is not required in floating roof tanks when the roof is floating.

The entrainment of tank atmospheres by stripping pumps or eductors should be avoided as far as possible.

7.5 LOADING OF CARGO

7.5.1 COMMENCEMENT OF LOADING

Before starting to load cargo, all necessary terminal and tanker valves in the loading system should be open. Loading should commence at a slow rate. The flow of oil should be under the control of the terminal in accordance with requests by the tanker and should not be increased until cargo flow is correctly established.

7.5.2 TOPPING OFF ON BOARD THE TANKER

When final tanks are being topped off the terminal should be requested to reduce the loading rate sufficiently to permit effective control of the flow. After topping off individual tanks, ullages should be checked from time to time to ensure that overflows do not occur due to leaking valves or incorrect operation.

The tanker's valves should not be closed against the shore, except in an emergency.

7.5.3 STOPPING LOADING BY THE TERMINAL

Many terminals require a 'standby' period for shutting off pumps and this should be well understood before loading commences. Where possible the final loading should be done by gravity. If pumps have to be used to the end their speed during the 'standby' time should be regulated so that shore control valves can be closed as soon as requested by the ship. Shore control valves should be closed before ship's valves.

The number of valves to be closed should be reduced to a minimum during the topping off period.

7.5.4 CHECKS AFTER LOADING

As soon as practicable after completion of loading, a responsible ship's officer should check that all valves in the cargo system are closed, that all appropriate tank openings are closed, and that pressure/vacuum relief valves are correctly set.

7.5.5 LOADING VERY HIGH VAPOUR PRESSURE CARGOES

Consideration should be given to the need for special precautions during loading when the true vapour pressure of the cargo is expected to exceed the following:

For natural gasoline type cargoes, for example pentanes plus (0·75 atmosphere or 10·8 pounds/square inch absolute).

For crude oils, with or without added gas, 1·0 bar (1·0 atmosphere or 14·5 pounds/square inch absolute).

For some intermediate cargoes (for example flash stabilized condensates, some distillation overhead products, and crude oils with abnormally low methane and ethane contents) TVP limits between these two values might be appropriate.

When cargo temperatures, crude oil stabilization conditions and Reid vapour pressures are known, true vapour pressures can be derived for checking against criteria of this kind.

Precautions which might be applied if it is agreed that they are required include:

Avoid loading when there is little or no wind.

Use very low initial flow rates into tanks.

Minimize the total loading time per tank.

Use very low topping off rates.

Avoid partial vacuum in the loading line.

Avoid venting through openings at deck level.

Avoid loading hot oil which has lain in shore lines exposed to the sun; if this is unavoidable direct this oil to tanks venting well clear of the superstructure.

Provide additional supervision to monitor gas dispersion and to ensure compliance with all safety requirements.

7.5.6 LOADING HEATED PRODUCTS

Excessive heat in a cargo, unless the ship is specially designed for carrying very hot cargoes, (e.g. a bitumen carrier), can do damage to a tanker's structure and to equipment such as valves, pumps and gaskets. The master may therefore refuse to load a cargo if he considers that it is too hot.

The following precautions help to alleviate the effects of loading a hot cargo:

The cargo should be spread throughout the ship as evenly as possible in order to dissipate excess heat and to avoid local heat stress.

The loading rate should be adjusted to maintain a reasonable temperature.

When hot cargo is being loaded the ambient conditions, particularly the temperature of the dock water, must be taken into consideration in order to avoid excessive stresses due to temperature differences.

Tanks and pipelines must be completely free of water before receiving any cargo that has a temperature above the boiling point of water.

7.5.7 LOADING OVERALL (LOADING FROM THE TOP)

There may be specific port or terminal regulations relating to loading overall.

Volatile petroleum or non-volatile petroleum having a temperature above its flash point should never be loaded or transferred overall.

Non-volatile petroleum having a temperature below its flash point may be loaded overall in the following circumstances:

If the tank concerned is gas free and provided no contamination by volatile petroleum can occur.

If prior approval is received from the master and from the terminal representative.

Ballast or slops should not be loaded or transferred overall in the presence of a flammable gas mixture.

The free end of the hose should be lashed inside the tank coaming to prevent movement.

7.6 DISCHARGE OF CARGO

7.6.1 START OF DISCHARGE

Discharge should start at a slow rate. Shore valves should be fully open to receiving tanks before the tanker's manifold valves are opened. The terminal should inform the tanker if non-return (check) valves are not fitted in the shore line. If there is a possibility that pressure might exist in the shore line, the tanker's manifold valves should not be opened until adequate pump pressure has been developed.

During discharge the flow of oil should be controlled by the tanker in accordance with requests from the terminal.

7.6.2 STRIPPING AND DRAINING OF CARGO TANKS

If during the discharge of the main bulk of cargo, a selected tank is used to receive the drainings of tanks being stripped, personnel should be alert to the fact that in the selected tank the ullage will be decreasing, so that great care should be taken to avoid an overflow and proper precautions should be taken in respect of the petroleum gas emitted.

7.6.3 SIMULTANEOUS BALLAST AND CARGO HANDLING

If ballasting of cargo tanks is carried out simultaneously with discharge of cargo, petroleum gas may be emitted from the tanks being ballasted, and proper precautions should be taken.

7.6.4 PRESSURIZING OF CARGO TANKS

When high vapour pressure petroleum, such as natural gasoline and certain crude oils, reaches a low level in cargo tanks the head of liquid is sometimes not enough to keep cargo pumps primed.

If an inert gas system is installed in the tanker this system can be used for pressurizing to improve pump performance. Alternatively air supplied by low pressure fans may be used. Steam or compressed air should not be used as a medium for pressurizing because of the static electricity hazard introduced.

7.7 INERTING ULLAGE SPACES IN CARGO TANKS

A full description of fixed inert gas systems and their operation during cargo and ballast handling is contained in Chapter 9.

7.8 CRUDE OIL WASHING

A full description of the requirements relating to crude oil washing is given in Section 8.4.

7.9 PIPELINE AND HOSE CLEARING AFTER CARGO HANDLING

The procedure for clearing the pipelines and hoses or arms between the shore control valve and the ship's manifold will depend on the shore facilities available and whether these include a slop tank or other receptacle. The relative heights of the ship and shore manifold may influence procedures.

Some portion of the system between the shore control valve and the ship's manifold is usually emptied or, in some cases, blown by air into the ship's tanks. Sufficient ullage should be left in final tanks to accept the drainings of hoses or arms. The hoses or arms used for highly viscous non-volatile grades of oil may have to be air blown to clear them, and the turbulence which air blowing causes is an additional factor necessitating sufficient ullage.

The use of air or inert gas for clearing hoses or loading arms after handling volatile static accumulator oils is not recommended, but if used the amount of air or inert gas entering the tank should be kept to a minimum.

Before hoses or arms are disconnected the drain cocks at the manifold should be opened into fixed drain tanks or portable drip pans with the vacuum breakers open.

After disconnection cargo manifolds should be blanked. Contents of portable drip pans must not be thrown overboard, but should be disposed of safely.

7.10 TRANSFERS BETWEEN VESSELS

7.10.1 SHIP TO SHIP TRANSFERS

In ship to ship transfers, both tankers should comply fully with the safety precautions required for normal cargo operations. If the safety precautions are not being observed on either vessel, the operations should not be started, or should be stopped.

A full description of the safety aspects of transfer operations are contained in the ICS/OCIMF 'Ship to Ship Transfer Guide (Petroleum)', to which reference should be made before starting the transfer.

7.10.2   SHIP TO BARGE TRANSFERS

In tanker to barge transfers of petroleum only authorized and properly equipped barges should be used. Precautions similar to those set out for ship to ship cargo transfers as described in the ICS/OCIMF 'Ship to Ship Transfer Guide (Petroleum)' should be followed. If the safety precautions are not being observed on either the barge or the tanker, the operations should not be started or should be stopped.

Special attention should be given to the supporting of the transfer hoses particularly to avoid chafe or kinking.

The rate of pumping from ship to barge should be controlled according to the size and nature of the receiving barge and well understood communications procedures should be established and maintained, particularly when the freeboard of the ship is high in relation to the barge.

If there is a large difference in freeboard between the ship and the barge, the barge crew should make allowance for the contents of the hose on completion of the transfer.

Arrangements should be made to release the barges in an emergency, having regard to other shipping or property in the vicinity. If the tanker is at anchor, it may be appropriate to drop the barge clear of the tanker, where it could be secured to wait for assistance.

Barges should be removed from alongside as soon as possible after completion of loading or discharging volatile petroleum.

7.10.3   SHIP TO SHIP TRANSFERS USING TERMINAL FACILITIES

Where a tanker on a berth is transferring cargo to another tanker on another berth through the shore headers and pipelines, the terminal should ensure that adequate communications and procedures are set up between the two tankers.

7.11   JETTISON OF CARGO

Jettison of cargo is an extreme measure justified only as a means of saving life at sea or for the safety of the vessel. A decision to jettison cargo should therefore not be taken until all the alternative options have been considered in the light of available information upon stability and floatation.

If it is necessary to jettison cargo the following precautions should be taken:

Engine room personnel should be alerted. Depending on the circumstances prevailing at the time, consideration should be given to changing over engine room intakes from high to low level.

Discharge should take place through the sea valve and where possible on the side opposite to the engine room intakes.

All non-essential inlets should be closed.

If discharge must be from deck level, flexible hoses should be rigged to extend below the water surface.

All safety precautions relating to normal operations which involve the presence of flammable gas in the vicinity of the deck must be observed.

A radio warning should be broadcast.

7.12   BALLAST HANDLING

7.12.1   BALLAST LOADING

The ballasting operation should be discussed and agreed with the terminal representative, who should be advised of the approximate time of commencement and the duration of ballasting both into segregated ballast tanks and into cargo tanks.

Before ballasting of non-gas free tanks is carried out alongside a terminal, the responsible officer should consult with the terminal representative and all safety checks and precautions as for loading volatile petroleum should be observed.

During ballasting of cargo tanks which have not been gas freed, gas is expelled which may be within the limits of flammability on mixing with air. This should therefore be vented through the recognized vent lines as during loading.

Ballast should not be loaded overall into non-gas free tanks.

7.12.2   SIMULTANEOUS BALLAST AND CARGO HANDLING

The agreement of the terminal representative should be obtained before the simultaneous handling of cargo and ballast, other than segregated ballast.

7.12.3   STARTING THE TANKER'S CARGO PUMPS TO BALLAST

When cargo pumps are used for ballasting, they should be operated so that on opening the sea suction valves no oil is allowed to escape overboard.

TABLE 7-1 *Requirement for static electricity precautions when ullaging, dipping and sampling*

				Are static precautions needed?	
Volatility classification	Electrostatic classification	Examples	Additional factors	Tank gas free	Tank non gas free
Non-volatile flash point 60°C (140°F) or above	Non-accumulators	Hard asphalts (bitumens) Black diesel oils Residual fuels	—	No	No
	Accumulators	Heavy gas oils Clean diesel oils High flash jet fuels (1) Lubricating oils	Oil temperature significantly below flash point	No	Yes
			Oil temperature near or above flash point	Yes	Yes
Volatile flash point below 60°C (140°F)	Non-accumulators	Crude oils Cut back asphalts (bitumens)	—	No	No
	Accumulators	Kerosenes Heating oils Kerosene type jet fuels (2)	Oil temperature significantly below flash point	No	Yes
		Gasoline type jet fuels (3) Naphthas White spirits	Oil temperature near or above flash point	Yes	Yes
		Motor gasolines Aviation gasolines Natural gasolines	High Vapour Pressure	No*	No*

*Except that metallic dipping, ullaging, and sampling equipment should be earthed.
(1) JP-5 (2) Avtur, Jet A-1, JP-1 (3) Avtag, Jet-B, JP-4

7.12.4   SEQUENCE OF VALVE OPERATIONS

The following procedures should be adopted when taking ballast into non-gas free or non-inerted tanks:

   The tank valves should be the first valves opened.

   The initial flow of ballast should be restricted so that the entrance velocity is less than 1 metre/second (3 feet/second) until the longitudinals are covered, or if there are no longitudinals, until the depth of the ballast in the tank is at least 1·5 metres (5 feet).

These precautions are required to avoid a geyser effect which may lead to the build up of an electrostatic charge in a mist or spray cloud near the point where the ballast enters the tank. When a sufficient charge exists, the possibility of a discharge and ignition cannot be excluded.

Chapter 8

Tank Cleaning and Gas Freeing

This Chapter deals with the procedures for cleaning and gas freeing cargo tanks and other enclosed spaces after the discharge of volatile petroleum or of non-volatile petroleum carried in a non-gas free tank, or when there is a possibility of flammable gas entering the tank or space. Safety precautions to be taken are set out, including those related to crude oil washing of cargo tanks.

8.1   **SUPERVISION AND PREPARATIONS**

8.1.1   SUPERVISION

A responsible officer should supervise all tank cleaning and gas freeing operations.

8.1.2   PREPARATIONS

Before and during tank cleaning and gas freeing operations, the responsible officer should be satisfied that all the appropriate precautions set out in Chapters 2 and 6 are being observed. All personnel on board should be notified that tank cleaning or gas freeing is about to begin.

If craft are alongside the tanker, their personnel should also be notified and their compliance with all appropriate safety measures should be checked.

Before starting gas freeing or tank cleaning at a terminal, the following additional measures should be taken:

The precautions in Chapter 4 should be observed as appropriate.

The appropriate personnel ashore should be consulted to ascertain that conditions are safe on the jetty and to obtain agreement that operations can start.

8.1.3   GAS FREEING AND TANK CLEANING CONCURRENTLY WITH CARGO HANDLING

Generally tank cleaning and gas freeing should not take place concurrently with cargo handling. If for any reason this is necessary, there should be close consultation with, and agreement, by the terminal representative.

However, crude oil washing and cargo discharge may take place concurrently, but the terminal representative should be advised (see Section 8.4).

8.1.4   TESTING OF TANK CLEANING HOSES

Hoses that are to be used in conjunction with portable tank cleaning machines should be tested with a low voltage ohm meter (not a high voltage insulation tester) for electrical continuity on each occasion before use.

8.1.5   TESTING AND CALIBRATION OF GAS MEASURING INSTRUMENTS

Before tank cleaning or gas freeing measuring instruments to be used in these operations should be calibrated and tested (see Chapter 17).

8.1.6   ENTRY INTO CARGO TANKS

No one should enter any cargo tank unless permission to do so has been received from the officer responsible and all appropriate precautions have been taken (see Chapter 10).

8.2   CARGO TANK WASHING AND CLEANING

8.2.1   TANK WASHING ATMOSPHERES

Tank washing may be carried out in any of the following atmospheres:

Atmosphere A — an atmosphere which is not controlled and which can thus be above, below, or within the flammable range.

Atmosphere B — an atmosphere made incapable of burning by the deliberate reduction of the hydrocarbon content to below the lower flammable limit (LFL).

For the purpose of this guide the readings given by a suitable combustible gas indicator should not exceed 50% LFL.

Atmosphere C — an atmosphere made incapable of burning by the introduction of inert gas and the resultant reduction of the overall oxygen content. For the purpose of this guide the oxygen content of the tank atmosphere should not exceed 8% by volume.

Atmosphere D — an atmosphere made incapable of burning by deliberately maintaining the hydrocarbon content of the tank above the upper flammable limit (UFL). A hydrocarbon content of at least 15% by volume should be attained before starting washing and maintained throughout washing.

8.2.2   WASHING IN AN UNCONTROLLED ATMOSPHERE (A)

Under Atmosphere A conditions, precautions must be taken to avoid ignition sources and all the following precautions should be observed:

(a)   Washing machines in use at any one time should be restricted in any one compartment to not more than 4 machines each having a flow rate not exceeding 35 cubic metres/hour, or not more than 3 machines each having a flow rate of between 35 and 60 cubic metres/hour. Washing machines having a flow rate greater than 60 cubic metres/hour should not be used in Atmosphere A.

For the purposes of this section a compartment is defined as any part of a tank sectionalized by a wash plate (swash) bulkhead.

(b)   All hose connections should be made up before the washing machine is introduced into the tank and should not be broken until after the machine has been removed from the tank. To drain the hose, a coupling may be partially opened and then tightened again before the machine is removed.

(c)   Recirculated water should not be employed for tank washing and chemical additive should not be used.

(d)   Wash water may be heated provided the temperature does not exceed 60°C (140°F); if water above 60°C is required for any reason (e.g. in preparation for drydocking), washing should be undertaken under Atmosphere B, C or D conditions. Alternatively the tank may be washed with water cooler than 60°C and then gas freed before subsequent washing with hotter water.

(e)   Steam should not be introduced into the tank.

(f)   The tank should be kept drained during washing. Washing should be stopped to clear any unusual build up of wash water.

(g)   Sounding and the introduction of other equipment should preferably be done through a sounding pipe.

If a sounding pipe is not used it is essential that any metallic components of the sounding or other equipment are bonded and securely earthed to the ship before introduction into the tank and remain earthed until removed. This precaution should be observed during washing and for 5 hours thereafter. The 5 hour delay can be reduced to 1 hour if the tank is continuously mechanically ventilated.

As examples during this period:

An interface detector of metallic construction may be used if earthed to the ship by means of a stout clamp or bolted metal lug.

A metal rod may be used on the end of a metal tape which is earthed to the ship.

A metal sounding rod suspended on a fibre rope should not be used even if the end at deck level is fastened to the ship because the rope cannot be completely relied upon as an earthing path.

Equipment made entirely of non-metallic materials may, in general, be used, for example:

A wooden sounding rod may be suspended on a rope without earthing.

Ropes made of synthetic polymers should not be used for lowering equipment into cargo tanks.

Further information on electrostatic precautions during tank washing is given in Chapter 19.

8.2.3   WASHING IN A TOO LEAN ATMOSPHERE (B)

The following precautions are recommended:

(a)   If the tank has a vent system which is common to other tanks, the tank should be isolated to prevent an ingress of gas from the other tanks.

(b)   The tank bottom should be flushed with water and stripped and the piping system, including cargo pumps, cross overs and discharge lines, should also be flushed with water.

(c)   Before washing, the tank should be ventilated to reduce the gas concentration of the atmosphere to 10% or less of the lower flammable limit (LFL). Gas tests should be made at various levels with due consideration for the possibility of local pockets of flammable gas. Mechanical ventilation and gas testing should continue during washing.

(d)   Washing should be discontinued if the gas concentration rises to 50% LFL; washing may be resumed when continued ventilation has reduced the gas concentration to 20% LFL.

(e)   If portable washing machines are used, all hose connections should be made up before the washing machine is introduced into the tank and should not be broken until after the machine has been removed from the tank. To drain the hose a coupling may be partially opened and then tightened again before the machine is removed.

(f)   The tank should be kept drained during washing; washing should be stopped to clear any unusual build up of wash water.

(g)   Recirculated water should not be used for tank washing.

(h)   Steam should not be introduced into the tank.

(i)   The same precautions relating to sounding and the introduction of other similar equipment should be taken as when washing in an Uncontrolled Atmosphere (A) (See paragraph 8.2.2 (g)).

(j)   Chemical additives may be employed.

(k)   Wash water may be heated above 60°C (140°F), but care must be taken to see that the gas concentration does not rise above 50% LFL (See paragraph 8.2.3 (d)).

8.2.4   WASHING IN AN INERT ATMOSPHERE (C)

None of the operating restrictions for washing in atmospheres A and B needs to be observed if the tank is inerted.

The requirements for the maintenance of an inert atmosphere during washing are set out in paragraph 9.2.7.

47

8.2.5 WASHING IN AN OVER RICH ATMOSPHERE (D)

The procedure for washing in an over rich atmosphere depends greatly on the properties of the particular cargo or medium used for achieving this condition, and on the ship layout. Reference should be made to special instructions issued by the owner.

None of the operating restrictions for washing in Atmospheres A and B needs to be observed if the atmosphere is maintained at too rich a level to burn. Special procedures and particular care are necessary to ensure that air does not enter the tank.

It should be confirmed by measurement that the hydrocarbon content of the tank atmosphere is at least 15% by volume throughout the washing operations.

8.2.6 FREE FALL

It is essential that slop handling procedures are adjusted so that a free fall of water or slops in the receiving tank does not occur at any time. The liquid level should always be such that the discharge inlets in the slop tank are covered to a depth of at least one metre.

8.2.7 SPRAYING OF WATER

The spraying of water into a tank containing a substantial quantity of a static accumulator oil could result in static electricity generation at the liquid surface, either by agitation or by water settling. Tanks which contain a static accumulator oil should always be pumped out before they are washed with water, unless the tank is kept in an inert condition.

8.2.8 STEAMING OF TANKS

Due to the hazard of static electricity, steam should not be introduced into any tank where a flammable atmosphere may exist.

8.2.9 LEADED GASOLINE

Unlike shore tanks which may contain leaded gasoline for long periods and which therefore present a hazard of tetraethyl lead (TEL) and tetramethyl lead (TML) very little risk is likely in a ship's tanks which normally alternate between different products and ballast. Ships employed in the regular carriage of leaded gasoline should at least flush the bottoms of the tanks after two successive cargoes to reduce the risk further.

8.2.10 REMOVAL OF SLUDGE, SCALE AND SEDIMENT

Before the removal by hand of sludge, scale and sediment, the tank atmosphere should be safe for entry, as described in paragraph 10.5.5, and precautions should be maintained throughout the period of work.

8.3 GAS FREEING

8.3.1 GENERAL

The following recommendations apply to cargo tank gas freeing generally (additional considerations apply when the tank has been inerted — these are given in Chapter 9):

The covers of tank openings should be kept closed until actual ventilation of the individual tank commences.

Any tank openings inside an enclosed or partially enclosed space should not be opened until after the tank pressure has been relieved to an area outside that space.

The piping system including cargo pumps, crossovers and the discharge lines should be flushed through with water and the tank stripped. Valves other than those used for ventilation should then be closed and secured.

If the vent system is common to other tanks, the tank should be isolated to prevent an ingress of gas from the other tanks.

Heating coils, if fitted, should be cleared with water or steam.

After ventilation the tank atmosphere should be tested at the bottom and at several depths through several tank openings using an approved combustible gas indicator. Ventilation should be suspended while these tests are being conducted. If satisfactory results are not obtained further ventilation should take place.

8.3.2   GAS FREE FOR RECEIVING CARGO

A tank which is required to be gas free for receiving cargo should be ventilated until tests confirm that the hydrocarbon gas concentration throughout the tanks does not exceed 40% LFL.

8.3.3   GAS FREE FOR ENTRY AND COLD WORK WITHOUT BREATHING APPARATUS

In order to be gas free for entry without breathing apparatus after the carriage of cargo, a tank or space should be ventilated until tests confirm that the hydrocarbon gas concentration throughout the compartment is not more than 1% LFL, i.e. a reading of nil should be obtained.

The full range of gas tests required before entry into a cargo tank is described in detail in Section 10.2. These include additional tests that should be made, as appropriate, to check the oxygen content, and for the presence of hydrogen sulphide, benzene and other toxic gases.

8.3.4   GAS FREE IN PREPARATION FOR HOT WORK

In addition to meeting the requirements for entry, a check should be made to ensure that no sludge or loose scale exists which, if disturbed or heated, could give off petroleum gas.

When the tanker is alongside a terminal, the terminal representative should be consulted as the issue of a Hot or Cold Work Permit may be required.

8.4   CRUDE OIL WASHING

8.4.1   GENERAL

In certain circumstances a crude oil tanker fitted with fixed washing equipment in the tanks directly connected to the cargo pumping system can use crude oil instead of water as the washing medium. This operation may take place either in port or at sea. It is most frequently carried out while the tanker is discharging cargo and it then enables redissolving of oil fractions adhering to the tank surfaces to take place so that these residues can be discharged with the cargo. There is then no need to water wash tanks during the ballast voyage for the removal of residues. Water washing or bottom flushing may be necessary if the tank is to be used for clean ballast.

Reference should be made to the ICS/OCIMF 'Guidelines for Tank Washing with Crude Oil' for full details of the procedure involved. The requirements for safety are in general the same as those in other cargo handling operations (see Chapters 6 and 7).

8.4.2   NOTIFICATION TO TERMINAL

When it is intended to carry out crude oil washing during cargo discharge the responsible officer should notify the terminal representative giving the anticipated effect on the overall discharge time.

8.4.3   TYPES OF WASHING MACHINES

Normally, only washing machines fixed in the tank should be used for crude oil washing. Portable equipment is not suitable and should not be used.

8.4.4   TANK ATMOSPHERE CONTROL

Compared with water, dry crude oil produces a much lower electrostatic space charge in the tank during the washing process. Nevertheless it is considered necessary to conduct crude oil washing only in atmospheres controlled to avoid a flammable gas mixture. By its nature crude oil washing makes impossible the achievement of a too lean atmosphere.

8.4.5   INERT GAS ATMOSPHERE

The usual method of controlling the tank atmosphere during crude oil washing is by inerting the tank. With this method the safety of the operation is independent of the characteristics of the crude oil, but the oxygen content of the tank must be maintained below 8% by volume as described in detail in Chapter 9.

8.4.6   OVER-RICH ATMOSPHERE

Crude oil washing has been carried out with the cargo tank atmosphere in an over-rich condition relying on gas evolution from the crude oil being used for washing. Not all crude oils are suitable for this method of atmosphere control and, in any event, very careful monitoring with special equipment is necessary to ensure that the over rich condition is achieved and maintained. This technique should not be used unless the personnel involved have received special training. It should only be used with the specific permission of the owner and the terminal.

8.4.7   PRECAUTIONS AGAINST LEAKAGE FROM THE WASHING SYSTEM

Before arrival in port, when it is intended to crude oil wash, a check should be made that the valves on all washing machines are securely shut. The tank washing system should be pressure tested and examined for leaks.

While crude oil washing is in progress the system must be kept under continuous observation so that any leak will be detected immediately and action can be taken to deal with it.

On completion of washing the system must be completely drained of oil. If it is necessary for the system to be cleaned it should be flushed through with water into appropriate tanks. If it is required to be gas free it should be ventilated in the same way as cargo lines.

8.4.8   AVOIDANCE OF OIL/WATER MIXTURES

Before crude oil washing is commenced any water which may have settled as a water bottom should be withdrawn from each tank. The slop tank, if it is to be used for the washing supply, should be completely discharged and refilled with dry crude oil.

8.4.9   EXCLUSION OF OIL FROM THE ENGINE ROOM

If any part of the tank washing system extends into the engine room it should be blanked off to prevent any oil entering the engine room.

If the tank wash water heater is fitted outside the engine room it should be effectively isolated.

8.4.10   TANK ENTRY

If it is necessary to enter a tank the full precautions given in Chapter 10 must be taken.

8.4.11   CARGO TANK BALLAST

After crude oil washing small quantities of cargo remain in the tanks, pumps and pipelines. However, ballast loaded into such tanks at this stage should have a low oil content compared with ballast loaded into unwashed tanks, and this ballast should be easier to process through the load-on-top system. The oil content can be further reduced by draining pumps and lines or by flushing them into a slop tank before ballast is loaded.

Before clean ballast is loaded tanks may require water washing or flushing. Pumps and lines should be flushed with water.

8.4.12   CONTROL OF ATMOSPHERIC EMISSIONS

During crude oil washing hydrocarbon gas is generated within the tank. When inert gas is in use its entry can be controlled so as to maintain a slight positive pressure well below the level at which the pressure/vacuum relief valves operate. By this means both the venting of hydrocarbon gas from the tank and the entry of air from outside the tank are prevented.

However, during the subsequent ballasting of cargo tanks their atmospheres are displaced, leading to hydrocarbon gas being expelled to the open air. The careful application of simultaneous ballasting and cargo discharge on suitably fitted ships minimizes this effect.

8.4.13   CAUTIONARY NOTICE

A notice should be displayed in the cargo and engine control rooms, on the bridge and on the notice boards of ships which use crude oil washing. The following is suggested:

          THE TANK WASHING LINES ON THIS SHIP
          MAY CONTAIN CRUDE OIL. ON NO ACCOUNT
          ARE VALVES ON THESE LINES TO BE
          OPENED BY UNAUTHORIZED PERSONNEL.

Chapter 9

Fixed Inert Gas Systems

This Chapter describes in general terms the points to watch in the operation of a fixed inert gas system in order to ensure the safety of operations, and the precautions to be taken to avoid hazards to health. Reference should be made to the manufacturer's instructions and the installer's diagrams for further details, and account taken of instructions given by the tanker owner in operating the system. Reference may also be made to the ICS/OCIMF 'Inert Flue Gas Safety Guide' for fuller details of design and operating procedures of typical inert gas systems. It is essential that there is close co-operation between the deck and engine departments throughout.

9.1   GENERAL

Hydrocarbon gas normally encountered in petroleum tankers cannot burn in an atmosphere containing less than 11% of oxygen by volume. Thus one way to provide protection against fire or explosion in the vapour space of cargo tanks is to keep the oxygen content below 8% by volume, which gives an adequate safety margin. A means of achieving this is by using a fixed inert gas system connected by piping to each tank, which reduces the air content of the tank and makes the atmosphere non-flammable.

On tankers inert gas may be produced by one of two main processes:

> Ships with main or auxiliary boilers normally use the flue gas which contains typically only 2-4% by volume of oxygen. This is scrubbed with sea water to cool it and to remove sulphur dioxide and particulates, and it is then blown into the tanks through a distribution system.

> On diesel and gas turbine engined ships the engine exhaust gas will contain too high an oxygen level for use as inert gas. An inert gas generating plant may then be used to produce gas by burning diesel or light fuel oil. The gas is scrubbed and used in the same way as boiler flue gas.

Inert gas may be introduced into tanks by one of two processes:

> Dilution, when the incoming inert gas mixes with the contents of the tank in order to form a homogeneous mixture throughout the tank, so that the concentration of the original gas decreases progressively. It is important for complete replacement of the original contents of the tank that the incoming inert gas has a sufficiently high entry velocity to reach the bottom of the tank. The inert gas system should also have the capability to achieve the required degree of gas replacement throughout the tank.

> Displacement, the basis of which is that the lighter inert gas enters at the top of the tank and forms a stable horizontal interface with the heavier gas being displaced from the bottom of the tank through a suitable piping arrangement. This method requires a relatively low entry velocity of the inert gas although, in practice because of mixing at the interface, more than one volume change is necessary.

It must be emphasized that the protection depends on the proper operation and maintenance of the entire inert gas system. It is of particular importance to ensure the correct functioning, at all times, of the non-return barriers, especially the deck water seal, and non-return valve between the machinery space and the deck distribution system, so that there is no possibility of petroleum gas or liquid petroleum passing back through the system to the machinery spaces.

Care must be taken, particularly during cargo handling, ballasting and tank cleaning operations,

51

to ensure that a positive pressure is maintained in cargo tanks at all times, and that no individual tank is exposed to excessive pressure or vacuum. This is especially necessary during the discharge of cargo.

A mixture of the inert gas and petroleum gas when vented and mixed with air can become flammable if the hydrocarbon content of the vented mixture is sufficiently high. Normal safety precautions for gases vented from a tank should not be relaxed when the inert gas system is in use. Similarly there should be no relaxation of fire prevention or fire extinguishing procedures or arrangements due to the presence of the inert gas system.

9.2 OPERATION OF AN INERT GAS SYSTEM

9.2.1 INERTING OF EMPTY TANKS

When inerting empty tanks which are gas free, for example following a dry dock or tank entry, inert gas should be introduced through the distribution system provided on the tanker, venting the tank contents to atmosphere. This operation should continue until the oxygen content throughout the tank is nowhere greater than 8% by volume. The oxygen level will not thereafter increase if a positive pressure is maintained by using the inert gas plant as necessary. If the tank is not gas free, the precautions against static electricity given in paragraph 9.2.6 should also be applied.

9.2.2 LOADING CARGO OR BALLAST INTO TANKS IN AN INERT CONDITION

The inert gas supply should be shut off and the tanks vented through the appropriate vent system. In the case of simultaneous ballasting and cargo discharge, venting to the atmosphere can be minimized by interconnecting the tanks through the inert gas mains.

9.2.3 LOADED PASSAGE

A positive pressure of inert gas may be maintained in the ullage space to prevent the ingress of air. If the pressure falls below a lower alarm level it may be necessary to start the inert gas plant to restore adequate pressure. Loss of pressure is normally associated with falling air or sea temperatures, ship movement caused by bad weather or leakage from tank openings.

9.2.4 DISCHARGE OF CARGO OR BALLAST

The inert gas supply should be maintained throughout cargo or ballast discharge operations, so that inert gas and not air enters the tank. If manual dipping of a tank is necessary, pressure may be reduced while sighting ports are open. However, care should be taken not to allow a negative pressure to develop since this would pull air into the tank. This may require reducing the cargo pumping rate. Throughout cargo discharge, particularly when the boiler load is either low or fluctuating, the oxygen content of the inert gas supply should be carefully monitored.

If the inert gas plant fails during the discharge, the positive pressure on the system can be rapidly lost, and discharge should be stopped before the tanks come under vacuum. Masters should be guided by the owner upon the acceptability of the resulting delay while the inert gas plant is being repaired. Discharge without the inert gas supply should not be resumed without prior consultation with the terminal representative. If it is decided to continue the discharge, air will be drawn into the tanks and the overall protection provided by the inert gas will be reduced or lost. It will be necessary to apply all the precautions needed in the absence of inert gas including the precautions against static electricity set out in paragraph 9.2.6.

9.2.5 BALLAST PASSAGE

During the ballast passage tanks other than those required to be gas freed should remain in the inert condition and under positive pressure to prevent an ingress of air. Whenever pressure falls to the lower alarm level the inert gas plant should be restarted to restore the pressure, care being taken to monitor the oxygen content of the inert gas delivered.

9.2.6 STATIC ELECTRICITY PRECAUTIONS

In normal operations, the presence of inert gas prevents the existence of flammable gas mixtures inside cargo tanks. However, mainly in the case of a failure of the inert gas system, hazards due to static electricity may arise. To avoid these hazards, the following procedures are recommended:

If the inert gas plant breaks down during discharge and air enters the tank, no dipping, ullaging, sampling or other equipment should be introduced into the tank for 30 minutes after the injection of inert gas has stopped. After 30 minutes equipment may be introduced provided that all metallic components are securely earthed.

During the re-inerting of a tank following a breakdown and repair of the inert gas system, or during the initial inerting of a non-gas free tank, no dipping, ullaging, sampling or other equipment should be inserted until it has been established that the tank is in an inert condition. This should be done by monitoring the efflux gas from the tank being inerted, when it is known that the efflux gas is fully representative of the gas condition throughout the tank. However, if it is necessary to introduce a gas sampling system into the tank for this purpose, there should be a wait of 30 minutes after stopping the injection of inert gas before insertion of the sampling system. Metallic components of the sampling system should be securely earthed.

9.2.7   TANK WASHING

Before starting tank washing, the tank atmosphere should be checked to ensure that the oxygen content does not exceed 8% by volume throughout the tank. During the whole of the washing operation a positive pressure should be maintained on the system. Any inert gas supplied to maintain this positive pressure should be carefully monitored.

If the oxygen content rises above 8% by volume in a cargo tank, or in the slop tank, or a negative pressure develops in a tank, the washing should be stopped and the tank purged with inert gas until the oxygen level is 8% by volume or less throughout.

9.2.8   GAS FREEING FOR ENTRY

All flushing and washing should be done while the tank is in an inert condition.

The tank should then be purged with inert gas to reduce the hydrocarbon content to 2% by volume or less so that during the subsequent gas freeing no portion of the tank atmosphere is brought within the flammable range. The hydrocarbon content may be measured with an appropriate meter designed to measure the percentage of hydrocarbon gas in an oxygen deficient atmosphere. The usual combustible gas indicator is not suitable for this purpose.

The tank should then be gas freed.

Before starting to gas free, the tank should be isolated from other tanks which may contain inert gas or flammable gas mixtures. When portable fans or fixed fans connected to the cargo pipeline system are used to introduce air into the tank, the inert gas inlet into the tank should be blanked or valved off. If the inert gas system fan is employed operating on fresh air, the line back to the inert gas source, and each tank inlet on the inert gas main into the tanks which are to be kept inerted, should be valved or blanked off.

To ensure dilution of toxic components of flue gas as well as other gases present to below their threshold limit values, gas freeing should continue until, firstly, tests with an oxygen meter show a steady oxygen reading of 21% by volume and, secondly, tests with a combustible gas indicator show less than 1% LFL.

Positive fresh air ventilation should be maintained throughout the period that men are working in the tanks.

When other tanks in an inert condition are adjacent or interconnected by a pipeline etc. to the tank being entered, personnel should be alert to the possibility of leakage of inert gas into the gas free tank through bulkhead fractures, defective valves etc. Risk of this occurring can be minimized by keeping the inert gas pressure just above the lower alarm limits.

9.3   PRECAUTIONS TO BE TAKEN TO AVOID HAZARDS TO HEALTH

9.3.1   INERT GAS ON DECK

If gases are vented at low level and the cargo hatches, ullage caps or other tank vents are used as outlets localized areas around these can contain levels of gases in harmful concentrations, and can also be depleted in oxygen. In these conditions work on deck should not be undertaken for prolonged periods except when measurements show the hydrocarbon gas content of the atmosphere in the working area to be below 1% LFL and the oxygen content 21% by volume.

There are some wind conditions which may bring gases back down onto the deck even from specially designed purge pipes, and if these conditions are suspected combustible gas indicator and oxygen meter checks of working areas on deck should be made.

9.3.2   ULLAGING AND INSPECTION OF TANKS FROM CARGO HATCHES

The low oxygen content of inert gas can rapidly cause asphyxiation. Care should therefore be taken to avoid standing in the path of vented gas.

9.3.3   ENTRY INTO CARGO TANKS

Entry into cargo tanks should be permitted only after they have been gas freed as described in paragraph 9.2.8. The safety precautions set out in paragraph 10.4.1 should be observed. Consideration should be given to carrying a personal oxygen deficiency alarm. If the hydrocarbon and oxygen levels specified in paragraph 9.2.8 cannot be achieved, entry should be permitted only in exceptional circumstances and when there is no practicable alternative. Personnel must wear breathing apparatus (see paragraph 10.4.4).

9.3.4   SCRUBBER AND CONDENSATE WATER

Inert gas scrubber effluent water is acidic. Condensate water which tends to collect in the distribution pipes, particularly the deck main, is often even more acidic than the effluent and is highly corrosive.

Care should be taken to avoid unnecessary skin contact with either effluent or condensate water. Particular care should also be taken to avoid all contact with the eyes and protective goggles should be worn.

Chapter 10

Entry into Enclosed Spaces

This Chapter describes the tests to be carried out to determine whether or not an enclosed space is safe for entry. The conditions for entry are set out as well as the precautions to be taken while work is being carried out in enclosed spaces. The Chapter also covers breathing apparatus for use in unsafe atmospheres and rescue from enclosed spaces.

10.1 **HAZARDS**

10.1.1   HYDROCARBON GAS

During the carriage and after the discharge of volatile petroleum, the presence of hydrocarbon gas should always be suspected in empty compartments for the following reasons:

Petroleum may have leaked into compartments, including pumprooms, cofferdams, permanent ballast tanks and tanks adjacent to those that have carried cargo.

Petroleum may remain on the sides and bottoms of tanks that have been discharged, even after cleaning and ventilation.

Sludge and scale in a tank which has been declared gas free may give off further gas if disturbed or subjected to a rise in temperature.

Petroleum may remain in cargo and ballast pipelines and pumps which are opened for renewal of gaskets, glands, etc.

The presence of gas should similarly be suspected in empty compartments if non-volatile petroleum has been loaded into non-gas free tanks.

10.1.2   OXYGEN DEFICIENCY

Lack of oxygen should always be suspected in compartments that have been closed for some time, particularly if they have contained water or have been subjected to damp or humid conditions. Entry should never be permitted without breathing apparatus until such compartments have been thoroughly ventilated and, where an oxygen meter is available, test readings indicate an oxygen level of 21% by volume throughout these spaces.

10.1.3   OTHER HAZARDS

These include the toxic hazards due to the presence of benzene and hydrogen sulphide for which appropriate tests and precautions should be taken. The risk of injury due to poor lighting, slippery surfaces, etc, should also be borne in mind, and appropriate precautions taken.

10.2 **GAS TESTS FOR ENTRY OR WORK**

10.2.1   GENERAL

Any decision to enter a compartment where there has been or there could be gas should be made only after investigation with approved gas testing equipment which has itself recently been checked.

It is essential that all gas testing equipment used is of an approved type, is correctly maintained and where appropriate is frequently checked against standard samples. Gas testing should be done by personnel who have been trained in the use of the equipment and are sufficiently knowledgeable to interpret correctly the results obtained.

Care should be taken to obtain a representative cross-section of the compartment by sampling at several depths and through as many deck openings as practicable. When tests are being carried out from deck level, ventilation should be stopped.

Where it has been decided that a tank is gas free, that decision applies to the condition of the tank only at the time of the tests and gives no assurance that the tank will remain in a gas free condition.

Even after a tank or compartment has been found to be gas free, local pockets of gas should always be suspected. Hence, when descending to the lower part of a tank or compartment further gas tests should be made. Regeneration of gas should always be considered as possible even after loose scale has been removed.

While men remain in a compartment ventilation should be continued and frequent gas tests appropriate to the work in hand or to any change in conditions should be made. In particular, tests should be made before each daily resumption of work or after any interruption or break in the work. Tests should be so arranged that a result representative of the condition of the entire space is obtained.

10.2.2 HYDROCARBON GAS

To be safe for entry whether for inspection, cold work or hot work, a reading of nil (and certainly no higher than 1% LFL) should be obtained on a combustible gas indicator (see paragraphs 8.3.3 and 8.3.4).

10.2.3 BENZENE

It is difficult to determine in practical terms the level at which benzene as a component of petroleum products starts to present a hazard, but, in the absence of statutory regulations or advice from the owners of the cargo, it is prudent to check for benzene vapour before entering tanks which have contained petroleum products such as motor gasolines, special boiling point products, solvents etc, to ensure that the threshold limit value (TLV) of 10 parts per million is not exceeded.

Tests for benzene at this concentration can only be made with a special indicator and not a combustible gas indicator (see Chapter 17).

10.2.4 HYDROGEN SULPHIDE

Although a tank which has contained sour crude or sour products will contain hydrogen sulphide, if the tank is washed and ventilated and tests for hydrocarbon gas show the quantity present to be less than 1% LFL, the threshold limit value for hydrogen sulphide of 10 parts per million will not be exceeded in the tank atmosphere.

10.2.5 OXYGEN DEFICIENCY

Before entry into any compartment or space which has been closed for any length of time, the atmosphere should be tested with an oxygen meter to check that the normal oxygen in air level of 21% by volume is present.

On a vessel fitted with an inert gas system, the atmosphere of any space or compartment which has been previously inerted, or is adjacent to an inerted tank, or is interconnected in any way with the inert gas system or an inerted tank, should be tested with an oxygen meter to check that there is no oxygen deficiency before entry.

10.2.6 TOXIC COMPONENTS OF FLUE GAS

The dilution of the toxic components of flue gas during gas freeing can be monitored by implication using the methods described in paragraph 9.2.8.

10.3 BREATHING APPARATUS

10.3.1 GENERAL

Breathing apparatus should be worn whenever entry is made into a space which contains toxic gas or smoke, or which is deficient in oxygen. It should also be worn if there is a possibility that any of these conditions may exist or occur during the period of occupation.

Breathing apparatus is designed to provide the wearer with an adequate supply of air. The air can either be carried by the user in portable cylinders or supplied through a hose from a source of air.

Gas masks and canisters of the type which depend on chemical absorbents to protect the wearer from poisonous gases do not give protection against petroleum gas in high concentrations nor against oxygen deficiency. Gas masks do not manufacture or provide oxygen. They should never be used instead of breathing apparatus.

10.3.2   FRESH AIR BREATHING APPARATUS

In its simplest form, breathing apparatus consists of a hose leading from a source of fresh air to the face mask worn by the user. Earlier outfits have a helmet fitting over the head of the user instead of a face mask and some of these are still in service. Air is usually forced along the supply hose by bellows or rotary pump.

When using this equipment the following precautions should be taken:

The air supply point must be in fresh air.

All hose couplings and terminal connections must be tight.

The face mask or helmet should be checked and adjusted to ensure that it is air tight.

The bellows or blower must be checked to ensure that it is delivering a positive pressure.

A positive pressure must be maintained to the mask or helmet throughout the period of use.

The total length of air hose used should not exceed 37 metres (120 feet).

The wearer should keep his air line clear of projections.

If the wearer has reason to suspect the efficiency of the equipment he should leave the compartment immediately.

10.3.3   SELF CONTAINED BREATHING APPARATUS

This consists of a portable supply of compressed air contained in a cylinder or cylinders attached to a carrying frame and harness, worn by the user. Air is provided to the user through a face mask which can be adjusted to give an air tight fit. A pressure gauge indicates the pressure in the cylinder and an audible alarm sounds when the supply is running low. Air is admitted to the face mask through a demand valve which opens when the wearer inhales. The demand valve can be by-passed giving an additional flow of air into the face mask. On non-positive pressure face masks the use of this bypass valve causes rapid depletion of the air cylinder and on these masks it should normally be kept closed.

When using the equipment the following precautions should be taken:

The face mask should be checked and adjusted to ensure it is air tight.

The pressure gauge should be checked before use.

The audible low pressure alarm should be checked before use.

The pressure gauge should be read frequently during use to check the air supply.

Ample time should be allowed for getting out of the hazardous atmosphere. In any event the wearer should leave immediately if the low pressure alarm sounds. It should be remembered that air supply duration depends on the weight of the user and the extent of his exertion.

If the wearer has reason to suspect the efficiency of the equipment he should leave the compartment immediately.

10.3.4   AIR LINE BREATHING APPARATUS

Air line breathing apparatus has been developed to enable compressed air equipment to be used for longer periods than would be possible using self contained equipment alone and to give easier access to confined compartments.

The apparatus consists of a face mask supplied with compressed air through a small diameter air hose. Air from a compressor is suitably filtered and its pressure is reduced to the design pressure required to supply air to the face mask. Because of the small diameter of the air hose, it is essential that the air pressure does not fall and the supply should be adjusted to maintain a constant pressure. If the compressor fails to maintain this pressure, the supply must be switched over to compressed air bottles provided for such an emergency. The user should then be signalled to leave the compartment.

The air line pressure gauge and the control for changing over to an alternative supply must be under the supervision of a responsible person who has received instruction in the procedure required.

It is recommended that a completely separate supply of clean air should be available under the direct control of the user.

When using the equipment the following precautions should be taken:

The face mask should be checked and adjusted to ensure that it is air tight.

The working air pressure should be checked before use.

The audible low pressure alarm should be tested before use.

The wearer should keep his air line clear of projections.

If the wearer has reason to suspect the efficiency of the equipment he should leave the compartment immediately, switching over to an alternative supply of air, if available.

The length of air hose used should not exceed 91 metres (300 feet).

10.3.5   MAINTENANCE

All types of breathing apparatus should be examined and tested by a responsible officer at regular intervals. Defects should be made good promptly and a record of repairs kept. Air bottles should be refilled as soon as possible after use. Masks and helmets should be cleaned and disinfected after use.

10.3.6   STOWAGE

Breathing apparatus should be stowed fully assembled in a place where it is readily accessible. Air bottles should be fully charged and adjusting straps slack. Units should be sited to be available for emergencies in different parts of the ship.

10.3.7   TRAINING

Practical demonstration and training in the use of breathing apparatus should be carried out to give personnel experience in its use. Only trained personnel should use self contained and air line breathing apparatus since incorrect or inefficient use can endanger the user's life.

10.4   CONDITIONS FOR ENTRY

10.4.1   ENCLOSED SPACES

No one should enter a cargo tank, cofferdam, double bottom or similar enclosed space without permission to do so from a responsible officer who has ascertained immediately before entry that the atmosphere there is in all respects satisfactory for entry. The officer responsible should ensure that:

Effective ventilation is maintained continuously while men are in the tank or compartment.

A responsible member of the crew is in constant attendance outside the compartment and knows how to raise the alarm in an emergency. In no circumstances should he enter the tank before help has arrived. The lines of communication for dealing with emergencies should be clearly established and understood by all concerned.

Lifelines and harnesses are ready for immediate use.

Approved breathing apparatus and resuscitating equipment are in an easily accessible position.

A separate means of access should be available where possible for use as an alternative means of escape in an emergency.

10.4.2 COFFERDAMS, DOUBLE BOTTOMS AND OTHER ENCLOSED SPACES

Before entry into these spaces, the oxygen content should be ensured in all cases by thorough ventilation and tests should be carried out with an oxygen meter if available.

Toxic gas should always be suspected in cofferdams and double bottoms into which volatile petroleum could have leaked. The same precautions as for entry into cargo tanks should therefore be observed.

10.4.3 PUMPROOMS

The precautions for entry set out in Section 2.15 should be observed.

10.4.4 NON-GAS FREE AND SUSPECT COMPARTMENTS

It is stressed that entry into tanks which are not gas free or are oxygen deficient should only be permitted in exceptional circumstances and when there is no practicable alternative. In this highly hazardous situation, the personnel must be well trained in the use of breathing apparatus and aware of the dangers of removing their breathing apparatus while in the hostile atmosphere.

When it is necessary to enter a tank or compartment where it is suspected that the atmosphere contains toxic gas or is deficient in oxygen, or that these conditions are likely to occur during the period of occupation, an officer should be responsible for continuous supervision of the operation and should ensure that:

Ventilation is provided where possible.

Personnel wear breathing apparatus and lifeline.

Means of communication are provided and a system of signals is agreed and understood by the personnel involved.

Spare sets of breathing apparatus and resuscitators are available outside the compartment.

Any essential work that is to be undertaken is carried out in a manner that will avoid creating an ignition hazard.

10.4.5 NOTICES

Suitable notices should be prominently displayed to inform personnel of the precautions to be taken when entering tanks or other enclosed spaces, and of any restrictions placed upon the permitted work.

10.5 WORK IN ENCLOSED SPACES

10.5.1 GENERAL

All the conditions for entry should be observed.

Before work is undertaken, a check should be made that no loose scale or sludge exists in the vicinity which, if disturbed or heated, could give off toxic or flammable gases. Effective ventilation should be maintained and, where practicable, directed over the area concerned.

10.5.2   **OPENING UP EQUIPMENT AND FITTINGS**

Whenever cargo pumps, pipelines, valves, or heating coils are to be opened, they should first be flushed with water. Even then there is a possibility that some cargo may remain which may be a source of further gas. Special care must therefore be taken whenever such equipment is opened up, and additional gas tests should be made.

10.5.3   **USE OF TOOLS**

Tools should not be carried by personnel, but lowered into compartments in a canvas bag or bucket to avoid their being dropped. Before any hammering or chipping is undertaken or any power tool is used, the responsible officer should be satisfied that there is no likelihood of there being petroleum gas in the vicinity. See Chapter 2 for general precautions relating to hand tools.

10.5.4   **ELECTRIC LIGHTS AND ELECTRICAL EQUIPMENT**

Unless a compartment is gas free for hot work, that is the gas concentration is less than 1% LFL, and all sludge, scale and sediment that might form a source of gas has been removed, no electric lights or electrical equipment should be taken into the compartment, other than approved air driven lamps, unless the lights or equipment are intrinsically safe, or are contained in an approved explosion proof housing (see Section 2.4).

In port, any local regulations concerning the use of electric lights or electrical equipment should be followed.

10.5.5   **REMOVAL OF SLUDGE, SCALE AND SEDIMENT**

Before work is started, tests with a combustible gas indicator should give a reading of nil (no higher than 1% LFL). Periodic gas tests should be made and continuous ventilation should be maintained throughout the period men are in the compartment.

There may be increases in gas concentration in the immediate vicinity of the work, and care should be taken to ensure that the atmosphere remains safe for personnel.

10.5.6   **COLD WORK**

To be safe for cold work, tests with a combustible gas indicator should give a reading of nil (no higher than 1% LFL) and it is advisable that any sludge, scale and sediment is removed from the area where, and below which, the work is to take place.

When cold work is to be undertaken alongside a terminal, the terminal representative should be consulted as the issue of a work permit may be required.

10.5.7   **HOT WORK**

Immediately before hot work is undertaken the compartment should be ventilated until tests with a combustible gas indicator give a reading of nil (no higher than 1% LFL). All sludge, scale and sediment should be removed from an area of at least 3 metres around the area of hot work (including reverse sides of frames, bulkheads etc). Other areas that may be affected by the hot work should be cleaned e.g. the area immediately below the place where the hot work is being undertaken.

Periodic gas tests should be made while the hot work is in progress and before re-starting work after it has been stopped. Continuous gas alarm detectors may be used as an additional safeguard. A suitably trained firewatcher should be in attendance in the compartment while any hot work is in progress.

All pipelines to a tank being worked on should be isolated, and adjacent tanks and spaces should be rendered safe by gas freeing, inerting, or filling with water. Other tanks which may not be gas free should be closed. Checks should be made that there is no ingress of flammable gases or liquids, toxic gases or inert gas from adjacent tanks or spaces by leakage into the working space. An adjacent bunker tank containing fuel may be considered safe as long as tests on the ullage space in the bunker tank with a combustible gas indicator give an essentially nil reading. If the hot work could cause heat transfer through a common bulkhead the adjoining space should either be filled with liquid to above the level at which work is being done, or inerted, or gas freed with all combustible residue on the bulkhead removed.

If hot work is to be done on any piping, valves, heating coils, or other equipment, they should first be flushed and opened to ensure that they are gas free.

Pumping of cargo or ballast, tank washing, and other operations which could produce flammable gas on deck should be stopped.

Adequate fire extinguishing equipment should be laid out ready for immediate use.

When alongside a terminal, no hot work should be allowed until the terminal representative has been consulted and approval obtained, as the issue of a hot work permit may be required (see paragraph 4.10.4).

At sea, consideration may be given to introducing a system for hot work permits (see paragraph 2.7.3).

10.6   RESCUE FROM ENCLOSED SPACES

When an accident involving injury to personnel occurs in an enclosed space, the first action should be to raise the alarm. Although speed is often vital in the interest of saving life, rescue operations should not be attempted until the necessary assistance and equipment have been obtained. There are many examples of lives being lost through hasty, ill prepared rescue attempts.

Preliminary organization is of great value in arranging a quick and effective response. Lifelines, breathing apparatus, resuscitation equipment and other items of rescue equipment should be kept ready for use and a trained emergency team should be available.

Whenever it is suspected that an unsafe impure atmosphere has been a contributing cause of the accident, breathing apparatus and, where practicable, lifelines should be worn by persons entering the space. A code of signals should be agreed in advance.

The officer in charge of the rescue should remain outside the space, where he can exercise the most effective control.

10.7   RESUSCITATION

Selected terminal and tanker personnel should be instructed in resuscitation techniques for the treatment of persons who have been overcome by toxic gases or fumes, or whose breathing has stopped from other causes such as electric shock or drowning.

Some ships are provided with special apparatus for use in resuscitation. This apparatus can be one of a number of different types. It is important that personnel are aware of its presence on board and that instructions are given in its use.

The apparatus should be stowed where it is easily accessible and it should not normally be locked up. The instructions provided with it should be clearly displayed in the following places:

    With the apparatus.

    In the officers' accommodation.

    In the hospital or medicine locker.

The apparatus and the contents of cylinders should be checked periodically.

Chapter 11

Combination Carriers

This Chapter sets out safety measures to be taken on combination carriers that are additional to those necessary for conventional tankers. In this context the term combination carrier refers to two main types, Oil/Bulk/Ore ships and Oil/Ore ships, and does not include other types of combination carriers, which may for example carry liquefied gas and petroleum or containers and general cargo.

11.1 TYPES OF COMBINATION CARRIERS

11.1.1 OIL/BULK/ORE (OBO)

The OBO ship is capable of carrying her full deadweight when trading as an ore carrier with cargoes of heavy ore concentrates. This type of ship is also designed to carry other types of dry bulk cargoes such as grain and coal, but in these cases she will not reach her full deadweight even though her total cubic capacity is in use.

Holds are usually arranged to extend the full breadth of the ship, with upper and lower hopper tanks and double bottom tanks. In some cases some holds have wing tanks.

Oil or dry bulk cargo is carried in the holds. Oil may in addition be carried in one or more sets of upper hopper tanks, and where there are wing tanks one set may also be used. Normally wing tanks for the carriage of oily slops are fitted aft of the cargo holds. Ballast may be carried in top and bottom hopper tanks and in double bottom tanks.

Conventional bulk carrier hatches, normally of the side rolling type, are fitted, with a special sealing arrangement.

11.1.2 OIL/ORE (O/O)

These ships are designed to carry their full deadweight when trading as a tanker and also when carrying heavy ore concentrates. They are not designed to carry light bulk cargoes.

Holds are fitted so as to extend approximately one half of the total breadth of the ship, and conventional wing tanks are incorporated with the main strengthening sections in these tanks, so allowing smooth sides in the centre holds. Hatches are generally one piece side rolling with a sealing arrangement similar to OBO ships.

11.2 SLACK HOLDS IN OBO SHIPS

11.2.1 GENERAL

Because of the broad beam and the size of the holds of OBO ships, the very large free surface in partially filled holds permits substantial movement of liquid which can result in:

Loss of stability.

'Sloshing'.

11.2.2 LOSS OF STABILITY

Particular care should be taken when loading or discharging liquid cargo from OBO ships to ensure that the total free surface effect of the cargo tanks and of any slack (partly filled) ballast tanks is kept within the safe limits of stability, otherwise a sudden and violent list can occur.

All ships are supplied with stability data, and loading and unloading instructions to comply with government requirements. These instructions should be carefully studied and followed. Generally it will be noted from these that no more than a specified number of holds or tanks should be slack at any one time.

Consideration should be given to the distribution of the deadweights along the ship taking account of the ship's longitudinal strength.

Before arriving in port, it is good practice to make out a programme for the loading or discharging sequence bearing in mind the free surface and load distribution as well as the trim if there are draught limitations.

Some OBO ships have a valve interlocking system which will only allow a safe number of tanks to have a free surface at once. As such systems can fail and in some cases be overridden, it is advisable to have an easily read notice exhibited at the loading and discharging control stations, and/or wheelhouse, stating the maximum number of holds that can be slack at any one time.

Terminal operators should appreciate that OBO ships are subject to loading rate limitations and to specific discharge procedures. If an OBO ship develops a list during loading, the terminal representative should investigate and collaborate with ship's personnel in deciding how the condition should be corrected.

On completion of loading of oil cargo, the number of slack holds should be at an absolute minimum. On occasions it may be necessary to reduce the quantity of cargo loaded in order to avoid slack holds. Particular attention should be paid to details given in the Stability Information Book.

11.2.3 'SLOSHING'

'Sloshing' is the movement of liquid when the vessel is rolling or pitching.

It can give rise to:

Structural damage caused by the slamming effect of the liquid against the ship's side or bulkheads.

An electrostatically charged mist in the ullage space in holds partially filled with a mixture of oil and water, such as dirty ballast or retained tank washings; this can occur even with only a gentle rolling motion.

A remote possibility of introducing compression ignition.

In order to eliminate these problems slack tanks (i.e. less than 90% full) should be avoided wherever possible. This may be difficult with an oil cargo, but it may be more readily achieved when the vessel is in ballast.

11.3 VENTING OF CARGO HOLDS

11.3.1 VENT SYSTEMS

The vent lines from the cargo holds may be led either to individual vent outlets fitted with high velocity vent valves or to a main gas line vent system which expels the petroleum gas through a riser at a safe height above the deck.

11.3.2 BLOCKAGE OF VENT LINES

Due to the movement of liquid within the cargo hold under rough sea conditions the possibility of liquid entering the vent line is greater than on a conventional tanker. Various trap systems may be incorporated, such as a U bend or a special valve, but the possibility of blockage should always be suspected after a rough voyage. This may also occur if the vessel has been in very hot weather which has caused the cargo to expand above the gas line outlet.

Drains are normally fitted in each gas line and these should be checked before discharging or loading of cargo commences or before transferring cargo, in order to ensure that the cargo hold is able to 'breathe'.

11.3.3   VENTING DURING CARRIAGE OF DRY BULK CARGOES

Before loading a dry bulk cargo all holds that have been used for the carriage of oil cargoes should be washed, gas freed and vented.

During the carriage of dry bulk cargoes the holds should be sealed from the main oil cargo pumping and gas venting system.

11.4   HATCH COVERS

11.4.1   SEALING

OBO and O/O ships' hatches have a much more onerous duty to perform when these ships are carrying liquid cargo than when carrying dry bulk cargo, as they are required to remain gas and liquid tight at all times, even when the ship is working in a seaway.

Regular attention should be given to the pulling down devices, for example by adjusting them and lubricating screw threads.

When closing the hatch covers, the closing devices should be evenly and progressively pulled down in the correct sequence to the manufacturer's instructions.

The cover joints should be examined for gas leakage when the compartment is loaded with liquid cargo and any gas or liquid leaks which cannot be stopped by adjusting the closing devices should be marked or noted so that the jointing material can be examined when opportune and the joint made good. Additional sealing using tape or a sealing compound may be necessary.

If the ship is fitted with an inert gas system the gas tightness of the hatch covers can affect the frequency of the topping up of the inert gas pressure in the compartments.

Most OBO or O/O ships use synthetic rubber for the sealing of hatches, and this material should be examined whenever a suitable opportunity occurs. It is also advisable to have on board a reasonable stock of jointing material of the correct sizes so that repairs can be carried out at sea.

11.4.2   RUBBING IN A SEAWAY

Generally the hatch covers on most OBO and O/O ships work when a ship is in a seaway and it is thus possible for the steel hatch cover to rub on the steel coaming. Investigations have shown that this is unlikely to provide a source of ignition for flammable gas. The joints between the hatch cover and hatch coaming should be cleaned before closing the covers down, especially after a dry bulk cargo has been carried. A compressed air hose with a suitable nozzle might be used for this purpose.

11.4.3   FOREIGN MATTER IN RUNWAYS

It is important to keep hatch cover runways clear of foreign matter to facilitate the opening and closing of the hatches. After rough clearing with a brush and shovel, runways can be cleaned using a compressed air hose or in some cases the washdeck hose.

11.5   TANK CLEANING OPENINGS

Due to the height of hatch coamings, which are partially filled on completion of loading a liquid cargo, all tank cleaning openings on the main deck have to withstand a positive pressure. It is essential therefore that the gaskets and tank cleaning covers make a perfect fit and the seats should be cleaned by wire brushing to ensure proper sealing prior to loading liquid cargo. In view of the positive pressure only bolted type covers are recommended and these should all be hardened down prior to loading a bulk liquid cargo.

11.6   TANK WASHING GUIDELINES

After discharging an oil cargo it may be necessary to wash the cargo holds and wing tanks before loading the next cargo. If the next cargo is to be oil then washing should be carried out in accordance with the guidelines given in Chapter 8. It is essential also to note the problems associated with slack holds described in Section 11.2.

If the next cargo is to be a dry bulk cargo it will be necessary to clean and gas free all the cargo holds in order to remove all traces of oil and sludge before arrival at the loading port. In so doing, appropriate precautions for entry into enclosed spaces, as described in Chapter 10, should be taken.

If the next cargo is to be a dry bulk cargo of high quality such as grain, sulphur, alumina etc it will be necessary to ensure a very high standard of cleanliness and in the case of bulk food stuffs the complete elimination of any taint in the cargo holds. In addition to conventional machine washing, extensive hand hosing and scraping will probably be necessary to remove all traces of sludge and oil from difficult spaces within the cargo hold.

Before the ship is cleared to load the dry bulk cargo an inspection will be necessary at the loading port and the degree of inspection will depend on the type of bulk cargo to be loaded.

11.7   CARRIAGE OF SLOPS WHEN TRADING AS A DRY BULK CARRIER

To enable them to land crude oil slops ashore using the ship's pumping system, many OBO and O/O ships are fitted with a pipe line and deck connection to receive a shore hose. This allows the crude oil slops to be landed to a barge or shore tank if these are available. This should always be done if the facilities exist. After discharge of slops ashore, the empty tanks should be cleaned and gas freed, or inerted.

If slops cannot be discharged and have to remain on board the following practices should be followed:

Collect all the crude oil slops into the slop tank specially designated for this purpose, cleaning and gas freeing the other tanks.

Fit blanking plates or some positive means of closure in all pipe lines, including common vent lines, leading to or from the slop tank to ensure that the slops and the slop atmosphere are isolated from other compartments.

Purge the partly filled slop tank with inert gas, and maintain a positive pressure within this tank at all times.

Do not use carbon dioxide in liquid form for providing the inert gas to the ullage space of the dirty slop tank because of the risk of static electricity generation.

The free fall of crude oil or crude oil slops into the slop tank should be avoided as this may cause electrostatic charge build up.

11.8   CONTAMINATION OF BALLAST TANKS ON OBO SHIPS

On OBO ships a serious operational problem occurs if there is leakage of oil from the cargo holds into the permanent ballast tanks.

The known weak points are as follows:

On vessels with vertically corrugated transverse bulkheads, cracks may occur in the welding seams between these bulkheads and the upper hopper tanks. On vessels where the upper hopper tanks and the lower hopper tanks are connected by trunkways or a pipe the contamination would therefore affect the lower hopper tank in addition to the area around the actual fracture. On vessels where the upper hopper tank is connected to the lower hopper tank by means of a pipe it may be advisable to install a valve in the drop line to confine oil contamination to the upper hopper tank.

In double skin vessels, leaks may be found in the upper welding seams of the longitudinal bulkhead between ballast tank and cargo tank abutting the sloped deckhead of the cargo tank.

Depending on the cargo carried it is essential not only to test the ballast tank for oil content but also the atmosphere for flammable mixtures and oxygen deficiency before entering and carrying out any repairs. Entry into such tanks should be in accordance with the provisions for entry into enclosed spaces in Chapter 10.

11.9   INERT GAS SYSTEMS

Inert gas systems may be fitted to combination carriers for use when trading as oil tankers. They should then be operated as described in Chapter 9.

An additional problem on combination carriers is that due to the large hatch covers there is a greater possibility of leakage of either petroleum gas or inert gas than with conventional tankers. There should be an adequate check system to minimise leakage and loss of inert gas.

11.10   VOID SPACES, DUCT KEELS AND PIPE TUNNELS

Between cargo holds a void space may be fitted through which various piping systems may be led and through which entry is necessary in order to gain access to tank valves and to double bottom tanks.

A single duct keel may be fitted along the centre line or on some ships two duct keels are fitted, one on either side. These carry all the piping for the ballast tanks and cargo holds.

Some duct keels and pipe tunnels may be fitted with wheel trolleys on rails to give easier access for personnel and equipment.

Due to the restricted natural ventilation all these spaces may be oxygen deficient. Furthermore they are adjacent to cargo holds and ballast tanks, and petroleum gas and inert gas could therefore leak into them.

Because these spaces may be difficult to enter and pass through, the precautions for entry into enclosed spaces given in Chapter 10 should be strictly applied to them. Additionally, it should be noted that the rescue of an unconscious person from such confined regions may be extremely difficult.

11.11   TESTING OF CARGO TANKS ON DRY BULK VOYAGE

Before loading a dry bulk cargo, any spaces which have previously contained oil and are not to be utilized for dry bulk cargo, e.g. wing tanks on an O/O carrier, should be cleaned and gas freed. These spaces should be regularly checked for petroleum gas on the loaded passage. If any gas is detected the space should either be gas freed and further cleaning carried out or inerted and segregated from other spaces.

11.12   CARGO CHANGEOVER CHECK LISTS

11.12.1   OIL TO DRY BULK CARGO

1. Flush all main suctions into cargo holds and tanks and strip dry.

2. Wash cargo holds and tanks including access trunks.

3. Gas free all cargo holds and tanks.

4. Hose off, blow through, disconnect and stow heating coils as required. Plug securing sockets as necessary.

5. Complete hand hosing and digging of holds and sumps to requirements of next cargo.

6. Drain cargo holds and suction wells.

7. Blank off main suctions to holds as necessary. Ensure stripping discharges to after hold are securely blanked.

8. Ensure sounding pipes to bilge wells are open and cleared of obstructions.

9. Fit main and stripping suction recess doors as necessary, also fit heating coil connecting pipe recess doors.

10. Wash cargo pipeline system thoroughly, including deck lines, bottom lines and pumproom.

11. Ensure gauging system, where fitted, is stowed or blanked as necessary to manufacturers' recommendations.

12. Drain, vent and prove gas free all gas lines and risers.

13. Blank off gas line to holds as necessary.

14. Set venting system to requirements of next cargo.

15. Check hatch cover sealing arrangements and holding down bolts.

16. Check ballast tanks, void spaces, cofferdams and pumprooms for flammable gas. Vent as necessary and prove gas free.

17. If slops are retained, ensure designated pipeline segregations are fitted, tanks fully inerted and relevant venting system adopted as necessary.

Cargo holds should not be used as slop tanks during cleaning due to the risk of sloshing. Holds containing dirty ballast should only be discharged when the ship is neither rolling nor pitching. Hatch covers should not be opened until the hold is gas free. All closing devices should be kept secured to prevent movement of the hatch covers.

11.12.2 DRY BULK CARGO TO OIL

1. Sweep holds clean and lift cargo remains out of hold for disposal.

2. Wash cargo remains off bulkheads with a high pressure water jet, stripping slowly to remove water, leaving solid residues.

3. Remove suction doors and attach securely to stowage positions.

4. Remove solid residues from the tank top and sumps, and prove that the stripping suction is clear.

5. Close off sounding pipes to sumps as required.

6. Remove blanks from main cargo suctions and stripping discharges to after hold.

7. Lower, secure in place, connect and prove tight heating coils as necessary.

8. Remove requisite blanks from gauging system and render fully operational.

9. Wash thoroughly all stripping lines to remove solid residues.

10. Open, clean and check all strainers in cargo system.

11. Check and clean hatch cover sealing arrangements, trackways etc.

12. Close hatches and check sealing and bolting down arrangements.

13. Remove blanks from gas lines as necessary.

14. Set venting system for next cargo.

15. Prove all valves and non-return valves in cargo system operational.

16. Inert holds prior to loading where applicable. During inerting process prove tightness of hatch covers, tank cleaning covers, access hatches and all openings into cargo spaces with soapy water solution.

Chapter 12

Packaged Cargoes

This Chapter provides guidance about the carriage on tankers of packaged petroleum and other flammable liquids and gases. It also refers to certain anti-knock compounds (tetraethyl lead and tetramethyl lead) which may be carried on petroleum tankers, but does not attempt to give guidance on the many hazardous chemical cargoes which may be shipped from time to time. Guidance on precautions to be taken when handling such cargoes may be obtained from the ICS Tanker Safety Guide (Chemicals) or from the shipper.

12.1   **DANGEROUS GOODS**

Dangerous goods are classified in Chapter VII of the International Convention for the Safety of Life at Sea.

The master should only permit aboard the ship packaged dangerous goods which have been declared by the shipper of the goods as being properly packaged, marked and labelled so that they comply with the appropriate provisions of the International Maritime Dangerous Goods (IMDG) Code.

The master should ensure that the dangerous goods loaded in the ship are properly stowed and segregated as recommended in the IMDG Code.

Before accepting the cargo the master should check that he has received adequate advice on any special properties relevant to entering an enclosed compartment containing the cargo, and on procedures for dealing with any leak, spill, inhalation, skin contact or fire.

12.2   **PETROLEUM AND OTHER FLAMMABLE LIQUIDS**

12.2.1   GENERAL

The following procedures should be observed in addition to the general safety precautions for handling bulk petroleum.

12.2.2   LOADING AND DISCHARGING

Packaged petroleum and other flammable liquids should not be handled during the loading of volatile petroleum in bulk except by permission of the responsible officer and the terminal representative.

12.2.3   PRECAUTIONS DURING HANDLING

The handling of packaged petroleum and other flammable liquids should be supervised by a responsible officer.

The following precautions should be taken:

Stevedores should comply with smoking restrictions and other safety regulations.

When permanent hatch protection is not fitted temporary protection should be provided to avoid the risk of sparks being caused by hoists striking the hatch coamings or sides or hold ladders.

All hoists should be the right size to pass through hatches with ample clearance.

Fibre rope slings, cargo nets, or drumhooks on wire rope or chain slings should be used for handling loose drums.

Goods should preferably be palletised and secured. Pallets should be lifted with pallet lifting gear with safety nets. If goods are not presented on pallets, cargo trays or fibre rope slings may be used. Cargo nets are liable to cause damage.

Loose gas cylinders should be handled with cargo nets of a sufficiently small mesh.

Each package should be inspected for leakage or damage before being stowed and any found defective should be rejected.

Drums should be lowered on to a platform of dunnage on deck or in the hold.

Drums must not be dragged across the deck or hold and should not be allowed to slide or roll free.

Cans and drums should be stowed with caps and end plugs uppermost.

Each tier should be separated by dunnage. The number of tiers in height which can be safely used in stowing drums or containers is limited by the thickness of metal of which the drum or container is manufactured. Advice should be obtained from the terminal.

Sufficient suitable dunnage should be used to prevent possible damage during the voyage.

Cargo should be secured to prevent any movement during the voyage.

During darkness, adequate approved lighting should be provided overside and in the hold.

Empty receptacles, unless gas free, should be treated in all respects as filled receptacles.

No materials liable to spontaneous combustion should be used as dunnage or should be stowed in the same compartment. Attention is drawn to the combustible nature of certain protective packings such as straw, wood shavings, bitumenised paper, felts and polyurethane.

On completion of the loading or discharge and prior to closing hatches, the hold should be inspected to check that everything is in order.

12.2.4   ENTRY INTO HOLDS

Before entry into any hold which contains, or which has contained, packaged petroleum and/or other flammable liquids, all precautions for entry into enclosed spaces should be taken (see Chapter 10). Holds should be ventilated during all cargo handling operations. If handling operations are interrupted and hatches closed, the atmosphere should again be tested before resuming work.

12.2.5   ELECTRICAL EQUIPMENT

The use of portable electrical equipment, other than approved air driven lamps, should be prohibited in holds or spaces containing packaged petroleum or other flammable liquids, or on deck or in spaces over or adjacent to such holds or spaces, unless the ship complies with the conditions for the use of such equipment on tankers (see paragraph 2.4.2).

12.2.6   SMOTHERING TYPE FIRE EXTINGUISHING SYSTEMS

When packaged petroleum or other flammable liquids are being handled, the control valves of any smothering system in the holds should be closed and precautions taken to prevent unauthorised or accidental opening of these valves. On completion of loading or discharging operations and when hatches have been secured, any fixed smothering system that has been closed should be returned to operational readiness.

12.2.7   FIRE FIGHTING PRECAUTIONS

In addition to the precautions outlined in paragraph 4.2.1 at least two fire extinguishers of the dry chemical type and fire hoses equipped with spray nozzles should be ready for use while cargo handling is taking place.

12.2.8   CENTRECASTLE AND FORECASTLE SPACES

Packaged petroleum or other flammable liquids should not be carried in the centrecastle and forecastle spaces or any other space unless such spaces have been specifically designed and classified for this purpose.

12.2.9   DECK CARGO

When drums or other receptacles are carried on deck they should be stowed:

In a single tier only unless properly secured in containers.

On end with caps or plugs uppermost.

Well clear of all deck fittings, including tank valve controls, fire hydrants, steam pipes, deck lines, tank washing openings and ladders.

Adequately dunnaged and properly secured to the vessel's structure.

12.2.10   BARGES

Barge personnel should comply with the requirements of Chapter 4, as appropriate, particularly with regard to smoking, naked lights and cooking appliances, and, if alongside a tanker, with any instructions referred to in paragraph 6.11.3. Barges containing packaged petroleum or other flammable liquids should be allowed to remain alongside a tanker during the hours of darkness only if adequate safe illumination is provided and there are means of ensuring compliance with smoking restrictions and other safety requirements.

12.3   LIQUEFIED GASES

In addition to the general precautions for handling packaged petroleum and other flammable liquids given in section 12.2, the following should apply:

Pressurized receptacles should be suitably protected against physical damage from other cargo, stores or equipment.

Pressurized receptacles should not be overstowed with other heavy cargo.

Pressurized receptacles should be stowed in such a position that the safety relief device is in communication with the vapour space within the receptacle.

Valves should be suitably protected against any form of physical damage.

Oxygen cylinders should be stowed separately from flammable gas cylinders.

Temperatures should be kept down and hold temperature should not be permitted to rise above 50°C (122°F). Hold temperatures should be constantly checked, and if they approach this level the following precautions should be taken:

Ventilate the cargo hold.

Spray the containers with water while loading or discharging operations are being carried out in the direct rays of the sun.

Rig an awning over the hold.

Wet down the deck.

Spray the containers in the hold if necessary.

12.4   TETRAETHYL LEAD (TEL) AND TETRAMETHYL LEAD (TML)

12.4.1   GENERAL

Extreme care is necessary in handling anti-knock compounds due to the toxic hazards arising from skin contact or vapour inhalation. It is essential that before handling packaged cargoes of TEL and TML advice is given to the vessel's master about the nature and properties of the substances and that the recommendations contained in handbooks issued by the manufacturing companies are strictly followed.

Chapter 13

Emergency Procedures

This Chapter deals with the preparation of plans both by the terminal and by the tanker to meet an emergency that may in any way concern the cargo or cargo handling, as well as the immediate action to be taken in such an emergency. Particular attention is paid to the procedures to be followed and the action to be taken in the event of a fire, because this is potentially the most extreme type of emergency likely to be encountered, but much of the guidance is applicable in other circumstances, and it should be read with this in mind. It does not cover rescue from enclosed spaces, for which see Chapter 10.

13.1   GENERAL

All tankers and terminals should have ready for immediate implementation procedures to be adopted in the event of an emergency. Frequently the emergency will be a fire but the procedures should also cover other hazardous situations such as hose or pipeline bursts, cargo overflow, collision between ships, or a man collapsed in a tank. Similarly, the equipment to be deployed will often be fire fighting equipment, but procedures should also cover other emergency equipment such as breathing apparatus, resuscitators, etc.

The procedures should be familiar to the personnel involved, who should clearly understand the action they would be required to take. This should include the sounding of alarms, the setting up of a control centre and the organisation of personnel to deal with the emergency.

13.2   TERMINAL EMERGENCY PLAN

13.2.1   PREPARATION

All terminals should develop a terminal emergency plan to cover all aspects of the action to be taken in the event of an emergency.

This plan should allow for urgent preventive action by those at the location of the emergency. If this initial action is not successful in containing and overcoming the incident it must be possible quickly to mobilize the entire resources of the terminal and of any other local sources of assistance so as to make a concentrated effort to deal with the incident.

13.2.2   CONTROL

It is essential that the terminal emergency plan should make absolutely clear the person, or persons in order of priority, who has overall responsibility for dealing with the emergency. The responsibility, under him, for the actions of the various parts of the terminal organisation which may be called upon to participate in the effort to contain and control the incident must also be clearly laid down. Failure to define lines of responsibility can easily lead to confusion and to the loss of valuable time.

At major terminals it is probable that a control centre will be set up at a convenient central point, not adjacent to the location of the incident — possibly in the main terminal office. Particularly in the case of major fires a secondary unit, the forward control, may be needed to take charge of operations at the site of the incident, under the overall command of the control centre.

13.2.3   COMMUNICATIONS

The control centre should be capable of directing, co-ordinating and controlling, either directly or through the forward control, all fire fighting and other emergency activities including advice to shipping, and for these purposes it must have a communications system linking it with:

Within the terminal:

> Fire service (ashore and afloat)
> Personnel
> Medical service

Outside the terminal:

> Fire service
> Medical service
> Harbour authorities
> Tugs and launches
> Pilots
> Police
> Other appropriate civil authorities.

It may not in practice be possible for small terminals to implement all the recommendations regarding communications which follow but they should endeavour to deploy a communications system adequate for their requirements, including a fire alarm.

Reliable communications are essential in dealing successfully with emergency situations. Because of their importance, consideration should be given to setting up a secondary system to take over if the main system is put out of action.

13.2.4   COMMUNICATIONS SYSTEM

There are three basic elements which the system should be able to handle:

> Terminal fire alarm.
> Summoning of assistance.
> Co-ordination and control of all fire fighting and emergency activities, including movement of vessels.

The communications system must have the flexibility to cover operations:

> On a tanker.
>
> On the jetty.
>
> On adjacent water.
>
> Elsewhere in the terminal.

Most of the equipment should therefore be portable or mobile, particularly that for use by the forward control; moreover it should be of a type approved for any location in which it may be used. It is recommended that the most satisfactory system to meet all the requirements is a UHF/VHF radiotelephone system. Tugs, water borne fire fighting equipment and designated rescue launches, if available, should be permanently fitted with UHF/VHF radio telephone equipment capable of operation on the channel designated for emergency use.

For communication links from the control centre, the following are typical suggestions:

Internal fire service	Special fire alarm and normal communication system.
Forward control	UHF/VHF radiotelephone; normal communication system in reserve.
Personnel and internal medical services	Normal communication system.
Fire fighting craft and rescue launches	UHF/VHF radiotelephone; via habour or port authorities as reserve.

74

Ships at berths	Normal UHF/VHF radiotelephone link used in cargo handling operations. There may be occasions when it would be helpful to station a terminal man with a portable radio on a tanker at a berth.
Civil authorities including fire services, police and medical services	Direct telephone link with failure alarm, UHF/VHF radio telephone or public telephone system.
Harbour authorities, pilots, tugs and other harbour craft	UHF/VHF radiotelephone or public telephone system.

13.2.5 COMMUNICATIONS DISCIPLINE

All personnel should understand and appreciate the necessity for strictly observing rules laid down for using communications in an emergency. They should receive frequent instruction on such requirements, which should include the following:

All sections should be allocated a call sign which should always be used to identify the section concerned.

Calls, announcements and conversations should be as brief as possible consistent with intelligibility.

Calls, announcements and conversations should be interrupted only when the demands of another section are vital to the outcome of the emergency operation.

Calls from the control centre should take priority over all other calls.

Only persons authorised to do so under the terminal emergency plan should use the communications system.

A log may be kept at the control centre possibly on a tape recorder.

13.2.6 FIRE FIGHTING EQUIPMENT PLAN

A fire fighting equipment plan showing clearly the location and particulars of all fire fighting equipment on or immediately adjacent to the berth should be permanently displayed on the berth.

13.2.7 ACCESS TO EQUIPMENT

Fixed and portable fire fighting equipment, resuscitation equipment, etc. should be kept free of obstructions at all times.

13.2.8 TRAFFIC MOVEMENT AND CONTROL

Jetty approaches and jetty heads should at all times be kept free of obstructions to the movement of vehicles. Packed cargo or stores for a ship should not be stacked on the jetty in the path of direct access in case of an emergency. Vehicles brought to a jetty or on a jetty approach should not be immobilized and ignition keys should not be removed.

During an emergency traffic into a terminal or onto berths must be strictly limited to vehicles required to deal with the emergency or to render assistance. When available, and if it is practicable, local police should be requested to exercise control well outside the terminal so that the roads which converge on the terminal are kept free for essential traffic movement.

13.2.9 MUNICIPAL AND PORT SERVICES

A terminal emergency plan should make the best possible use of the services which can be relied upon to be available. In such circumstances success in dealing with an emergency could depend upon the degree of co-operation achieved and upon prior combined training carried out with these services. Frequent opportunities should be taken to have combined exercises simulating terminal emergencies.

If a terminal is located in an area where a concentration of industry exists it may be practicable to sponsor the setting up of a mutual assistance plan.

13.2.10   POLICE AND FIRE SERVICES

Any emergency requiring assistance beyond the resources of the terminal should be reported to the local police and the local fire services, as appropriate.

13.2.11   PILOTS

In an emergency the local pilotage organisation may be called upon, at short notice, to produce a number of pilots to advise in handling ships not involved, if partial or total evacuation of jetties is decided upon.

13.2.12   TUGS

If available, tugs may be required in an emergency to:

Assist in fighting a fire.

Unberth the ship involved in the emergency.

Unberth other ships in the area.

Tugs equipped with special fire fighting appliances may not be available during an emergency for unberthing operations.

Tugs with fire fighting equipment should be inspected regularly to ensure that the equipment and foam compound stocks are in good condition.

Tugs which come under the command of the control centre during an emergency should be fitted with a communications system which can be integrated with the system of the control centre.

13.2.13   RESCUE LAUNCHES

A launch or launches, if available, should be detailed in an emergency to act as:

Rescue launches for the recovery of personnel who may be in the water.

Evacuation launches for personnel trapped on a tanker or on a berth.

Launches detailed for these duties should have the following equipment:

A communications system capable of being integrated into the control centre system.

Fixed or portable searchlights for night operations.

Blankets, as personnel recovered from the water are likely to be suffering from cold and shock.

Portable boarding ladders to facilitate entry into the launch; men in the water may have little or no reserve energy and may be unable to help themselves.

Self contained breathing apparatus.

The crews of the launches should receive instruction in rescuing survivors from the water, bearing in mind that they may be seriously injured or suffering from extensive burns. They should also receive instruction in artificial respiration.

13.2.14   MEDICAL FACILITIES

Terminal and outside medical facilities should be alerted at once depending upon the nature of the emergency. As soon as possible they should be informed of:

Nature and location of the emergency.

Likelihood of casualties.

Whether medical staff are required at the location of the emergency.

As soon as details of casualties are known, these should be passed to the appropriate medical authorities, with names if available.

13.2.15 HARBOUR AUTHORITIES

The local harbour authority, if there is one, should be informed of any emergency involving the terminal, or ships berthed or moored at the terminal, with details of:

Nature and extent of emergency.

Name of ship or ships involved, with locations.

Nature of assistance required.

This information will be required to enable the harbour authority to decide whether to restrict navigation within the port area or to close the port.

13.2.16 EMERGENCY REMOVAL OF TANKER FROM BERTH

If a fire on a tanker or on a berth cannot be controlled it may be necessary to consider whether or not the tanker should be removed from the berth. Planning for such an eventuality may require consultation between a port authority representative or harbour master, the responsible terminal official, the master of the tanker and the senior local authority fire officer. The plan should stress the need to avoid precipitate action which might increase, rather than lessen, the danger to the tanker, the terminal, other ships berthed nearby and other adjacent installations.

If it is necessary to remove a tanker which may be on fire from a berth the circumstances may be such that the ship's crew is unable to assist. The terminal emergency plan should therefore make provision for manpower for closing valves, disconnecting hoses or arms, unmooring the tanker and for operating fire fighting equipment without assistance from the tanker's personnel.

The terminal plan should cover:

Designation of the person or persons in order of priority who have the authority to decide whether to remove from or retain at her berth a tanker which is on fire.

Action to be taken with respect to ships at other berths.

Designation of safe locations to which a tanker on fire can be moved under controlled conditions if it is decided to move the ship.

The decision on whether to remove a tanker under controlled conditions, or to retain it at the berth can involve:

Capability of fire fighting equipment at the terminal and readily available from nearby sources.

Availability of tugs for removal of the tanker from the berth.

Ability of the tanker to move under her own power.

Availability of safe locations to which a tanker on fire can proceed or be towed and possibly beached.

Availability of adequate fire fighting equipment and personnel to fight a fire if a tanker is towed to a safe location, which will probably be remote.

Proximity of other ships at the terminal.

Shipping and other facilities in the area and possibility of closure of the port for a period.

Relative investment and earning capacity of the tanker and of the terminal facilities that could become inoperative or be destroyed by the fire.

13.2.17 TRAINING AND DRILL

The extent of training of terminal personnel in fire prevention and fire fighting may depend upon whether there is a permanent fire fighting unit attached to the terminal or to a plant nearby, or whether arrangements have been made for speedy assistance from an outside source.

Selected terminal personnel should receive instruction in the use of the fire fighting and emergency equipment available at the terminal. All personnel working at terminals should receive instruction in fire prevention and in basic fire fighting techniques. Periodic refresher training should be provided, supplemented by fire drills.

Crews of tugs which can be used for fire fighting should receive instruction and training in fighting oil fires in co-operation with land based fire fighting services. In order to utilise fully the tugs' fire fighting equipment and potential during an emergency it may be necessary to supplement the crew with trained shore personnel. Opportunities should be provided at frequent intervals for combined practices involving the tugs and shore fire fighting services.

Opportunities may arise whereby a combined fire practice or conference can be arranged between shore personnel and crew members of a tanker at a berth, without imposing operational delay on either the terminal or the tanker. This would help to make the tanker personnel familiar with the fire fighting equipment ashore. Shore personnel would also have the opportunity of becoming familiar with the types and locations of fire fighting equipment on board and of being instructed on any design features on tankers which may require special attention in case of fire.

13.3 TANKER EMERGENCY PLAN

13.3.1 PREPARATION

Planning and preparation are essential if personnel are to deal successfully with emergencies on board tankers. The master and other officers should consider what they would do in the event of various types of emergency, such as fire in cargo tanks, fire in the engine room, the collapse of a man in a tank, the ship breaking adrift from her berth, the emergency release of the tanker from her berth, etc.

They will not be able to foresee in detail what might occur in all such emergencies, but nevertheless good pre-planning will result in quicker and better decisions and a well organised reaction to the situation.

13.3.2 EMERGENCY ORGANISATION

An emergency organisation should be set up which will take action in the event of an emergency. The purpose of this organisation will be in each situation to:

Raise the alarm.

Locate and assess the incident and the possible dangers.

Organise manpower and equipment.

The following suggestions are for guidance in planning an emergency organisation. Four elements should be considered, namely, a command centre, an emergency party, a back-up emergency party and an engineering group.

(a) Command centre

There should be one group in control of the emergency action with the master or the senior officer on board in charge. The command centre should have means of internal and external communication.

(b) Emergency party

This group should be under the command of a senior officer and should assess the emergency and report to the command centre on the situation, and advise what action should be taken and what assistance should be provided, either from on board or, if the ship is in port, from ashore.

(c) Back up emergency party

The back up emergency party under the command of an officer should stand by to assist the emergency party as requested by the command centre and provide back up services, e.g. equipment, stores, medical services etc.

(d) Engineering group

This group should be under the command of the chief engineer or the senior engineering officer on board and should provide emergency engineering assistance as requested by the command centre. The prime responsibility for dealing with any emergency in the main machinery spaces will probably rest with this group. It may be called on to provide additional manpower elsewhere if circumstances so dictate.

13.3.3   PRELIMINARY ACTION

The person who discovers the emergency should raise the alarm and pass on information about the situation to the officer on duty, who should alert the emergency organisation. While this is being done, those on the scene can attempt immediate measures to control the emergency until the emergency organisation takes effect.

Each group in the emergency organisation should have a designated assembly point, as should those persons not directly involved as members of any group. These personnel should stand by to act as directed.

13.3.4   SHIP'S FIRE ALARM SIGNAL

At a terminal the sounding of the ship's fire alarm system should be supplemented by a series of long blasts of the ship's whistle, each blast of not less than 10 seconds duration, or by some other locally required signal.

13.3.5   FIRE FIGHTING EQUIPMENT PLANS

Fire fighting equipment plans should be displayed permanently in prominent positions showing clearly, for each deck, the location and particulars of the fire fighting equipment.

13.3.6   INSPECTION AND MAINTENANCE

Fire fighting equipment should always be ready for immediate use and be checked frequently. Inspection of all fire fighting and other emergency equipment should be carried out by a responsible officer, and any maintenance work should be done without delay. As soon as possible after an incident there should be a thorough check of all the equipment used. All breathing apparatus used should be checked and bottles recharged, foam systems should be flushed through, etc.

13.3.7   TRAINING AND DRILL

Ship's personnel should be familiar with the theory of fire fighting described in Chapter 21, and should receive instruction in the use of fire fighting and emergency equipment. Practices and drills should be arranged at intervals to ensure that they retain their familiarity with the equipment.

If an opportunity arises for a combined fire practice or conference with shore personnel at a terminal (see paragraph 13.2.17) the master should make an officer available to show the shore personnel the locations of portable and fixed fire fighting equipment on board and also to instruct them on any design features of the ship which may require special attention in case of fire.

13.4   FIRE ON A TANKER AT SEA

Ship's personnel who discover an outbreak of fire should immediately raise the alarm, indicating the location of the fire. The ship's fire alarm should be operated as soon as possible thereafter.

Personnel in the vicinity of the fire should apply the nearest suitable extinguishing agent to limit the area of the fire, to extinguish it and thereafter to prevent re-ignition. If they are unsuccessful, their actions should very quickly be superseded by the operation of the tanker's emergency plan.

Any cargo or ballast operations should be stopped immediately and then all valves should be closed.

All doors, openings and tank apertures should be closed as soon as possible and mechanical ventilation should be stopped. Decks, bulkheads and other structures in the vicinity of the fire, and adjacent tanks containing petroleum or which are not gas free, should be cooled with water.

The tanker should be manoeuvred so as to enable the fire to be restricted and attacked from windward.

13.5 FIRE AT A TERMINAL — ON A TANKER OR ASHORE

13.5.1 ACTION BY SHIP'S PERSONNEL

If the fire is on board a tanker, the ship's personnel should take the same action, as appropriate, as if the tanker were at sea. The terminal should be informed without delay of the outbreak of fire on the tanker. The tanker's engines should be brought to standby. In addition it may be necessary for designated ship's personnel to stand by to disconnect hoses or metal arms.

13.5.2 ACTION BY TERMINAL PERSONNEL

If there is a fire at a terminal or on a tanker at a jetty, terminal personnel should immediately raise the alarm if this has not already been done. The terminal emergency plan should then be implemented and the terminal fire alarm system operated as soon as possible.

In the case of fire on a tanker the terminal representative should immediately contact the senior deck officer on board to ascertain what assistance can be rendered by shore equipment or by shore personnel. Shore personnel should stop cargo operations to all ships on berths at the jetty involved, close all valves, be prepared to disconnect hoses or metal arms and to assist in fighting the fire.

Details of the fire, whether on a tanker or ashore, should be passed to the control centre as soon as possible. Essential information should be given to the control centre such as:

> Name and location of tanker or tankers involved.
>
> Nature of fire.
>
> Nature of immediate assistance required.
>
> Nature of casualties, if any.

All ships at the terminal should be informed of the emergency and consideration should be given to the following:

> Whether to stop cargo operations and then to close valves on some or all tankers.
>
> Whether to stand by to disconnect hoses or metal arms on some or all tankers.
>
> Whether to put ships' engines on standby and to be prepared to unberth ships.

13.6 METHODS OF DEALING WITH FIRES

In all cases of fire, speed of attack and in raising the alarm are essential.

Although absolute rules cannot be laid down, the following are the initial actions recommended for different types of fire. Much fuller information is given in Chapter 21.

> Fire from minor spillage of oil on deck or jetty:
> Use dry chemical powder or foam extinguishers, or water fog or water spray.

Fire from large spillage of oil on deck or jetty:
Use dry chemical powder and follow up with foam or water fog or water spray. Surrounding risks should be cooled with water spray.

Fire from spillage of oil on surrounding waters:
Emulsify the oil with water jets or apply foam, as appropriate.

Electrical fires:
Switch off and electrically isolate the affected equipment; use carbon dioxide, halon or dry chemical extinguishers.

Fire in accommodation involving combustible material such as bedding:
Use water spray, close all doors and ports of affected and adjacent accommodation and stop all mechanical ventilation of accommodation. Continue water spray to avoid re-ignition. Breathing apparatus may be required.

Fire at sighting or ullage ports:
Direct dry chemical powder, foam jets or heavy water spray horizontally across the tank opening until it is possible to close it.

Fire in cargo tanks:
Use foam, or steam smothering if fitted, although the latter may be slow and hence not very effective. In the case of heavy oils use water fog or water spray.

Mast riser fire:
Cut off the gas supply to the fire if possible or inject steam at the base of the mast riser.

Major fire in pumproom or engine room:
Close down the pump room or engine room and stop mechanical ventilation. Use the ship's fixed fire fighting equipment. Use water sprays to cool the decks and structures in the vicinity.

Part II

Technical Information

Chapter 14

Basic Properties of Petroleum

This Chapter describes the physical and chemical properties which have the most bearing on the hazards arising in handling petroleum liquids. These properties are vapour pressure, the flammability of the gases evolved from the liquids and the density of these gases.

14.1 VAPOUR PRESSURE

14.1.1 TRUE VAPOUR PRESSURE

All crude oils and the usual petroleum products are essentially mixtures of a wide range of hydrocarbon compounds (i.e. chemical compounds of hydrogen and carbon). The boiling points of these compounds range from $-162°C$ $(-260°F)$ (methane) to well in excess of $+400°C$ $(+750°F)$, and the volatility characteristics of any particular mixture of compounds depend primarily on the quantities of the lower boiling point (more volatile) constituents.

The tendency of a crude oil or petroleum product to produce gas is characterized by the vapour pressure. When a petroleum mixture is transferred to a gas free tank or container it commences to vaporize, that is, it liberates gas into the space above it. There is also a tendency for this gas to re-dissolve in the liquid, and an equilibrium is ultimately reached with a certain amount of gas evenly distributed throughout the space. The pressure exerted by this gas is called the equilibrium vapour pressure, usually referred to simply as the vapour pressure.

The vapour pressure of a pure compound depends only upon its temperature. The vapour pressure of a mixture depends both upon its temperature and upon the volume of the gas space into which vaporization occurs, that is, it depends upon the ratio of gas to liquid by volume.

The True Vapour Pressure (TVP) or bubble point vapour pressure is the equilibrium vapour pressure of a mixture when the gas/liquid ratio is effectively zero. It is the highest vapour pressure which is possible at any specified temperature.

As the temperature of a petroleum mixture increases its TVP also increases. If the TVP exceeds atmospheric pressure the liquid commences to boil.

The TVP of a petroleum mixture provides a good indication of its ability to give rise to gas. Unfortunately it is a property which is extremely difficult to measure, although it can be calculated from a detailed knowledge of the composition of the liquid. For crude oils it can also be estimated from the stabilisation conditions, making allowance for any subsequent changes of temperature or composition. In the case of products reliable correlations exist for deriving TVP from the more readily measured Reid Vapour Pressure and temperature.

14.1.2 REID VAPOUR PRESSURE

The Reid Vapour Pressure (RVP) test is a simple and generally used method for measuring the volatility of petroleum liquids. It is conducted in a standard apparatus and in a closely defined way. A sample of the liquid is introduced into the test container at atmospheric pressure so that the volume of the liquid is one fifth of the total internal volume of the container. The container is sealed and immersed in a water bath where it is heated to 100°F (37·7°C). After the container has been shaken to bring about equilibrium conditions rapidly, the rise in pressure due to vaporization is read on an attached pressure gauge. This pressure gauge reading gives a close approximation, in bars or in pounds per square inch absolute, to the vapour pressure of the liquid at 100°F.

RVP is useful for comparing the volatilities of a wide range of petroleum liquids in a general way. It is, however, of little value in itself as a means of estimating the likely gas evolution in specific situations mainly because the measurement is made at the standard temperature of 100°F and at a fixed gas/liquid ratio. For this purpose TVP is much more useful; as already mentioned in some cases correlations exist between TVP, RVP and temperature.

14.2 FLAMMABILITY

14.2.1 GENERAL

In the process of burning, hydrocarbon gases react with the oxygen in the air to produce carbon dioxide and water. The reaction gives enough heat to form a visible flame which travels through the mixture of hydrocarbon gas and air. When the gas above a liquid hydrocarbon is ignited the heat produced is usually enough to evaporate sufficient fresh gas to maintain the flame, and the liquid is said to burn; in fact it is the gas which is burning and is being continuously replenished from the liquid.

14.2.2 FLAMMABLE LIMITS

A mixture of hydrocarbon gas and air cannot be ignited and burn unless its composition lies within a range of gas in air concentrations known as the 'flammable range'. The lower limit of this range, known as the lower flammable limit (LFL) is that hydrocarbon concentration below which there is insufficient hydrocarbon gas to support and propagate combustion. The upper limit of the range, known as the upper flammable limit (UFL), is that hydrocarbon concentration above which there is insufficient air to support and propagate combustion.

The flammable limits vary somewhat for different pure hydrocarbon gases and for the gas mixtures derived from different petroleum liquids. Very roughly the gas mixtures from crude oils, motor or aviation gasolines and natural gasoline type products can be represented respectively by the pure hydrocarbon gases propane, butane and pentane. The following Table gives the flammable limits for these three gases. It also shows the amount of dilution with air needed to bring a mixture of 50% by volume of each of these gases in air down to its LFL; this type of information is very relevant to the ease with which gases from the different liquids disperse to a non-flammable concentration in the atmosphere.

Gas	Flammable limits % vol. hydrocarbon in air		Number of dilutions by air to reduce 50% by volume mixture to LFL
	Upper	Lower	
Propane	9·5	2·2	23
Butane	8·5	1·9	26
Pentane	7·8	1·5	33

In practice the lower and upper flammable limits of oil cargoes carried in tankers can, for general purposes, be taken as 1% and 10% by volume respectively.

14.2.3 EFFECT OF INERT GAS ON FLAMMABILITY

When an inert gas, typically flue gas, is added to a hydrocarbon gas/air mixture the result is to increase the lower flammable limit hydrocarbon concentration and to decrease the upper flammable limit concentration. These effects are illustrated in Fig. 14-1, which should be regarded only as a guide to the principles involved.

Every point on the diagram represents a hydrocarbon gas/air/inert gas mixture, specified in terms of its hydrocarbon and oxygen contents. Hydrocarbon air mixtures without inert gas lie on the line AB the slope of which reflects the reduction in oxygen content as the hydrocarbon content increases. Points to the left of AB represent mixtures with their oxygen content further reduced by the addition of inert gas.

The lower and upper flammability limit mixtures for hydrocarbon gas in air are represented by the points C and D. As the inert gas content increases the flammable limit mixtures change as indicated by the lines CE and DE, which finally converge at the point E. Only those mixtures represented by points in the shaded area within the loop CED are capable of burning.

On such a diagram changes of composition due to the addition of either air or inert gas are represented by movements along straight lines directed either towards the point A (pure air), or

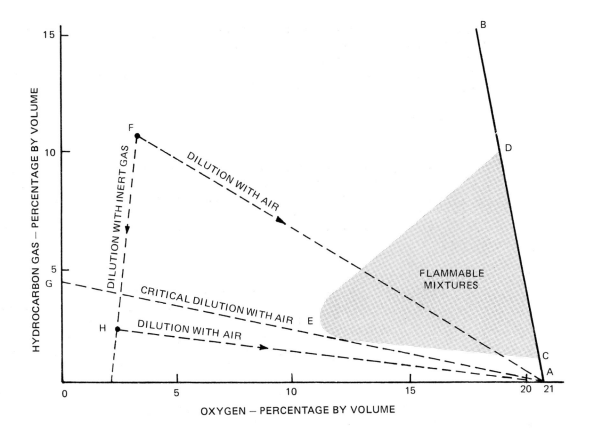

Fig. 14-1. *Flammability composition diagram—hydrocarbon gas/air/inert gas mixture*

This diagram is illustrative only and should not be used for deciding upon acceptable gas compositions in practical cases.

towards a point on the oxygen content axis corresponding to the composition of the added inert gas. Such lines are shown for the gas mixture represented by the point F.

It is evident from Fig. 14-1 that as inert gas is added to hydrocarbon/air mixtures the flammable range progressively decreases until the oxygen content reaches a level, generally taken to be about 11% by volume, when no mixture can burn. The figure of 8% by volume specified in this guide for a safely inerted gas mixture allows a margin beyond this value.

When an inerted mixture, such as that represented by the point F, is diluted by air its composition moves along the line FA and therefore enters the shaded area of flammable mixtures. This means that all inerted mixtures in the region above the line GA go through a flammable condition as they are mixed with air, for example during a gas freeing operation. Those below the line GA, such as that represented by point H, do not become flammable on dilution. Note that it is possible to move from a mixture such as F to one such as H by dilution with additional inert gas, i.e. purging.

14.2.4   TESTS FOR FLAMMABILITY

Since hydrocarbon gas/air mixtures are flammable within a comparatively narrow range of concentrations of hydrocarbon gas in air, and concentration in air is dependent upon vapour pressure, it should in principle be possible to evolve a test for flammability by measuring vapour pressure. In practice the very wide range of petroleum products and the range of temperatures over which they are handled has prevented the development of one simple test for this purpose.

Instead the oil industry makes use of two standard methods. One is the Reid Vapour Pressure test, which has already been described, and the other is the Flash Point test, which measures flammability directly.

14.2.5   FLASH POINT

In this test a sample of the liquid is gradually heated in a special pot and a small flame is repeatedly and momentarily applied to the surface of the liquid. The flash point is the lowest liquid temperature at which the small flame initiates a flash of flame across the surface of the liquid, thereby indicating the presence of a flammable gas/air mixture above the liquid. This gas/air mixture corresponds closely to the lower flammable limit mixture.

There are many different forms of flash point apparatus but they fall into two classes. In one the surface of the liquid is permanently open to the atmosphere as the liquid is heated and the result of such a test is known as an 'open cup flash point'. In the other class the space above the liquid is kept closed except for brief moments when the initiating flame is introduced through a small port. The result of this class of test is termed a 'closed cup flash point'.

Because of the greater loss of gas to atmosphere in the open cup test the open cup flash point of a petroleum liquid is always a little higher (by about 6°C or 10°F) than its closed cup flash point. The restricted loss of gas in the closed cup apparatus also leads to a much more repeatable result than can be obtained in open cup testing. For this reason the closed cup method is now more generally favoured and is used in this guide in the classification of petroleum. Open cup test figures, however, may still be found in the legislation of various national administrations, in classification society rules and other such documents.

14.2.6   FLAMMABILITY CLASSIFICATION OF PETROLEUM

There are many schemes for dividing the complete range of petroleum liquids into different flammability classes based on flash point and vapour pressure and there is a considerable variation in these schemes between countries. Usually the basic principle is to consider whether or not a flammable equilibrium gas/air mixture can be formed in the space above the liquid when the liquid is at ambient temperature.

Generally in this guide it has been sufficient to group petroleum liquids into two categories entitled non-volatile and volatile defined in terms of flash point as follows:

Non-volatile

Flash point of 60°C (140°F) or above as determined by the closed cup method of test. These liquids produce, when at any normal ambient temperature, equilibrium gas concentrations below the lower flammable limit. They include residual fuel oils, heavy gas oils and diesel oils. Their RVP's are below 0·007 bar (0·1 pounds/square inch absolute) and are not usually measured.

Volatile

Flash point below 60°C (140°F) as determined by the closed cup method of testing. Some petroleum liquids in this category are capable of producing an equilibrium gas/air mixture within the flammable range when in some part of the normal ambient temperature range, while most of the rest give equilibrium gas/air mixtures above the upper flammable limit at all normal ambient temperatures. Examples of the former are jet fuels and kerosenes and of the latter gasolines and most crude oils. In practice gasolines and crude oils are frequently handled before equilibrium conditions have been attained and gas/air mixtures in the flammable range may then be present.

The choice of 60°C (140°F) as the flash point criterion for the division between non-volatile and volatile liquids is to some extent arbitrary. Since less stringent precautions are appropriate for non-volatile liquids it is essential that under no circumstances is a liquid capable of giving a flammable gas/air mixture ever inadvertently included in the non-volatile category. The dividing line must therefore be chosen to make allowance for such factors as the misjudging of the temperature, inaccuracy in the flash point measurement and the possibility of minor contamination by more volatile materials. The closed cup flash point figure of 60°C (140°F) makes ample allowance for these factors and is also compatible with the definitions adopted internationally by the Intergovernmental Maritime Consultative Organization (IMCO) and by a number of regulatory bodies throughout the world.

A consequence of the margin of safety incorporated in the 60°C (140°F) flash point criterion is that some of the lower vapour pressure members of the volatile category may in some circumstances be handled at temperatures below their flash points so that the gas concentrations associated with them are below the lower flammable limit. Relaxations of static electricity precautions which take advantage of this are mentioned in Chapter 19 and specified in detail in

Chapter 7. These Chapters also deal with relaxations of static electricity precautions which are possible with volatile cargoes of high vapour pressure, such as gasolines, because the gas concentrations immediately above their surfaces are above the upper flammable limit.

14.3   DENSITY OF HYDROCARBON GASES

The densities of the gas mixtures evolved from the normal petroleum liquids, when undiluted with air are all greater than the density of air. Layering effects are therefore encountered in cargo handling operations and can give rise to hazardous situations.

The following table gives gas densities relative to air for the three pure hydrocarbon gases, propane, butane and pentane, which represent roughly the gas mixtures that are produced, respectively, by crude oils, by motor or aviation gasolines and by natural gasolines. These figures are not significantly changed if inert gas is substituted for air.

Gas	Density relative to air		
	Pure hydrocarbon	50% by volume Hydrocarbon/50% by volume air	Lower flammable limit mixture
Propane	1·55	1·25	1·0
Butane	2·00	1·5	1·0
Pentane	2·5	1·8	1·0

It will be seen that the density of the undiluted gas from a product such as motor gasoline is likely to be about twice that of air, and that from a typical crude oil about 1·5 times. These high densities, and the layering effects that result from them, are only significant while the gas remains concentrated. As they are diluted with air the densities of the gas/air mixtures from all three types of cargo approach that of air, and at their lower flammable limits are indistinguishable from it.

Chapter 15

Toxicity of Petroleum and Associated Substances

The toxicity hazards of petroleum and its products are described in this Chapter, together with those of inert gas. Although not strictly a matter of toxicity, the effects of oxygen deficiency are also described.

15.1 GENERAL

The toxic hazards to which personnel are exposed in tanker operations arise almost entirely from contact with gases of various kinds.

A convenient guide to the toxicities of gases in air is provided by their Threshold Limit Values (TLVs). The TLV of a gas is the highest concentration in air, expressed in parts per million by volume (ppm), to which it is believed that a person can be exposed for eight hours a day for an indefinitely long period without danger to health. TLVs are kept under regular review and the values quoted in this guide are those agreed at the American Conference of Governmental and Industrial Hygienists in 1976.

15.2 LIQUID PETROLEUM

15.2.1 INGESTION

The risk of swallowing significant quantities of liquid petroleum during normal tanker and terminal operations is very slight. Petroleum has low oral toxicity to man, but when swallowed it causes acute discomfort and nausea. There is then a possibility that liquid petroleum may be drawn into the lungs during vomiting and this can have serious consequences, especially with higher volatility products such as gasolines and kerosenes.

15.2.2 SKIN CONTACT

Many petroleum products, especially the more volatile ones, cause skin irritation and remove essential oils from the skin, leading to dermatitis. They are also irritating to the eyes. Certain heavier oils can cause serious skin disorders on repeated and prolonged contact.

Direct contact with petroleum should always be avoided by wearing the appropriate protective equipment, especially gloves and goggles.

15.3 HYDROCARBON GASES

The main effect of hydrocarbon gas mixtures on personnel is to produce narcosis. The symptoms include headache and eye irritation, with diminished responsibility and dizziness similar to drunkenness. At high concentrations these lead to paralysis, insensibility and death.

There are considerable variations in the toxicities of different pure components of hydrocarbon gas mixtures, but a TLV of about 250 ppm, corresponding to about 2% LFL, is considered to be applicable for the mixtures encountered during the operations associated with the transportation of petroleum liquids.

The human body can tolerate concentrations somewhat greater than the TLV for short periods; the following are typical effects at higher concentrations:

0·1% vol. (1,000 ppm) Irritation of the eyes within one hour.

91

0·2% vol. (2,000 ppm)	Irritation of the eyes, nose and throat, dizziness and unsteadiness within half an hour.
0·7% vol. (7,000 ppm)	Symptoms as of drunkenness within 15 minutes.
1·0% vol. (10,000 ppm)	Rapid onset of 'drunkenness' which may lead to unconsciousness and death if exposure continues.
2·0% vol. (20,000 ppm)	Paralysis and death occur very rapidly.

The smell of hydrocarbon gas mixtures is very variable, and in some cases the gases may dull the sense of smell. The impairment of smell is especially serious if the mixture contains hydrogen sulphide. The absence of smell should therefore never be taken to indicate the absence of gas.

The TLV concentration is considerably below the lower flammable limit and combustible gas indicators cannot be expected to measure concentrations of this order accurately.

15.4 BENZENE AND OTHER AROMATICS

The aromatic group of hydrocarbons includes benzene, toluene and cumene. The carriage of these aromatics in their pure form is outside the scope of this guide, but they are also components of such cargoes as gasolines, jet fuels and blendstocks. The vapour from aromatics is, in general, more harmful than that from the majority of hydrocarbons, but benzene, in particular which has a TLV of 10 ppm, presents a chronic health hazard after long term exposure.

Benzene should not be confused with 'benzine' which is a term loosely used to describe gasolines in general. The benzene content of many cargoes is relatively low, but there are some gasoline blendstocks which can have much higher levels e.g. a steam-cracked spirit. Consideration should be given to applying suitable safeguards to avoid undue inhalation of vented gases, particularly during loading.

Before personnel enter enclosed spaces where the presence of benzene is suspected, the concentration of this compound should be reduced as far as practicable. Gas tests should be made using instruments designed to detect the presence of benzene at low levels. Combustible gas indicators cannot be used for this purpose.

15.5 HYDROGEN SULPHIDE

Hydrogen sulphide (H_2S) has a disagreeable smell of rotten eggs; it rapidly deadens the sense of smell, however, and dangerous concentrations often cannot be detected by smell. Hydrogen sulphide paralyses the respiratory system; its action is dramatically rapid and an individual exposed to high concentrations collapses instantly, apparently dead. Rescuers wearing breathing apparatus should remove the victim immediately to fresh air and artificial respiration should be applied. Resuscitators should be readily available whenever oils containing hydrogen sulphide are handled.

The TLV of hydrogen sulphide is 10 ppm. The effects of the gas at concentrations in air in excess of the TLV are:

50–100 ppm	Eye and respiratory tract irritation after exposure of one hour.
200–300 ppm	Marked eye and respiratory tract irritation after exposure of one hour.
500–700 ppm	Dizziness, headache, nausea, etc within 15 minutes, loss of consciousness and possible death after 30–60 minutes exposure.
700–900 ppm	Rapid unconsciousness, death occurs a few minutes later.
1,000–2,000 ppm	Instantaneous collapse and cessation of breathing.

It is important to distinguish between concentrations of hydrogen sulphide in the atmosphere, expressed in ppm by volume, and concentrations in liquid petroleum expressed in ppm by weight. For example a crude oil containing 70 ppm (by weight) hydrogen sulphide has been shown to give rise to a concentration of 7,000 ppm (by volume) in the gas stream leaving an ullage port above the crude tank.

15.6   **GASOLINES CONTAINING TETRA ETHYL LEAD OR TETRA METHYL LEAD**

The amounts of tetra ethyl lead (TEL) or tetra methyl lead (TML) normally added to gasolines are insufficient to render the gases from these products significantly more toxic than those from unleaded gasolines. The effects of the gases from leaded gasolines are therefore similar to those described for hydrocarbon gases in Section 15.3.

15.7   **INERT GAS**

15.7.1   TOXIC CONSTITUENTS

The main hazard associated with inert gas is its low oxygen content. However, inert gas produced by combustion either in a steam raising boiler or in a separate inert gas generator contains trace amounts of various toxic gases which may increase the hazard to personnel exposed to it.

The precautions necessary to protect personnel against these toxic hazards are contained in paragraph 9.2.8. These precautions do not include requirements for direct measurement of the concentration of these trace constituents of flue gas because gas freeing the atmosphere of a cargo tank from a hydrocarbon gas concentration of about 2% by volume to 1% LFL, or until a steady 21% by volume oxygen reading is obtained, is sufficient to dilute these constituents to below their TLVs.

15.7.2.   NITROGEN OXIDES

Fresh flue gases contain typically about 200 ppm by volume of mixed nitrogen oxides (NO_x). The majority is nitric oxide (NO) which is not removed by water scrubbing. Nitric oxide reacts slowly with oxygen forming nitrogen dioxide (NO_2). As the gas stands in tanks the total concentration of nitrogen oxides falls over a period of 1-2 days to a level of 10-20 ppm by solution of the more soluble nitrogen dioxide in free water, or by condensation, to give nitrous and nitric acids. Further decrease below this level is very slow.

Nitric oxide is a colourless gas with little smell at its TLV of 25 ppm. Nitrogen dioxide is even more toxic with a TLV of 5 ppm.

15.7.3   SULPHUR DIOXIDE

Flue gas produced by the combustion of high sulphur content fuel oils contains typically about 2,000 ppm of sulphur dioxide (SO_2). Inert gas system water scrubbers remove this gas with an efficiency which depends upon the design and operation of the scrubber, giving inert gas with sulphur dioxide content usually between 2 and 50 ppm.

Sulphur dioxide produces irritation of the eyes, nose and throat and may also cause breathing difficulties in sensitive people. It has a distinctive smell at its TLV of 5 ppm.

15.7.4   CARBON MONOXIDE

Carbon monoxide (CO) is normally present in flue gas at a level of only a few parts per million, but abnormal combustion conditions and slow running can give rise to levels in excess of 200 ppm. Carbon monoxide is an odourless gas with a TLV of 50 ppm. It is insidious in its attack, which is to restrict oxygen uptake by the blood, causing a chemically induced form of asphyxiation.

15.8   **OXYGEN DEFICIENCY**

The oxygen content of the atmosphere in enclosed spaces may be low for several reasons. The most obvious one is if the space is in an inert condition, so that the oxygen has been displaced by carbon dioxide or nitrogen. Also, oxygen can be removed by chemical reactions such as rusting or the hardening of paints or coatings.

As the amount of available oxygen decreases below the normal 21% by volume breathing tends to become faster and deeper. Symptoms indicating that an atmosphere is deficient in oxygen may give inadequate notice, except to trained personnel. Most persons would fail to recognise the danger until they are too weak to be able to escape without help. This is especially so when escape involves the exertion of climbing.

While individuals vary in susceptibility, all will suffer impairment if the oxygen level falls to 16% by volume.

Exposure to an atmosphere containing less than 10% oxygen content by volume inevitably causes unconsciousness; the rapidity of onset of unconsciousness increases as the availability of oxygen diminishes, and death will result unless the victim is removed to the open air and resuscitation is applied.

An atmosphere containing less than 5% oxygen by volume causes immediate unconsciousness with no warning other than a gasp for air. If resuscitation is delayed for more than a few minutes irreversible damage is done to the brain even if life is subsequently restored.

Chapter 16

Hydrocarbon Gas Evolution and Dispersion

The gases evolved and vented during cargo handling and associated operations are reviewed. The dispersion of these gases in the atmosphere is illustrated by reference to the results of wind tunnel experiments. Finally the Chapter describes the problems which may be encountered with high true vapour pressure cargoes and the special precautions that may be taken.

16.1   INTRODUCTION

During many cargo handling and associated operations petroleum gas is expelled from cargo tank vents in sufficient quantity to give rise to flammable gas mixtures in the atmosphere outside the tanks. In this guide a major objective is to avoid the conjunction of such a flammable gas mixture and a source of ignition. In many cases this is achieved either by eliminating the source of ignition or by ensuring that there are barriers, such as closed doors and ports, between the gas and unavoidable sources of ignition.

However, it is impossible to cover every possibility of human error and every adverse combination of circumstances. An additional safeguard is introduced if operations can be arranged so that petroleum gas issuing from vents is dispersed sufficiently well to avoid flammable gas mixtures reaching those areas where sources of ignition may exist.

Gas concentrations external to cargo tanks present a flammability problem with the high vapour pressure members of the volatile category, the main types of which are represented by the following:

Crude oil.

Motor and aviation gasolines.

Natural gasolines.

Amongst the high vapour pressure distillate cargoes are the wide range of light distillate feedstocks (LDFs) and naphthas.

The gases from these petroleum liquids are denser than air and this has an important bearing on how they behave both within and outside the tanks (see Section 14.3.)

The gas which is vented is formed within the tanks, and the way in which it is formed has an important bearing on both the concentration when vented and on the length of time during which a high concentration is vented. Amongst the situations which lead to gas evolution are loading, standing of cargo in full or part filled tanks (including slop tanks), evaporation of tank residues after discharge and crude oil washing.

16.2   GAS EVOLUTION AND VENTING

16.2.1   EVOLUTION DURING LOADING

As a high vapour pressure petroleum cargo enters an empty gas free tank there is a rapid evolution of gas. Because of its high density the gas forms a layer at the bottom of the tank which rises with the oil surface as the tank is filled. Once it has been formed the depth of the layer increases only slowly over the period of time normally required to fill a tank, although ultimately an equilibrium gas mixture is established throughout the ullage space.

The amount and concentration of gas forming this layer at the beginning of loading depends upon many factors, some of which are:

The true vapour pressure (TVP) of the cargo.

The amount of splashing as the oil enters the tank.

The time required to load the tank.

The occurrence of a partial vacuum in the loading line.

The hydrocarbon gas concentration in the layer varies with distance above the liquid surface. Very close to the surface it has a value close to that corresponding to the TVP of the adjoining liquid. For example if the TVP is 0·75 bar (0·75 atmosphere or 10·8 pounds/square inch absolute), the hydrocarbon gas concentration just above the surface is about 75% by volume. Well above the surface the hydrocarbon gas concentration is very small, assuming that the tank was originally gas free. In order to consider further the influence of gas layer depth it is necessary to define this depth in some way.

When considering dispersion of gases outside cargo tanks, only high gas concentrations in the vented gas are relevant. For this purpose, therefore, the gas layer depth will be taken as the distance from the liquid surface to the level above it where the gas concentration is 50% by volume. It should be remembered that hydrocarbon gas will be detectable at heights above the liquid surface several times the layer depth defined in this way.

Most high vapour pressure cargoes give rise to a gas layer with a depth in these terms of less than 1 metre (3 feet). Its precise depth depends upon the factors listed above, and most of the advice with respect to vented gas given in this guide is intended for such cargoes. However, gas layers greater than 1 metre in depth may be encountered if the cargo TVP is great enough. Cargoes giving rise to these deeper gas layers may require special precautions (see Section 16.6.)

16.2.2   VENTING DURING LOADING

Once the dense hydrocarbon gas layer has formed above the surface of the liquid, its depth, as defined in paragraph 16.2.1, increases only very slowly. As the liquid rises in the tank the hydrocarbon gas layer rises with it. Above this layer the atmosphere originally present in the tank persists almost unchanged and it is this gas which in the early stages of loading enters the venting system. In an initially gas free tank, therefore, the gas vented at first is mainly air (or inert gas) with a hydrocarbon concentration below the LFL. As loading proceeds, the hydrocarbon content of the vented gas rises.

Concentrations in the range 30%–50% by volume are quite usual in the vent gas towards the end of loading, although the very high concentration immediately above the liquid surface remains in the final ullage space on completion of loading.

Subsequently evaporation continues until an equilibrium hydrocarbon gas concentration is established throughout the ullage space. This may be very high indeed, depending upon the cargo composition and temperature; values as high as 90%–95% by volume have been observed with crude oils. However, this gas is not vented other than by breathing of the tank, and thus only intermittently. When the oil is discharged this very dense gas mixture travels to the bottom of the tank with the descending liquid surface and may contribute to the gas vented during the next operation in the tank.

If the tank is not initially gas free the hydrocarbon gas concentration in the vent gas during loading depends upon the previous history of the tank and the following examples can be given:

In an unwashed crude oil tank loaded soon after discharge of a previous cargo there is a layer of highly concentrated gas at the bottom of the tank, with hardly any hydrocarbon gas above it. This gas is expelled immediately ahead of the layer which is formed as fresh cargo enters the tank.

In an unwashed crude oil tank after a long ballast voyage there is a homogeneous hydrocarbon gas concentration of up to 10% by volume throughout the tank. When the tank is next loaded this is the gas that is expelled until the concentrated gas layer immediately above the liquid surface begins to exert its influence. Thereafter this layer dominates the vent gas composition which is then not appreciably different from what it would have been in an initially gas free tank.

In a crude oil tank that has been washed or sprayed with crude oil but not subsequently purged with inert gas or gas freed a uniform gas concentration exists throughout the tank. Depending on the crude oil used and its temperature this concentration is usually well above the flammable range and may be as high as 40% by volume. This mixture is displaced from the tank throughout the subsequent loading until the possibly even richer gas adjacent to the liquid surface approaches the top of the tank.

Shortly after the discharge of a motor or aviation gasoline cargo, there is a layer at the bottom of the tank where concentrations of 30%–40% by volume hydrocarbon have been measured. This gas enters the vent system immediately ahead of the concentrated layer formed by the next cargo if loaded at this stage.

In motor or aviation gasoline tanks that have been battened down after discharge and not gas freed, uniform hydrocarbon gas concentrations as high as 40% by volume have been measured throughout the tanks. This concentration is expelled to the vent system through-out the next loading until the concentrated layer above the liquid surface approaches the top of the tank.

Note that in all loading operations, whether the tank is initially gas free or not, very high gas concentrations enter the venting system as the loading is being completed.

16.2.3 BALLASTING

The atmosphere in cargo tanks before ballasting is similar to that in a tank before the loading of oil cargo. High gas concentrations can therefore be expected to enter the venting system:

In the final stages of ballasting when this takes place soon after the discharge of a crude oil cargo.

Throughout a ballasting operation after crude oil washing or spraying. The prolonged venting of this high concentration can be minimized by using a common vent line during simultaneous ballasting and cargo discharge on suitably equipped ships.

In the final stages of ballasting when this takes place soon after discharge of a motor or aviation gasoline cargo.

Throughout a ballasting operation in tanks left standing without gas freeing after the discharge of motor or aviation gasoline.

16.2.4 GAS FREEING

In a gas freeing operation air is delivered into the tank where it mixes with the existing atmosphere in the tank and also tends to mix together any layers that may be present. The resultant mixture is expelled to the outside atmosphere. Because the process is one of continuous dilution with air the highest hydrocarbon concentration is vented at the beginning of gas freeing and decreases thereafter. For example, gas freeing of crude oil washed tanks can give concentrations as high as 40% by volume to begin with; gas freeing of a motor or aviation gasoline tank after standing would be similar, but in other circumstances the concentrations to be vented are much lower even at the commencement of the operation.

16.2.5 INERT GAS PURGING

If inert gas purging is being carried out by the displacement method, any dense concentrated hydrocarbon layer at the bottom of the tank is expelled in the early stages, followed by the remainder of the tank atmosphere as it is pressed downwards by the inert gas. If there is a uniformly high concentration throughout the tank, for example after crude oil washing, the hydrocarbon concentration of the vented gas remains high throughout the purging process until the inert gas reaches the bottom of the tank.

If inert gas purging is being carried out by the dilution method, the gas concentration at the outlet is highest at the beginning of the operation and falls continuously as it proceeds.

Whether the hydrocarbon gas at the outlet is mixed with air or with inert gas has no bearing on the dispersion of the gas after it has left the outlet.

16.3   **GAS DISPERSION**

As the hydrocarbon gas produced during loading, ballasting, gas freeing or inert gas purging issues from the vent or vents on the tanker it immediately commences to mix with the atmosphere. The hydrocarbon concentration is progressively reduced until, at some distance from the vent, it passes below the lower flammable limit. At any point beyond this it ceases to be of concern as a flammability hazard, because it cannot be ignited. Thus, there exists in the vicinity of any vent a flammable zone in space within which the gas concentration is above the lower flammable limit.

There is a potential danger of fire and explosion if this flammable zone reaches any location where there may be sources of ignition, such as:

Superstructures and deckhouses which the gas can enter through doors, ports or ventilation intakes.

The cargo deck, which, although it is usually regarded as free of sources of ignition, is a work area and thoroughfare.

A jetty alongside which, although it is usually regarded as free of sources of ignition, is a work area and thoroughfare.

16.4   **VARIABLES AFFECTING DISPERSION**

16.4.1   THE DISPERSION PROCESS

A mixture of hydrocarbon gas and air (or inert gas) issuing vertically from an outlet rises under its own momentum as a plume above the outlet. If there is no wind the plume remains vertical but otherwise it is bent over in the downwind direction. The rise of the plume due to its momentum is opposed by a tendency to sink because its density is greater than that of the surrounding air.

The flow velocity of the issuing gas is at its maximum as it passes through the outlet, and decreases as air is drawn into the plume. This air decreases the hydrocarbon gas concentration and hence the gas density in the plume. The progressive decreases in velocity, hydrocarbon concentration and density, together with the wind speed and other meteorological factors, determine the final shape of the plume and hence of the flammable zone due to the issuing gas.

16.4.2   WIND SPEED

For many years it has been recognised that the dispersion of hydrocarbon gas/air mixtures is inhibited by low wind speeds. This recognition is based upon experience on tankers and little experimental work has been done to obtain quantitative information on the effect of wind speed. However, measurements at Middle East terminals during loading operations with high vapour pressure cargoes have shown that hydrocarbon gas concentrations at or above the LFL can be detected at distances of at least 15 metres (50 feet) from a vent when the wind speed is low. The reported speeds below which this occurred varied between about 0·9 metres/sec (2 miles per hour) and about 3·6 metres/sec (8 miles per hour). Much depends upon the quantity of gas being vented and how it is vented, but experience at terminals seems to suggest that at wind speeds above about 5 metres/sec (11 miles per hour) dispersion is sufficient to avoid flammability risks.

16.4.3   RATE OF FLOW OF GAS

As the rate of flow of a hydrocarbon gas/air mixture of fixed composition is increased through a given opening several effects come into play. In the first place the rate of emission of the hydrocarbon constituent increases in proportion to the total gas flow rate and therefore the distance the plume travels before it is diluted to the LFL should be greater. On the other hand the higher the velocity the more efficient is the mixing of the initially hydrocarbon rich gas with the air and this tends to counterbalance the first effect.

In addition, at low rates of total gas flow the initial momentum of the plume may not be enough to counteract the tendency of the plume to sink because of its initially high density.

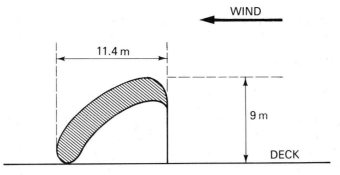

(a) Total Gas Flow 9·2 cubic metres/minute (325 cubic feet/minute) Approximate Loading Rate 465 tonnes/hour

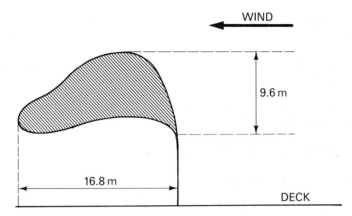

(b) Total Gas Flow 27·6 cubic metres/minute (975) cubic feet/minute) Approximate Loading Rate 1400 tonnes/hour

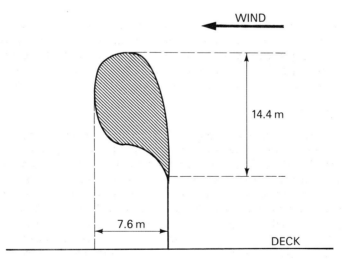

(c) Total Gas Flow 46 cubic metres/minute (1625 cubic feet/minute) Approximate Loading Rate 2300 tonnes/hour

Fig. 16-1. *The effect of gas flow rate on flammable zone*

Illustrations based upon wind tunnel data

Gas mixture	50% by volume propane in air
Diameter of opening	254 millimetres (10 inches)
Wind speed	1·1 metres/second (2·5 miles per hour)

The results of the interaction of these different processes at low wind speed are illustrated in Fig. 16-1. The gas mixture used in obtaining these diagrams was 50% by volume propane and 50% by volume air and is typical of that to be expected when topping off a crude oil cargo. At the lowest flow rate (Fig. 16-1(a)) the density effect predominates and the gas sinks back towards the deck. At the highest flow rate (Fig. 16-1(c)) mixing is far more efficient and there is no tendency for the plume to sink.

The flammable zones generated by the same operations with motor or aviation gasolines would be similar but with a more pronounced density effect, and this effect would be even more pronounced with a natural gasoline type cargo. Also, the greater dilution required to reach the lower flammable limit with motor or aviation gasolines (see paragraph 14.2.2) would tend to make the flammable zones larger than with crude oils, and this effect would be even more pronounced with the natural gasolines. Thus, the dispersion problem becomes progressively worse in going from crude oils through motor or aviation gasolines to natural gasoline type cargoes.

16.4.4   CONCENTRATION OF HYDROCARBON GAS

With a constant total rate of flow of gas, changes in hydrocarbon concentration have two effects. The rate of emission of hydrocarbon gas increases in proportion to the concentration so that, other things being equal, the extent of the flammable zone increases. Also, the initial density of the gas mixture as it issues from the opening becomes greater so that there is a greater tendency for the plume to sink.

At low concentrations, therefore, flammable zones similar to Fig. 16-1(c) are to be expected but they are likely to be small because of the relatively small amount of hydrocarbon gas. As the concentration increases the flammable zone tends to assume such shapes as Fig. 16-1(b) and 16-1(a) as the increasing density exerts its influence; in addition the overall size of the zone becomes greater due to the greater rate of emission of hydrocarbon gas.

16.4.5   CROSS SECTIONAL AREA OF THE OPENING

The area of the opening through which the hydrocarbon gas/air mixture issues determines, for a given volumetric rate of flow, the linear flow velocity and hence the efficiency of the mixing of the plume with the atmosphere. Effects of this kind occur, for example, in gas freeing. If fixed turbo-blower fans are used the mixture is usually vented through a stand pipe with a cross-sectional area small enough to give a high velocity and to encourage dispersion in the atmosphere. Small portable blowers normally have to be operated against a low back pressure, and it is usual to exhaust the gas through an open tank hatch. The efflux velocity is then very low with the outlet close to the deck, circumstances which encourage the gas to remain close to the deck.

16.4.6   THE DESIGN OF THE VENT OUTLET

The outlets from the venting systems on tankers take many forms. Some are simple openings so that the mixture flows out unimpeded in a vertical direction. In other designs louvres or cowls may be installed which have the effect of diverting the direction of flow either sideways or downwards. As an example of the effect of such devices Fig. 16-2 shows the result of installing a simple flat plate baffle just above a vent outlet. In this example the vent outlet is well above the deck; if it were lower extensive areas of the deck would be covered with a flammable gas mixture.

16.4.7   POSITION OF THE VENT OUTLET

If vent outlets are situated near structures such as deckhouses the shape of the flammable zone is influenced by turbulence produced in the air as it passes over them. A diagram illustrating the kind of eddies formed is given in Fig. 16-3. It shows how, on the upwind side, there are downward eddies below a level indicated by the line X-X and how, above and in the lee of the structure, there is a tendency for turbulent air to form eddies close to the structure. These movements can adversely affect the efficient dispersion of hydrocarbon gas.

If the rate of flow of gas is low there are marked effects in the lee of structures; examples are given in Fig. 16-4(a) and (b) which show a clear tendency for the gas to be pulled back towards and against the downwind end of the structure. Figure 16-4(c) shows the behaviour of gas from a similar vent upwind of the structure. The flammable zone in this case is little affected by the presence of the structure; both the eddies and the density of the issuing gas contribute to the downwind, downward migration of the gas.

100

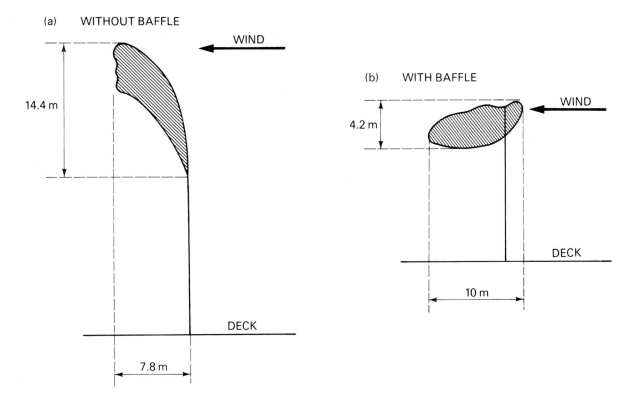

Fig. 16-2. *The effect of baffling a vent outlet on flammable zone*

Illustrations based upon wind tunnel data

Gas mixture	50% by volume propane in air
Diameter of opening	254 millimetres (10 inches)
Wind speed	1·1 metres/second (2·5 miles per hour)
Total gas flow	60 cubic metres/minute (2100 cubic feet/minute)
Approximate loading rate	3000 tonnes/hour

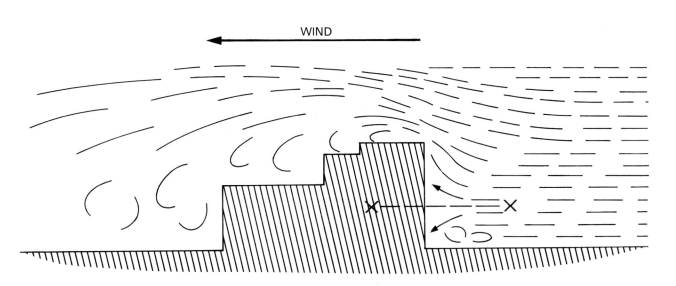

Fig. 16-3. *Pattern of air flow over a deck house*

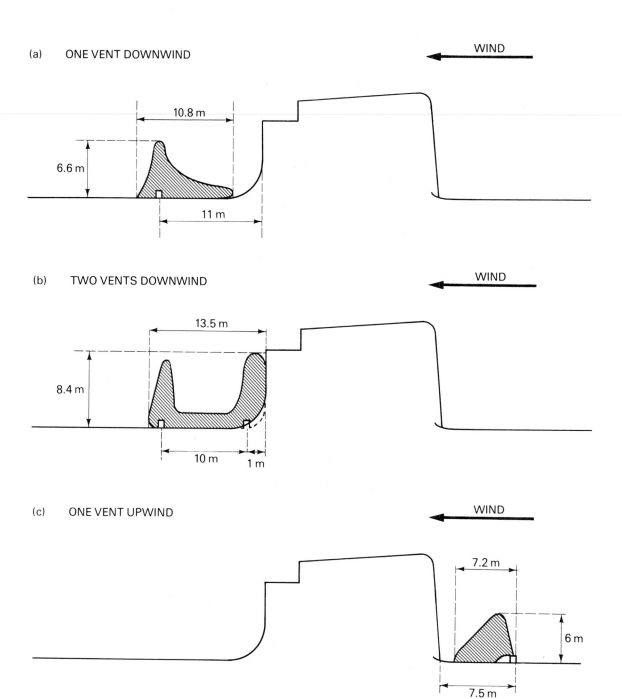

(a) ONE VENT DOWNWIND

WIND

10.8 m

6.6 m

11 m

(b) TWO VENTS DOWNWIND

WIND

13.5 m

8.4 m

10 m   1 m

(c) ONE VENT UPWIND

WIND

7.2 m

6 m

7.5 m

Fig. 16-4. *Flammable zones from vents near a deck house*

Illustrations based upon wind tunnel data

Gas mixture	50% by volume propane in air
Diameter of openings	152 millimetres (6 inches)
Wind speed	1·1 metres/second (2·5 miles per hour)
Total gas flow per opening	6·7 cubic metres/minute (233 cubic feet/minute)
Approximate loading rate per opening	330 tonnes/hour

If the efflux velocity from a vent near structure is high, it can overcome the influence of eddies. For example, Figure 16-5(a) shows the flammable zone from a vent situated only about 1·5 metres (5 feet) upwind of a deckhouse; the plume is almost vertical and only just touches the deckhouse. However, a somewhat lower rate of loading would have resulted in serious impingement of the zone upon the deckhouse. Fig. 16-5(b) illustrates the effect of an additional

102

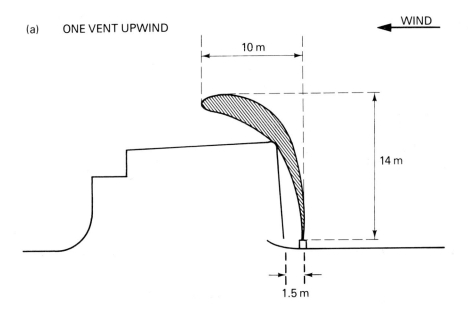

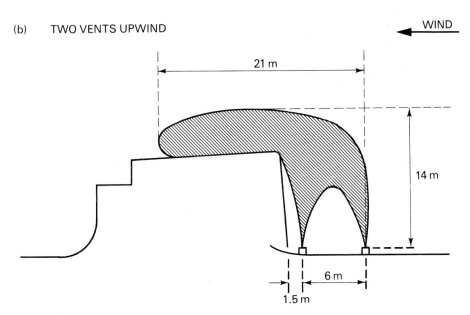

Fig. 16-5. *Flammable zones from vents near a deck house*

Illustrations based upon wind tunnel data

Gas mixture	50% by volume propane in air
Diameter of openings	152 millimetres (6 inches)
Wind speed	1·1 metre/second (2·5 miles per hour)
Total gas flow per opening	20 cubic metres/minute (700 cubic feet/minute)
Approximate loading rate per opening	1000 tonnes/hour

vent which doubles the amount of gas released. Partly as the result of eddies and partly due to a denser combined plume the flammable zone is in close contact with the top of the deckhouse.

16.5   **MINIMIZING DISPERSION HAZARDS**

The overall objective is to reduce to a minimum the number of occasions on which a flammable gas mixture may reach locations where there might be a source of ignition, despite all the normal precautions.

GAS LAYER DEPTH — DEPTH WITH HYDROCARBON GAS CONCENTRATION
OF 50% BY VOLUME OR MORE

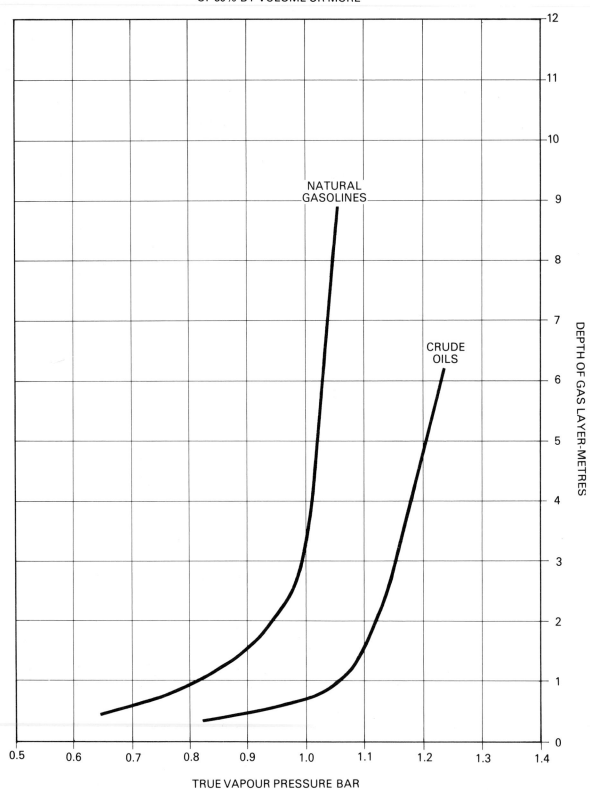

Fig. 16-6. *Relationship between depth of gas layer and true vapour pressure*

If the vent is situated well away from a large structure such as a deckhouse, it will be seen from Section 16.4 that the risk of a flammable mixture reaching either the deck or the structure is least if the gas is vented at high velocity. Variable orifice vents have been designed to achieve this over a wide range of loading rates.

If the vent is near a structure, there is a greater possibility of gas impingement on it and the presence of the structure has effects on the dispersion of the gas. However, even if such impingement does take place the risk of an ignition should be very small if all the normal precautions have been taken to control sources of ignition and to prevent entry of gas into accommodation.

There is, nevertheless, a residual risk and it is necessary to consider what can be done to make it even smaller. This is a matter of judgement depending upon the precise situation. If it is felt that the extent of impingement is not acceptable, the alternative actions that could be taken are either to increase or to decrease the rate of efflux of gas.

An increase of efflux velocity has the objective of ensuring that the plume of gas rises completely clear of the deck and the structure. However, such an increase may not be possible and, even if it is, wind speed and direction variations may be sufficient to make it unreliable.

A decrease in the efflux velocity tends to decrease the extent of impingement on structures at the expense of having more flammable gas on or near the cargo deck. This would be justified if it were considered that there is a greater probability of unexpected sources of ignition on or within structures than on the open deck. The situation is further complicated because in many cases the rate of efflux of gas would be decreased by reducing the loading rate into the tank concerned, so that the presence of gas at low level would be continued for a longer period than if no change were made.

In very adverse conditions, for example if there is little or no wind, it may be justifiable to discontinue the operation.

THE LOADING OF VERY HIGH VAPOUR PRESSURE CARGOES

GAS EVOLUTION

This Chapter has so far dealt with gas evolution and dispersion from high vapour pressure cargoes which give rise to concentrated hydrocarbon gas layers of depth 1 metre (3 feet) or less when loaded (see paragraph 16.2.1). Cargoes yielding layers of greater depth are sometimes encountered. The main ones are crude oils which may have their vapour pressures increased by the addition of extra gas, such as butane, and some natural gasolines, by-products of LNG/LPG production, which are sometimes known as pentanes plus.

Examples of the variation of gas layer depth (to the 50% vol concentration level) related to TVP are shown in Fig. 16-6 for typical natural gasolines and crude oils; there are some cargoes with intermediate properties, for example flash stabilised condensates, some distillation overhead products and crude oils with abnormally low methane and ethane contents.

The natural gasoline curve in Fig. 16-6 is for a series of blends of different TVPs and the crude oil curve is for a series produced by adding increasing amounts of butane to a crude oil. Below a gas layer depth of about 1 metre the dependence of depth on TVP is not very marked for either type of cargo. At greater TVP's it becomes progressively steeper, indicating that in this range a small increase in TVP could cause a very large increase in gas evolution.

Boiling commences when the TVP exceeds 1 bar (1 atmosphere). In the case of the natural gasoline blends this coincides quite closely with the steep increase in gas layer thickness. However with the crude oil/butane blends the steep increase does not occur until a TVP significantly above 1 bar is reached. Crude oils may be stabilised so that their TVP are near, or somewhat above, 1 bar as they enter the ship. In practice therefore some boiling may therefore occur even without butanisation, but the gas evolution is not necessarily excessive.

In boiling, gas bubbles form below the surface of the liquid, but only down to a depth at which the total pressure (atmospheric plus hydrostatic) is equal to the TVP. The consequent loss of gas in this region may lead to a local fall in TVP; moreover the latent heat required to evaporate the gas results in cooling which also reduces the TVP. The reduction in TVP due to both these causes in the liquid near the surface tends to delay boiling despite the fact that the TVP of the bulk of the liquid is above 1 bar.

This is the reason why crude oils can be handled with their TVPs somewhat above 1 bar. It does not apply to the same extent to the natural gasoline type of product because the gaseous constituents in a crude oil are only a small proportion of the total, whereas a natural gasoline usually consists almost entirely of potentially gaseous components. This means that the availability of gas, where boiling is taking place, is far greater with the natural gasolines than with crude oils. Natural gasolines suffer hardly any decrease of TVP due to gas depletion when they begin to boil, and boiling is much more likely to continue in their case than in the case of crude oils.

16.6.2   SPECIAL PRECAUTIONS WITH VERY HIGH VAPOUR PRESSURE CARGOES

When unusually deep gas layers are encountered very high concentrations of gas, approaching 100% by volume, may be vented for prolonged periods during loading. Excessive amounts of gas may then be detected on or around the tanker which may call for special precautions to be taken.

Curves of the kind given in Fig. 16-6 suggest that TVP at the loading temperature of the cargo should be used as the criterion for determining when special precautions are necessary. The RVP of a cargo gives very little guidance unless the temperature of the cargo when loaded is also specified. However, it has proved to be difficult to select TVP criteria because they depend ultimately on subjective judgements of acceptable gas situations on ships. As a general guide the available information suggests that consideration should be given to the need for special precautions when the TVP is expected to exceed the following values:

For natural gasoline type cargoes, for example pentanes plus, 0·75 bar (0·75 atmosphere or 10·8 pounds/square inch absolute).

For crude oils, with or without added gas, 1·0 bar (1·0 atmosphere or 14·5 pounds/square inch absolute).

For some intermediate cargoes, for example flash stabilised condensates, some distillation overheads products and crude oils with abnormally low methane and ethane contents, TVP limits between these two values might be appropriate.

Precautions that might then be applied are given in section 7.5.5.

Chapter 17

Gas Indicators

This Chapter describes the principles, use and limitations of portable instruments for measuring concentrations of hydrocarbon gas in inerted and non-inerted atmospheres, of other toxic gases and of oxygen. Certain fixed installations are also described. For all instruments reference should also be made to the manufacturer's instructions.

17.1   MEASUREMENT OF HYDROCARBON CONCENTRATION

The Catalytic Filament Combustible Gas (CFCG) Indicator is used for measuring small concentrations of hydrocarbon gases below the lower flammable limit (LFL) in atmospheres containing an amount of oxygen sufficient to support combustion. The scale is graduated in either % LFL or % LEL.

Two types of instruments are available commercially for measuring hydrocarbon gas concentrations in excess of the LFL or in oxygen deficient (inerted) atmospheres — the Non-Catalytic Filament Gas Indicator and the Refractive Index Meter.

17.2   CATALYTIC FILAMENT COMBUSTIBLE GAS INDICATOR

17.2.1   OPERATING PRINCIPLE

The sensing element of a CFCG indicator is usually a metal filament heated by an electric current. In some instruments the filament is replaced by a ceramic pellet coated with a catalyst (a pellister) but the mode of action is the same. When a mixture of a combustible gas with air is drawn over the filament the gas oxidises on the hot filament and makes it hotter. This increases its resistance and the change of resistance provides a measure of the concentration of combustible gas in the mixture.

A simplified diagram of the electrical circuit of a CFCG indicator is shown in Fig. 17-1. It is a Wheatstone bridge with the sensor filament forming one arm of the bridge.

The indicator is made ready for use by balancing the bridge with the filament at the correct operating temperature in contact with fresh air, so that the meter reading is zero. The increased resistance of the sensor filament brought about by combustion of the sample mixture throws the bridge out of balance and causes the meter to deflect by an amount proportional to the combustible gas concentration. The deflection is shown on a scale calibrated to read 0% – 100% LFL. Some instruments incorporate additional circuitry to give a second, expanded, range 0% – 10% LFL. To maintain consistent readings the voltage across the bridge must be kept constant and a control is provided for this purpose.

Another arm of the bridge consists of a second filament identical with the sensor filament and the two are mounted close to each other in the instrument. The second filament, however, remains permanently in contact with pure air and the arrangement provides automatic compensation for the effect of ambient temperature changes on the instrument reading. The resistances in the other two arms of the bridge are made from an alloy the electrical resistance of which is practically independent of temperature.

In taking a measurement the manufacturer's detailed instructions should be followed. After the instrument has been initially set at zero with fresh air in contact with the sensor filament, a sample is drawn into the meter by means of a rubber aspirator bulb or a pump. The reading is taken when the pointer has ceased to rise on the scale.

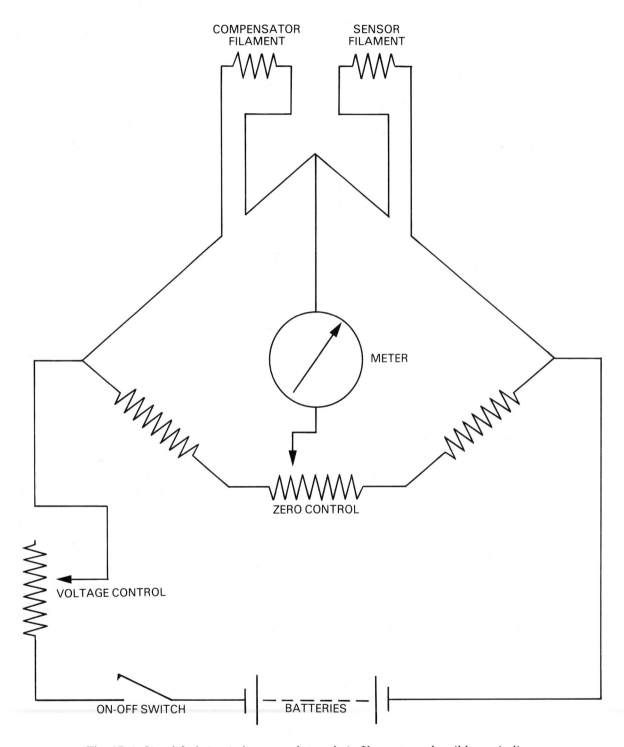

Fig. 17-1. *Simplified circuit diagram of a catalytic filament combustible gas indicator*

108

The out of balance voltage across the meter is proportional to hydrocarbon concentration up to 2–3 times the LFL although the reading cannot go beyond 100% LFL. If the concentration is more than about 3 times the LFL there is insufficient oxygen in the mixture to burn the hydrocarbon gas completely. The response of the instrument to such a concentration is that the needle initially deflects to the maximum on the scale and then falls back to a reading near zero. Continuous observation of the needle is necessary to avoid overlooking this kind of response. Prolonged operation with such a gas mixture causes the deposition of carbonaceous matter on the sensor filament and may alter the response of the instrument. In such cases the response of the instrument should be checked.

For the same reason the instrument does not give a reliable reading with atmospheres deficient in oxygen, such as those in inerted tanks. The meter should not be used if the oxygen concentration is less than 11% by volume.

Non-hydrocarbon gases, such as hydrogen sulphide or carbon monoxide, or gases from lead compounds, which may be present in a tank atmosphere, can affect the meter response, but only if they are present in very high concentrations.

The instrument is normally fitted with a filter to remove solid particles and liquid. It will not indicate the presence of combustible mists (such as lubricating oils) or dusts.

17.2.2   INSTRUMENT CHECK PROCEDURES

The instrument is set up to read correctly in the factory using a combustible gas/air mixture the composition of which should be indicated on the label fixed to the instrument.

The response should be checked periodically, say every month, depending on the frequency of use of the instrument and exposure to poisoning gases. Such a check should also be made after replacing a filament. Test kits for use in the field are available for this purpose providing a mixture of a hydrocarbon gas in air (such as 50% LFL butane in air). At intervals the instrument should be checked more thoroughly in a laboratory equipped with suitable gas blending facilities.

17.2.3   PRECISION OF MEASUREMENT

The response of the instrument depends upon the composition of the hydrocarbon gas mixture and in practice this composition is not known. The calibration of the instrument is such that the response is usually on the safe side for the gases encountered in tanker operations.

Factors that can affect the measurements are large changes in ambient temperature and excessive pressure of the tank atmosphere being tested, leading to high flow rates which in turn affect the filament temperature. To avoid the effect of gas flow rate it is recommended practice to take a reading when there is no flow, i.e. between two squeezes of the rubber aspirator bulb.

Use of dilution tubes which enable catalytic filament indicators to measure concentrations in overrich hydrocarbon/air mixtures is not recommended.

17.2.4   OPERATIONAL FEATURES

Only instruments fitted with flashback arrestors in the inlet and outlet of the detector filament chamber should be used. They are essential to prevent the possibility of flame propagation from the combustion chamber; a check should therefore always be made that they are fitted properly in their place.

Some authorities insist that PVC covers be fitted around meters with aluminium cases to avoid the risk of incendive sparking from the effect of impact with rusty steel.

When hydrocarbons are being measured no filters should be used other than the cotton filter inserted in the gas inlet of the detector to remove solid particles or liquid from the gas sample, although a water absorbent material may be necessary in the sampling line if the gas is very wet (see Section 17.10.)

17.3   NON-CATALYTIC HEATED FILAMENT GAS INDICATOR

17.3.1   OPERATING PRINCIPLE

The sensing element of this instrument is a non-catalytic hot filament. The composition of the surrounding gas determines the rate of loss of heat from the filament, and hence its temperature and resistance.

The sensor filament forms one arm of a Wheatstone bridge. The initial zeroing operations balance the bridge and establish the correct voltage across the filament, thus ensuring the correct operating temperature. During zeroing the sensor filament is purged with air or inert gas free from hydrocarbons. As in the CFCG indicator, there is a second identical filament in another arm of the bridge which is kept permanently in contact with air and acts as a compensator filament.

The presence of hydrocarbon changes the resistance of the sensor filament and this is shown by a deflection on the bridge meter. The rate of heat loss from the filament is a non-linear function of hydrocarbon concentration and the meter scale reflects this non-linearity.

The non-catalytic filament is not affected by gas concentrations in excess of its working scale. The instrument reading goes off the scale and remains in this position as long as the filament is exposed to the rich gas mixture.

17.3.2   INSTRUMENT CHECK PROCEDURES

The checking of a non-catalytic heated filament instrument requires the provision of gas mixtures of a known total hydrocarbon concentration.

The carrier gas may be nitrogen or carbon dioxide or a mixture of these. Since this type of instrument may be required to measure accurately either low concentrations (1% – 3% by volume) or high concentrations (greater than 10% by volume) it is desirable to have either two test mixtures, say 2% and 15% by volume or one mixture between these two numbers, say 8% by volume. Gas mixtures may be obtained in small aerosol-type dispensers or small pressurized gas cylinders.

17.4   REFRACTIVE INDEX METER

17.4.1   OPERATING PRINCIPLES

This is an optical device depending on the difference between the refractive indices of the gas sample and air.

In this type of instrument a beam of light is divided into two, and these are then recombined at the eyepiece. The recombined beams exhibit an interference pattern which appears to the observer as a number of dark lines in the eyepiece.

One light path is through chambers filled with air. The other path is via chambers through which the sample gas is pumped. Initially the latter chambers are filled with air and the instrument is adjusted so that one of the dark lines coincides with the zero line on the instrument scale. If a gas mixture is then pumped into the sample chambers the dark lines are displaced across the scale by an amount proportional to the change of refractive index. The displacement is measured by noting the new position on the scale of the line which was used initially to zero the instrument. The scale may be calibrated in concentration units or it may be an arbitrary scale whose readings are converted to the required units by a table or graph. The response of the instrument is linear and a one point test with a standard mixture at a known concentration is sufficient for checking purposes.

The instrument is normally calibrated for a particular hydrocarbon gas mixture. As long as the use of the instrument is restricted to the calibration gas mixture it provides accurate measurements of gas concentrations.

The measurement of the concentration of hydrocarbon gas in an inerted atmosphere is affected by the carbon dioxide present when flue gas is used for inerting. In this case the use of sodalime as an absorbent for carbon dioxide is recommended, provided the reading is corrected appropriately.

The refractive index meter is not affected by gas concentrations in excess of its scale range. The instrument reading goes off the scale and remains in this position as long as the gas chambers are filled with the gas mixture.

110

17.4.2 INSTRUMENT CHECK PROCEDURES

A mixture of a known hydrocarbon, e.g. butane in nitrogen at a known concentration, should be used to check the instrument. If the hydrocarbon test gas differs from the original calibration gas the indicated reading should be multiplied by the appropriate correction factor before judging the accuracy and stability of the instrument.

17.5 FIXED FLAMMABLE GAS DETECTION INSTALLATIONS

Fixed installations have been employed to a limited extent in a few petroleum tankers to monitor the flammability of the atmosphere in spaces such as pipe tunnels in double bottoms. Two general arrangements have been developed for fixed monitoring installations.

In one arrangement a multiplicity of sensing devices is distributed throughout the spaces to be monitored. Signals are taken sequentially from them by a central control.

The other arrangement incorporates the gas measurement system in the central control. Samples of the atmospheres to be checked are drawn sequentially, usually by vacuum pump, through sample lines to the central gas measurement system. It is important to ensure that there is no leakage of air into the system which would dilute the samples and cause misleading readings.

17.6 MEASUREMENT OF LOW CONCENTRATIONS OF TOXIC GASES

The only portable instruments suitable for use in tankers to measure very low concentrations of toxic gases are chemical tube devices.

Such an instrument consists of a sealed glass tube containing a proprietary filling which is designed to react with a specific gas and to give a visible indication of the concentration of that gas. To use the device the seals at each end of the glass tube are broken, the tube is inserted in a bellows-type fixed volume displacement hand pump, and a prescribed volume of gas mixture is drawn through the tube at a rate fixed by the rate of expansion of the bellows. A colour change occurs along the tube and the length of discolouration, which is a measure of the gas concentration, is read off a scale integral with the tube. In some versions of these instruments a hand operated injection syringe is used instead of a bellows pump.

It is important that all the components used for any measurement should be from the same manufacturer. It is not permissible to use a tube from one manufacturer with the handpump from another manufacturer. It is also important that the manufacturer's operating instructions should be carefully observed.

Since the measurement depends on passing a fixed volume of gas through the glass tube, if an extension hose is used it should be placed between the glass tube and the hand pump.

The tubes are designed and intended to measure concentrations of the specified gas *in air*. Thus measurements made in a ventilated tank, in preparation for tank entry, should be of acceptable accuracy. Measurements made with mixtures containing substantial concentrations of hydrocarbons or other components may be less reliable due to interferences. If such measurements are necessary then the manufacturer should be consulted for guidance.

The accuracy of the method varies somewhat from one tube to another. Manufacturers must guarantee the standards of accuracy laid down in national standards, and tanker operators should consult the regulatory authority appropriate for their ship's flag.

17.7 MEASUREMENT OF OXYGEN CONCENTRATIONS

Oxygen analysers normally used at terminals and on tankers are likely to be easily portable, although fixed installations are in use on vessels fitted with inert gas systems.

The portable analysers are normally used to determine whether an atmosphere, for example inside a cargo tank, may be considered fully inerted, or safe for entry. The fixed types of analysers are used for monitoring the oxygen content of the boiler uptakes and the inert gas main.

The following are the most common types of oxygen analysers in use:

Paramagnetic sensors.

Electrolytic sensors.

Selective chemical absorption liquids.

All analysers, regardless of type should be used strictly in accordance with the manufacturer's instructions. If so used, and subject to the limitations listed below, the analysers may be regarded as reliable.

17.8   USE OF OXYGEN ANALYSERS

17.8.1   PARAMAGNETIC SENSORS

The analyser readings are directly proportional to the pressure in the measuring cell. The unit is calibrated at a specific atmospheric pressure and the small error due to atmospheric pressure variations can be corrected if required. Reading errors can be more significant during pressure variations using some gas sampling arrangements, but can be avoided by reducing the sampling pressure to atmospheric during readings. Continuous samples should be supplied to the instrument by positive pressure. They should not be drawn through the analyser by negative pressure as the measuring pressure becomes uncertain.

The filter disc should be cleared or replaced when an increase in sample pressure is required to maintain a reasonable gas flow through the analyser. The same effect is produced if the filter becomes wet due to insufficient gas drying. The need for filter cleaning or replacement should be checked regularly.

17.8.2   ELECTROLYTIC SENSORS

Certain gases may affect the sensor and give rise to false readings. Sulphur dioxide, fluorine, chlorine, bromine, iodine and oxides of nitrogen interfere if they are present in concentrations of more than 0·25% by volume. Mercaptans and hydrogen sulphide can poison the sensor if their levels are greater than 1% by volume. This poisoning does not occur immediately but over a period of time; a poisoned sensor drifts and cannot be calibrated in air. In such cases reference should be made to the manufacturer's instructions.

17.8.3   SELECTIVE CHEMICAL ABSORPTION LIQUID

The use of this type for checking the condition of the ullage space in a loaded compartment is not recommended, because of the effect of high concentrations of hydrocarbon gases on the reagents.

17.8.4   MAINTENANCE, CALIBRATION AND TEST PROCEDURES

As these analysers are of vital importance, they should be carefully maintained and tested strictly in accordance with manufacturer's instructions.

It is essential that each time an instrument is to be used, a check is made of batteries (if fitted), zero setting and calibration. During use frequent checks should be made to ensure accurate readings are obtained at all times. Calibration is simple on all analysers, using atmospheric air as standard. Zero calibration can be checked with nitrogen or carbon dioxide.

17.8.5   PERSONAL OXYGEN MONITORS

Personal oxygen monitors which are capable of continuously measuring the oxygen content of the atmosphere are available. They should automatically provide an audible and visual alarm when the atmosphere becomes deficient in oxygen, say less than 19% by volume, giving the wearer adequate warning of unsafe conditions. These should be tested at regular intervals.

17.9   GAS SAMPLE LINES AND SAMPLING PROCEDURES

17.9.1   GAS SAMPLE LINES

The material and condition of sample lines can affect the accuracy of gas measurements.

Metal tubes are unsuited to most cargo tank gas measurements and flexible lines must be used.

The gases from crude oils and many petroleum products are composed essentially of paraffinic hydrocarbons and there are a number of suitable materials available for flexible sample tubing. The problem of material selection is more difficult for those gases containing substantial proportions of aromatic hydrocarbons, in particular, xylene. It is recommended that in such cases suppliers of sample tubing should be asked to provide test data showing the suitability of their product for the purposes for which it will be employed.

Sample tubing which is cracked or blocked, or which has become contaminated with cargo residues, greatly affects instrument readings. Users should check the condition of the tubing regularly and replace defective tubing.

17.9.2   SAMPLING PROCEDURES

Every cargo tank has 'dead spots' where the rate of change of gas concentration during ventilation or purging is less than the average in the bulk of the tank. The location of these dead spots depends on the positions of the inlet and outlet through which ventilating air or inert gas is admitted and expelled and also on the disposition of the structural members in the tank. Generally, but not invariably, the dead spots are to be found within the tank bottom structure.

The differences in gas concentration between the bulk volume of the tank and the dead spots vary depending on the operating procedures in use. For example, the powerful water jets produced by fixed washing machines are excellent mixing devices which tend to eliminate major differences in gas concentration between one location in the tank and another. Similarly, the introduction of ventilating air or the inert gas purge as powerful jets directed vertically downwards from the deck head produces good mixing and minimises variations in concentration.

17.10   FILTERS IN SAMPLE LINES

Cotton filters are normally used in hydrocarbon meters of either the catalytic or non-catalytic filament types, and additional filters are not normally needed. In extremely wet conditions, e.g. tank washing, excessive water can be removed from the gas sample using materials that retain water but do not affect the hydrocarbons. Suitable materials are granular anhydrous calcium chloride or sulphate. If required soda asbestos selectively retains hydrogen sulphide without affecting the hydrocarbons. However, it also retains carbon dioxide and sulphur dioxide and must not be used in tanks inerted with scrubbed flue gas.

Filters are best made of 200 – 300 millimetres (8 – 12 inches) lengths of flexible PVC tubing about 12 millimetres (0·5 inch) internal diameter with the absorbent confined between glass wool plugs.

The use of water retaining filters is essential with oxygen meters, particularly the paramagnetic type, because the presence of water vapour in the sample can damage the measuring cell.

Chapter 18

Electrical Equipment and Installations

In this Chapter a description is given of the different approaches to the classification of dangerous areas on board tankers and hazardous areas in terminals for the purposes of electrical installations and equipment. General guidance is given on the safety precautions to be observed during maintenance and repair of electrical equipment. The standards for, and the installation of, electrical equipment do not come within the scope of this safety guide.

18.1   DANGEROUS AND HAZARDOUS AREAS

18.1.1   DANGEROUS AREAS IN A TANKER

In a tanker, certain areas are defined by government departments and classification societies as being dangerous for the installation or use of fixed electrical equipment, either at all times or only during loading, ballasting, tank cleaning or gas freeing operations. These areas are described in International Electrotechnical Commission Publication 79 which refers to the types of electrical equipment which can be installed in them.

18.1.2   HAZARDOUS AREAS AT A TERMINAL

At a terminal, account is taken of the probability of a flammable gas mixture being present by grading hazardous areas into three zones:

Zone 0

An area in which a flammable gas mixture is continuously present or is present for long periods.

Zone 1

An area in which there is likely to be a flammable gas mixture under normal operating conditions.

Zone 2

An area in which the presence of a flammable gas mixture is unlikely, but if it does it is likely to be present for only a short period.

18.1.3   APPLICATION OF HAZARDOUS AREA CLASSIFICATIONS TO A TANKER AT A BERTH

When a tanker is at a berth it is possible that an area in the tanker which is regarded as safe may fall within one of the hazardous zones of the terminal. If such a situation should arise, and if the area in question contains unapproved electrical equipment then such equipment may have to be isolated whilst the tanker is at the berth.

18.2   ELECTRICAL EQUIPMENT AND INSTALLATIONS

18.2.1   ELECTRICAL EQUIPMENT AND INSTALLATIONS ON BOARD SHIP

Electrical equipment and installations in tankers will be in accordance with classification society or national requirements, or the recommendations of the International Electrotechnical Commission. Additional recommendations in respect of the use of temporary electrical installations, and portable electrical equipment are given in Sections 2.4, 4.8 and 10.5.

18.2.2 ELECTRICAL EQUIPMENT AND INSTALLATIONS AT TERMINALS

At terminals, the types of electrical equipment and methods of installation will normally be governed by national requirements and, where applicable, by the recommendations of the International Electrotechnical Commission.

18.3 INSPECTION AND MAINTENANCE OF ELECTRICAL EQUIPMENT

18.3.1 GENERAL

All apparatus, systems and installations, including cables, conduit and the like should be maintained in good condition. To ensure this they should be regularly inspected.

Correct functional operation does not necessarily imply compliance with the required standards of safety.

18.3.2 INSPECTIONS AND CHECKS

All equipment, systems and installations should be inspected when first installed. Following any repair, adjustment or modification those parts of the installation which have been disturbed should be checked.

If at a terminal there is at any time a change in the area classification or in the characteristics of the flammable material handled, a check should be made to ensure that all equipment is of the correct group and temperature class and continues to comply with the requirements for the revised area classification.

18.3.3 INSULATION TESTING

Insulation testing should be carried out only when no flammable gas mixture is present.

18.3.4 ALTERATIONS TO EQUIPMENT, SYSTEMS AND INSTALLATIONS

No modification, addition or removal should be made to any approved equipment, system or installation at a terminal without the permission of the appropriate authority, unless it can be verified that such change does not invalidate the approval.

No modification should be made to the safety features of equipment which relies on the techniques of segregation, pressurizing, pruging or other methods of ensuring safety, without the permission of the engineer responsible.

When equipment in a terminal hazardous zone is permanently withdrawn from service, the associated wiring should be removed from the hazardous zone or should be correctly terminated in an enclosure appropriate to the area classification.

When equipment in a terminal hazardous zone is temporarily removed from service, the exposed conductors should be correctly terminated as above, or adequately insulated, or solidly bonded together and earthed. The cable cores of intrinsically safe circuits should either be insulated from each other or bonded together and insulated from earth.

18.3.5 PERIODIC MECHANICAL INSPECTIONS

During inspections of electrical equipment or installations particular attention should be paid to the following:

Cracks in metal, cracked or broken glasses, or failure of cement around cemented glasses in flameproof or explosion proof enclosures.

Covers of flameproof enclosures to ensure that they are tight, no bolts are missing, and no gaskets are present between mating metal surfaces.

Each connection to ensure that it is properly connected.

Possible slackness of joints in conduit runs and fittings.

Clamping of armouring of cable.

Stresses on cables which might cause fracture.

18.4   ELECTRICAL REPAIRS, MAINTENANCE AND TEST WORK AT TERMINALS

18.4.1   GENERAL

As a general safety precaution the use of mechanical lock off devices and safety tags is strongly recommended.

18.4.2   COLD WORK

Work should not be carried out on any apparatus or wiring, nor should any flameproof or explosion proof enclosure be opened, nor the special safety characteristics provided in connection with standard apparatus be impaired, until all voltage has been cut off from the apparatus or wiring concerned. The voltage should not be restored until work has been completed and the above safety measures have been fully reinstated. Any such work, including changing of lamps, should be done only by an authorised person.

18.4.3   HOT WORK

For the purpose of repairs, alterations or carrying out tests, it is permissible to use soldering apparatus or other means involving flame, fire, or heat, or to use industrial type apparatus in any terminal hazardous area, provided that the area has first been made safe and certified gas free by an authorized person and is maintained in that stage as long as the work is in progress. When such hot work is considered necessary on a berth at which a tanker is moored or on a tanker berthed at a terminal, the joint agreement of the terminal and tanker should first be obtained and a Hot Work Permit issued.

It is also permissible to restore voltage to apparatus for testing during a period of repair or alteration subject to the same conditions.

Chapter 19

Static Electricity

This Chapter deals with the generation of static electricity during the loading and discharging of cargo and during tank cleaning. In addition the Chapter deals with ship to shore and ship to ship electric currents.

19.1 **PRINCIPLES OF ELECTROSTATIC HAZARD**

19.1.1 GENERAL

Static electricity presents fire and explosion hazards during the handling of petroleum, and tanker operations are no exception. Certain operations can give rise to accumulations of electric charge which may be released suddenly in electrostatic discharges with sufficient energy to ignite flammable hydrocarbon/air mixtures; there is, of course, no risk of ignition unless a flammable mixture is present. There are three basic stages leading up to a potential static hazard: charge separation, charge accumulation and electrostatic discharge. All three of these stages are necessary for an electrostatic ignition.

19.1.2 CHARGE SEPARATION

Whenever two dissimilar materials come into contact charge separation occurs at the interface. The interface may be between two solids, between a solid and a liquid or between two immiscible liquids. At the interface charge of one sign (say positive) moves from material A to material B so that materials A and B become respectively negatively and positively charged. Whilst the materials stay in contact and immobile relative to one another, the charges are extremely close together. The voltage difference between the charges of opposite sign is then very small, and no hazard exists.

The charges can be widely separated by many processes, such as:

The flow of liquids (e.g. petroleum or mixtures of petroleum and water) through pipes or fine filters.

The settling of a solid or an immiscible liquid through a liquid (e.g. rust or water through petroleum).

The ejection of particles or droplets from a nozzle (e.g. steaming operations).

The splashing or agitation of a liquid against a solid surface (e.g. water washing operations or the initial stages of filling a tank with oil).

The vigorous rubbing together and subsequent separation of certain synthetic polymers (e.g. the sliding of a polypropylene rope through PVC gloved hands).

When the charges are separated a large voltage difference develops between them. Also a voltage distribution is set up throughout the neighbouring space and this is known as an electrostatic field. As examples, the charge on a charged petroleum liquid in a tank produces an electrostatic field throughout the tank both in the liquid and in the ullage space, and the charge on a water mist caused by tank washing produces a field throughout the tank.

If an uncharged conductor is present in an electrostatic field it has approximately the same voltage as the region it occupies. Furthermore the field causes a movement of charge within the conductor; charge of one sign is attracted by the field to one end of the conductor and an equal charge of opposite sign is left at the opposite end. Charges separated in this way are known as induced charges and as long as they are kept separate by the presence of the field they are capable of contributing to an electrostatic discharge.

19.1.3	CHARGE ACCUMULATION

Charges which have been separated attempt to recombine and to neutralize each other. This process is known as charge relaxation. If one, or both, of the separated materials carrying charge is a very poor electrical conductor recombination is impeded and the material retains or accumulates the charge upon it. The period of time for which the charge is retained is characterized by the relaxation time of the material, which is related to its conductivity; the lower the conductivity the greater is the relaxation time.

If a material has a comparatively high conductivity the recombination of charges is very rapid and can counteract the separation process, and consequently little or no static electricity accumulates on the material. Such a highly conducting material can only retain or accumulate charge if it is insulated by means of a poor conductor, and the rate of loss of charge is then dependent upon the relaxation time of this less conducting material.

The important factors governing relaxation are therefore the electrical conductivities of the separated materials and of any additional materials which may be interposed between them after their separation.

19.1.4	ELECTROSTATIC DISCHARGES

Electrical breakdown between any two points, giving rise to a discharge, is dependent upon the strength of the electrostatic field in the space between the points. This field strength, or voltage gradient, is given approximately by dividing the difference in voltage between the points by their distance apart. A field strength of about 3,000 kilovolts per metre is sufficient to cause breakdown of air or petroleum gases.

The field strength near protrusions is greater than the overall field strength in the vicinity and discharges therefore generally occur at protrusions. A discharge may occur between a protrusion and the space in its vicinity without reaching another object. These single electrode discharges are rarely, if ever, incendive in the context of normal tanker operations.

The alternative is a discharge between two electrodes adjacent to each other. Examples are:

Between sampling apparatus lowered into a tank and the surface of a charged petroleum liquid.

Between an unearthed object floating on the surface of a charged liquid and the adjacent tank structure.

Between unearthed equipment suspended in a tank and adjacent tank structure.

Two electrode discharges may be incendive if various requirements are met. These include:

A discharge gap short enough to allow the discharge to take place with the voltage difference present, but not so short that any resulting flame is quenched.

Sufficient electrical energy to supply the minimum amount of energy to initiate combustion.

The nearly instantaneous release of this energy into the discharge gap.

Whether the last requirement can be fulfilled depends to a large extent on the conductivity of the electrodes. In order to consider this further it is necessary to classify solids and liquids into three groups.

The first group is the conductors. In the case of solids these are the metals, and in the case of liquids they are the whole range of aqueous solutions, including sea water. The human body, consisting of about 60% water, is effectively a liquid conductor. The important property of conductors is that not only are they incapable of holding a charge unless insulated, but that if they are insulated and an opportunity for an electrical discharge occurs all the charge available is almost instantaneously released into the discharge.

Discharges between two conductors very frequently occur as sparks, and are much more energetic and potentially dangerous than those occurring between objects, one of which is not a conductor. In the latter case discharges often take a more diffuse and much less dangerous form known as corona or brush discharge rather than a spark.

The second group is the non-conductors, which have such low conductivities that once they have received a charge they retain it for a very long period. Alternatively they can prevent the loss of charge from conductors by acting as insulators. Charged non-conductors are of primary concern because they can transfer charge to, or induce charge on, neighbouring insulated conductors which may then give rise to sparks. Very highly charged non-conductors may themselves contribute directly to incendive sparks.

Liquids are considered to be non-conductors when they have conductivities less than 100 picoSiemens/metre (pS/m) giving relaxation times greater than 0·2 seconds; they are often known as static accumulators. In the case of petroleum, clean oils (distillates) frequently fall into this category. An antistatic additive is a substance which is deliberately added to a petroleum distillate to raise its conductivity above 100 pS/m.

The solid non-conductors are highly insulating materials such as polypropylene, PVC, nylon and many types of rubber. They become more conductive as their surfaces are contaminated with dirt or moisture.

The third group is a range of liquids and solids with conductivities intermediate between those of the first two groups. The liquids have conductivities exceeding 100 pS/m and are often known as static non-accumulators. Examples are black oils (containing residual materials) and crude oils, which typically have conductivities in the range 10,000 – 100,000 pS/m. Some chemicals, for example alcohols, are also static non-accumulators.

The solids in this intermediate category include such materials as wood, cork, sisal and naturally occurring organic substances generally. They owe their conductivity to their ready absorption of water and they become more conductive as their surfaces are contaminated by moisture and dirt. In some cases thorough cleaning and drying may lower their conductivities sufficiently to bring them into the non-conductive range.

If materials in the intermediate conductivity group are not insulated from earth, their conductivities are normally sufficiently high to avoid accumulation of an electrostatic charge. However, their conductivities are normally low enough to inhibit production of energetic sparks.

The incendivity of a discharge depends upon so many other factors in addition to conductivity that generalizations beyond this are impossible and it is necessary to rely upon practical experience to indicate when it is acceptable to use them.

Under normal conditions gases are highly insulating and this has important implications with respect to mists and particulate suspensions in air and other gases. Charged mists are formed during the ejection of wet steam from a nozzle, while using tank washing machines, and during crude oil washing. Although the liquid, for example water, may have a very high conductivity, the relaxation of the charge on the droplets is hindered by the insulating properties of the surrounding gas. Fine particles present in inert flue gas and created during discharge of pressurized liquid carbon dioxide are frequently charged. The gradual charge relaxation which does occur is the result of the settling of the particles or droplets and, if the field strength is high, of corona discharge at protrusions which supplies a neutralizing charge of the sign opposite to that on the suspension.

In summary, electrostatic discharges can arise as a result of accumulations of charge on:

Liquid or solid non-conductors, for example a static accumulator oil, say a kerosene, pumped into a tank, or a polypropylene rope.

Electrically isolated liquid or solid conductors, for example mists, sprays or particulate suspensions in air, or a metal rod hanging on the end of a synthetic fibre rope.

For materials with intermediate conductivities the risk of electrostatic discharge is small, particularly if current practices are adhered to, and the chance of their being incendive is even smaller.

19.2 GENERAL PRECAUTIONS AGAINST ELECTROSTATIC HAZARDS

The most important countermeasure that must be taken to prevent an electrostatic hazard is to bond all metal objects together; bonding eliminates the risk of discharges between metal objects, which can be very energetic and dangerous. To avoid discharges from conductors to earth, it is normal practice to include bonding to earth (earthing or grounding). On ships, bonding to earth is effectively accomplished by connecting metallic objects to the metal structure of the ship, which is naturally earthed through the sea.

Some examples of objects which might be electrically insulated in hazardous situations and which must therefore be bonded are:

Ship/shore hose couplings and flanges if more than one length of non-conducting hose or pipe is used in a string.

Portable tank cleaning machines.

Conducting manual ullaging and sampling equipment.

The float of a permanently fitted ullage device if it lacks an earthing path through the metal tape.

The most certain method of bonding and earthing is by means of a metallic connection between the conductors. This method should be used whenever possible, although for electrostatic purposes an adequate bond can in principle be made using a material of intermediate conductivity.

Certain objects may be insulated fortuitously during tanker operations.

Some examples are:

A metal object such as a can floating in a static accumulating liquid.

A loose metal object while it is falling in a tank during washing operations.

Since there is no question of deliberately bonding such objects every effort should be made to remove them from the tank. This necessitates careful inspection of tanks, particularly after shipyard repairs.

19.3 ELECTROSTATIC HAZARDS WHEN HANDLING STATIC ACCUMULATOR OILS

19.3.1 PUMPING OIL INTO TANKS

Petroleum distillates often have electrical conductivities less than 100 picoSiemens/metre so that they fall into the category of accumulators.

Since their conductivities are not normally known all distillates must be treated as static accumulators unless they contain an antistatic additive (see paragraph 19.3.4.) During and for some time after entry into the tank a static accumulator oil may carry sufficient charge to constitute a hazard.

The charge may arise through one or more of several different processes:

Flow of the oil through the pipeline system into the tank. The production of charge depends, for a given conductivity, on the lengths and diameters of the pipes in the system and on the linear flow rate of the liquid through these pipes. Charge generation is enhanced if water droplets are suspended in the oil as it flows through the pipes.

Flow through a micropore filter of the kind used for aircraft jet fuels. These filters have the ability to charge fuels to a very high level probably because all the fuel is brought into intimate contact with the filter surface.

Turbulence and splashing in the early stages of pumping the oil into an empty tank.

The settling of water droplets, rust or other particles entering the tank with the oil or stirred up by it in the tank.

122

The generally accepted method for controlling electrostatic generation in the initial stages of loading is to restrict the flow rate of the static accumulator oil into the tank until all splashing and surface turbulence in the tank has ceased.

At the commencement of loading an empty tank the linear velocity in the branch line to each individual cargo tank should not exceed 1 metre/second (3 feet/second). The reasons for such a low rate are:

It is at the beginning of filling a tank that there is the greatest likelihood of water being mixed with the oil entering the tank; mixtures of oil and water constitute a most potent source of static electricity.

It minimizes the extent of turbulence and splashing as oil enters the tank; this helps to reduce the generation of static electricity and also reduces the dispersal of any water present, so that it more quickly settles out to the bottom of the tank where it can lie relatively undisturbed when the loading rate is subsequently increased.

During subsequent loading the limitations on flow rate imposed by present design of pipeline systems coupled with precautions in the introduction of dipping, ullaging and sampling equipment (see section 19.6) and the avoidance of electrically isolated conductors, have been sufficient to maintain operational safety. If markedly different pipeline or pumping systems were to be introduced enabling higher flow rates or velocities to be achieved then flow rate limitations might have to be imposed throughout loading.

The limitation on the initial loading rate applies for static accumulator oils whenever a flammable gas mixture may be present. These situations are fully described in Section 7.4 and are summarized in Table 7-1.

It is not uncommon during loading to encounter water from such operations as water washing, ballasting or line flushing and care should be taken to avoid excess water and unnecessary mixing. For example, cargo tanks and water flushed lines should be drained before loading and water should not be permitted to accumulate in tanks. Lines should not be displaced with water back into a tank containing a static accumulator oil.

Coarse filters are sometimes used in tanker operations. These generate an insignificant amount of charge provided that they are kept clean. However, if micropore filtration is used on the jetty sufficient time must be allowed for the charge to relax before the liquid reaches the tank. It is desirable for the liquid to spend a minimum of 30 seconds in the piping downstream of the filter.

19.3.2   FIXED EQUIPMENT IN CARGO TANKS

Fixed equipment such as washing machines or high level alarms suspended from the top of a tank may act as probes. When loading static accumulator oils, such probes may cause electrostatic discharges to the approaching liquid surface if they are not properly installed to prevent this.

19.3.3   AIR RELEASE IN THE BOTTOM OF TANKS

If air or inert gas is blown into the bottom of a tank containing a static accumulator oil a strong electrostatic field can be generated especially in the presence of water or particulate matter. Accordingly precautions should be taken to minimize the amount of air or inert gas entering tanks containing static accumulator oils.

19.3.4   ANTISTATIC ADDITIVES

If the oil contains an effective antistatic additive it is no longer a static accumulator. Although, strictly, this means that the precautions applicable to an accumulator can be relaxed, it is still advisable to adhere to them in practice unless it is certain that the conductivity is above 100 picoSiemens/metre.

19.4   OTHER SOURCES OF ELECTROSTATIC HAZARDS

19.4.1   FREE FALL IN TANKS

Loading or ballasting overall delivers charged liquid to a tank in such a manner that it can break up into small droplets and splash into the tank. This may produce a charged mist as well as increasing the petroleum gas concentration in the tank. Restrictions upon loading or ballasting overall are given in paragraph 7.5.7.

WATER MISTS

The spraying of water into tanks, for instance during water washing, gives rise to electrostatically charged mist. This mist is uniformly spread throughout the tank being washed. The electrostatic levels vary widely from tank to tank both in magnitude and in sign.

When washing is started in a dirty tank the charge in the mist is initially negative, reaches a maximum negative value, then goes back through zero and finally rises towards a positive equilibrium value. It has been found that, among the many variables affecting the level and polarity of charging, the characteristics of the wash water and the degree of cleanliness of the tank have the most significant influence. The electrostatic charging characteristics of the water are altered by recirculation or by the addition of tank cleaning chemicals; both of these may cause very high electrostatic levels in the mist. The size and number of washing machines in a tank affect the rate of change of charge but they have little effect on the final equilibrium value.

The charged mist droplets created in the tank during washing give rise to an electrostatic field which is characterized by a distribution of potential (voltage) throughout the tank space. The walls and structure are at earth (zero) potential; the space potential increases with distance from these surfaces and is highest at points furthest from them. The field strength, or voltage gradient, in the space is greatest near the tank walls and structure, more especially where there are protrusions into the tank. If the field strength is high enough electric breakdown occurs into the space giving rise to corona. Because protrusions cause concentrations of field strength a corona occurs preferentially from such points. A corona injects a charge of the opposite sign into the mist and is believed to be one of the main processes limiting the amount of charge in the mist to an equilibrium value. The corona discharges produced during tank washing are not strong enough to ignite the hydrocarbon/air mixtures that may be present.

Under certain circumstances discharges with sufficient energy to ignite hydrocarbon/air mixtures can occur from unearthed conducting objects already within, or introduced into, a tank filled with charged mist. Examples of such unearthed conductors are a metal sounding rod suspended on a non-conducting rope or a piece of metal falling through the tank space. Primarily by induction an unearthed conductor within a tank can acquire a high potential when it comes near an earthed object or structure, particularly if the latter is in the form of a protrusion. The unearthed conductor may then discharge to earth giving rise to a spark capable of igniting a flammable hydrocarbon/air mixture.

The processes by which unearthed conductors give rise to ignitions in a mist are fairly complex and a number of conditions must be satisfied simultaneously before an ignition can occur. These conditions include the size of the object, its trajectory, the electrostatic level in the tank and the geometrical configuration where the discharge takes place.

As well as solid unearthed conducting objects an isolated slug of water produced by the washing process may similarly act as a spark promoter and cause an ignition. Experiments have shown that high capacity, single nozzle fixed washing machines can produce water slugs which, due to their size, trajectory and duration before breaking up, may satisfy the criteria for producing incendive discharges. On the other hand there is no evidence of such water slugs being produced by portable types of washing machine.

Following extensive experimental investigations and using the results of long-term experience the tanker industry has drawn up the tank washing guidelines set out in Chapter 8. These guidelines are aimed at preventing excessive charge generation in mists and at controlling the introduction of unearthed conducting objects when there is charged mist in the tank. The guidelines apply to tanks of all sizes because it has been found that the maximum space potential, which is the best indicator of the electrostatic hazard, is practically independent of tank size.

Charged mists very similar to those produced during tank washing occur from time to time in partly ballasted holds of OBOs. Due to the design of these ships there may be violent impacts of the ballast against the sides of the hold when the ship rolls in even a moderate sea. The impacts also give rise to free flying slugs of water in the tank, so that if the atmosphere of the tank is flammable all the elements for an ignition are present. The most effective counter-measure is to have tanks either empty or fully pressed up so that the violent wave motion in the tank cannot take place.

19.4.3   STEAM

Steaming can produce mist clouds which may be electrostatically charged. The effects and possible hazards from such clouds are similar to those described for the mists created by water washing, but the introduction of steam can cause very much higher levels of charging than those produced by water washing. The time to reach maximum charge levels is also very much less. For these reasons steam should not be injected into cargo tanks where there is any risk of the presence of a flammable atmosphere.

19.4.4   INERT GAS

Small particulate matter carried in inert gas can be electrostatically charged. The charge separation originates in the combustion process and the charged particles are capable of being carried through the scrubber, fan and distribution pipes into the cargo tanks. The electrostatic charge carried by the inert gas is usually small but levels of charge have been observed well above those encountered with water mists formed during washing. Because the tanks are normally in an inert condition, the possibility of an electrostatic ignition has to be considered only if it is necessary to inert a tank which already contains a flammable atmosphere or if a tank already inerted is likely to become flammable because the oxygen content rises as a result of ingress of air. Precautions are then required during dipping, ullaging and sampling (see paragraph 19.5.5.)

19.4.5   DISCHARGE OF CARBON DIOXIDE

During the discharge of pressurized liquid carbon dioxide the rapid cooling which takes place can result in the formation of particles of solid carbon dioxide which become charged on impact and contact with the nozzle and thereby can lead to incendive sparks. Carbon dioxide should therefore not be injected into cargo tanks or pump rooms which may contain unignited flammable gas mixtures.

19.4.6   CLOTHING AND FOOTWEAR

A person who is insulated from earth by the high resistance of his footwear or the surface on which he is standing can become electrostatically charged. This charge can arise from contact charging associated with his clothing especially if the clothing is removed. In some circumstances a spark passing to earth from his body could sometimes have sufficient energy to ignite flammable gas mixtures.

Experience over a very long period indicates that electrostatic discharges caused by clothing and footwear do not present a significant hazard in the oil industry. This is especially true in a marine environment where surfaces rapidly become contaminated by deposits of salt and moisture which reduce electrical resistances, particularly at high humidities.

19.4.7   SYNTHETIC MATERIALS

An increasing number of items manufactured from synthetic materials are being offered for use on board ships. It is important that those responsible for their provision to tankers should be satisfied that, if they are to be used in flammable atmospheres, they will not introduce electrostatic hazards.

19.5   DIPPING, ULLAGING AND SAMPLING

19.5.1   GENERAL

There is a possibility of discharges whenever equipment is lowered into cargo tanks within which there may be electrostatic charges either in the liquid contents or on water or oil mists or on inert gas particulates. If there is any possibility of the presence of a flammable hydrocarbon/air mixture precautions must be taken to avoid incendive discharges throughout the system.

19.5.2   EQUIPMENT

If any form of dipping, ullaging or sampling equipment is used in a possibly flammable atmosphere where an electrostatic hazard exists or can be created it is essential at all times to avoid the presence of an unearthed conductor. Metallic components of any equipment to be lowered into a tank should be securely bonded together and earthed to the ship before introduction and remain earthed until after removal. It should be remembered that the operator handling the equipment is also a conductor, and should not be insulated from the ship. In most practical situations at sea there is a conducting path between the operator and the ship.

125

The suitability of equipment made wholly or partly of non-metallic components depends upon the conductivities of the materials employed and their manner of use. Thus, in the case of non-conductors it is known that a significant electrostatic charge can be generated when a polypropylene rope runs rapidly through a PVC-gloved hand. For this reason only natural fibre ropes should be used for dipping, ullaging and sampling. Non-conducting materials may be acceptable in other circumstances — for example, a sample bottle holder made of a synthetic plastic — but those responsible for the provision of such equipment to ships must be satisfied that they are safe to use. It is essential in all cases that non-conducting components do not lead to the insulation of any metal components from earth.

A material of intermediate conductivity, such as wood or natural fibre, generally has sufficient conductivity intrinsically, or as a result of water absorption, to avoid the accumulation of electrostatic charge. There should be a leakage path to earth from such materials so that they are not totally insulated but this need not have the very low resistance normally provided for the bonding and earthing of metals. In practice on ships such a path usually occurs naturally either by direct contact with the ship or by indirect contact through the operator of the equipment.

19.5.3   STATIC ACCUMULATOR OILS

It is wise to assume that during and immediately after loading the surface of a non-conducting liquid (static accumulator) may be at a high potential. It has already been said that metallic dipping, ullaging and sampling equipment should be bonded and earthed. There is therefore a possibility of a discharge between the equipment and the liquid surface as the two approach each other. Such discharges can be incendive, and therefore no dipping, ullaging or sampling with metallic equipment should take place whilst a static accumulator is being loaded when there is any possibility of the presence of a flammable gas mixture. Moreover there should be a delay of 30 minutes after the completion of loading of each tank before commencing these operations; this is to allow the settlement of water or particulate matter in the liquid and the dissipation of any electrical potential due to settling.

The situations where these restrictions for metallic equipment should be applied are fully described in Section 7.4 and are summarized in Table 7-1.

Discharges between the surface of a static accumulator and non-metallic objects have not in practice been found to be incendive. Dipping, ullaging or sampling with such equipment is therefore permissible at any time provided that it complies with the conditions described in paragraph 19.5.2.

The potential within a metal sounding pipe is always low due to the small volume and to shielding from the rest of the tank. Dipping, ullaging and sampling within a metal sounding pipe is therefore permissible at any time even with metallic equipment.

19.5.4   WATER MISTS DUE TO WASHING

The important requirement is that there should be no unearthed metallic conductor in the tank, and that none should be introduced whilst the charged mist persists, that is during washing and for 5 hours after the completion of the operation. Earthed and bonded metallic equipment can be used at any time because any discharges to the water mist take the form of non-incendive corona. The equipment can contain or consist entirely of non-metallic components; both intermediate conductors and non-conductors are acceptable although, for example, the use of polypropylene ropes should be avoided (see paragraph 19.5.2.) It is absolutely essential, however, that all metallic components are securely earthed. If there is any doubt about earthing, the operation should not be permitted.

Operations in a sounding pipe are safe at any time in the presence of a wash water mist.

19.5.5   INERT GAS

Precautions are not normally required against static electricity in the presence of inert gas because the gas prevents the existence of a flammable gas mixture. However, as mentioned in paragraph 19.4.4, very high electrostatic potentials are possible due to particulates in suspension in inert gas and if it is believed that the tank is for any reason no longer in an inert condition, dipping, ullaging and sampling operations should be restricted. Occasions when restrictions would be required are in the event of breakdown of the inert gas system during discharge, leading to the ingress of air, reinerting of a tank after such a breakdown, and initial inerting of a tank containing a flammable gas mixture.

Because of the very high potential that may be carried on inert gas particulates it is not wise to assume that corona discharges from introduced conducting equipment will be non-incendive. Therefore, no object should be introduced until the initially very high potential has had a chance to decay to a more tolerable level; a wait of 30 minutes after stopping the injection of inert gas is sufficient for this purpose. After 30 minutes equipment may be introduced subject to the same precautions as for water mists caused by washing.

19.6   EARTHING, BONDING AND CATHODIC PROTECTION

19.6.1   EARTHING AND BONDING PRACTICE

Earthing and bonding minimize the danger arising from:

Faults between electrically live conductors and non-current carrying metal work.

Atmospheric discharges (lightning).

Accumulations of electrostatic charge.

Earthing is achieved by the establishment of an electrically continuous low resistance path between a conducting body and the general mass of the earth. Earthing may occur inherently through intimate contact with the ground or water, or it may be provided deliberately by means of an electrical connection between the body and ground.

Bonding occurs where a suitable electrically continuous path is established between conducting bodies. Bonding may be effected between two or more bodies without involving earthing but more commonly earthing gives rise to bonding with the general mass of the earth acting as the electrical connection. Bonding may arise by construction through the bolting together of metallic bodies, thus affording electrical continuity, or may be effected by the provision of an additional bonding conductor between them.

Most earthing and bonding devices intended to protect against electrical faults or lightning are permanently installed parts of the equipment which they protect and their characteristics must conform to the national standards in the country concerned or to classification societies' rules, where relevant. Earthing and bonding to guard against static electricity is often associated with movable equipment and must be established whenever the equipment is set up.

The acceptable resistance in the earthing system depends upon the type of hazard that it is required to guard against. To protect electrical systems and equipment the resistance value is chosen so as to ensure the correct operation of the protective device (e.g. cut out or fuse) in the electrical circuit. For lightning protection the value depends on national regulations, and is typically in the range of 5 – 25 ohms. To avoid the accumulation of static electricity the earth resistance value should not be less than 1 megohm and in most cases may be considerably higher.

19.6.2   SHIP TO SHORE ELECTRIC CURRENTS

The subject of ship to shore currents is quite separate from static electricity. However, it is hoped that by considering ship to shore currents in conjunction with the discussion of the principles of static electricity it will be possible to dispel at least some of the confusion that frequently arises between them.

Large currents can flow in electrically conducting pipework and flexible hose systems between the ship and shore. The sources of these currents are:

Cathodic protection of the jetty or the hull of the ship provided by either a D.C. impressed current system or by sacrificial anodes.

Stray currents arising from galvanic potential differences between ship and shore or leakage effects from electrical power sources.

An all metal loading or discharge arm provides a very low resistance connection between ship and shore and there is a very real danger of an incendive arc when the ensuing large current is suddenly interrupted during the connecting or disconnecting of the arm at the tanker manifold. Similar arcs can occur with flexible hose strings containing metallic connections between the flanges of each length of hose. It is therefore becoming common practice to insert an insulating flange within the length of the loading arms and at the connection of flexible hose strings to the shore pipeline system. An alternative solution with flexible hose strings is to include in each string one length only of hose without internal bonding. The insertion of such a resistance completely blocks the flow of current through the loading arm or the hose string. At the same time the whole system remains earthed either to the ship or to the shore.

In the past it was usual deliberately to connect ship and shore systems by a bonding wire via a flame proof switch before the cargo connection was made and to maintain this bonding wire in position until after the cargo connection was broken. The use of this bonding wire had no relevance to electrostatic charging. It was an attempt to short circuit the ship/shore electrolytic/ cathodic protection systems and to reduce the ship/shore voltage to such an extent that currents in hoses or in metal arms would be negligible. However, because of the large current availability and the difficulty of achieving a sufficiently small electrical resistance in the ship/ shore bonding wire, this method has been found to be quite ineffective for its intended purpose. The use of ship/shore bonding wires is therefore being abandoned in favour of the insulating flanges described above.

Insulating flanges should be designed to avoid accidental short circuiting. A typical design of an insulating flange arrangement is shown in Appendix D. Points to be borne in mind when fitting an insulating flange are:

When the ship to shore connection is wholly flexible, as with hose, the insulating flange should be inserted at the jetty end where it is not likely to be disturbed.

When the connection is partly flexible and partly metal arm the insulating flange should be connected to the metal arm.

For all metal arms care should be taken to ensure that, wherever it is convenient to fit the flange, it is not short-circuited by guy wires.

Current flow can also occur through any other electrically conducting path between ship and shore, for example mooring wires or a metallic ladder or gangway. If there is a risk of the presence of a flammable gas mixture when such a conducting path is broken, then some form of insulation should be incorporated to prevent the flow of current.

Switching off cathodic protection systems of the impressed current type either ashore or on the ship is not, in general, considered to be a feasible method of minimising ship/shore currents in the absence of an insulating flange or hose. A jetty which is handling a succession of ships would need to have its cathodic protection off almost continuously and would therefore lose its corrosion resistance. Further, if the jetty system remains on, it is probable that the difference of potential between ship and shore will be less if the ship also keeps its cathodic protection system energised. In any case the polarization in an impressed current system takes many hours to decay after the system has been switched off, so that the ship would have to be deprived of full protection not only whilst alongside but also for a period before arrival in port. Only if the jetty is without an insulating flange and is devoid of cathodic protection, should consideration be given to switching off the ship's system.

19.6.3   SHIP TO SHIP ELECTRIC CURRENTS

The principles for controlling arcing during ship to ship transfer operations are the same as in ship to shore operations.

In ships dedicated to ship to ship transfers an insulating flange or a non-conducting length of hose should be used in the hose string. It is essential, however, that when transferring static accumulator oils these measures are not taken by both ships, leaving an insulated conductor between them upon which an electrostatic charge could accumulate. For the same reason, when such a ship is involved in ship to shore cargo transfers care should be taken to ensure that there is no insulated conductor between ship and shore through, for example, the use of two insulating flanges on one line.

In the absence of insulation between the ships the electrical potential between them should be reduced as much as possible. If both have properly functioning impressed current cathodic protection systems this is probably best achieved by leaving them running. Likewise if one has a sacrificial system and the other an impressed system, the latter should remain in operation. However, if either ship is without cathodic protection, or its impressed system has broken down, consideration should be given to switching off the impressed system, if any, on the other well before the two ships come together.

Chapter 20

Pressure Surge

This Chapter contains a brief explanation of the phenomenon of pressure surge in pipelines and discusses the ways in which it can be prevented.

20.1 INTRODUCTION

A pressure surge is generated in a pipeline system when there is an abrupt change in the rate of flow of liquid in the line. In tanker operations it is most likely to occur as a result of one of the following during loading:

Closure of an automatic shut down valve.

Slamming shut of a shore non-return valve.

Slamming shut of a butterfly type valve.

Rapid closure of a power operated valve.

If the total pressure generated in the pipeline exceeds the strength of any part of the pipeline system upstream of the valve there may be a rupture leading to an extensive spill of oil.

20.2 GENERATION OF PRESSURE SURGE

When a pump is used to convey liquid from a feed tank down a pipeline and through a valve into a receiving tank, the pressure at any point in the system while the liquid is flowing has three components:

The pressure on the surface of the liquid in the feed tank. In a tank with its ullage communicating to atmosphere this pressure is that of the atmosphere.

The hydrostatic pressure at the point in question.

The pressure generated by the pump, which is highest at the pump outlet and falls steadily down the line and through the valve to the receiving tank.

Of these three components, the first two are constant and need not be considered in the following description although they are always present and make their contributions to the total pressure.

Rapid closure of the valve superimposes an additional transient pressure which is due to the sudden conversion of the kinetic energy of the moving liquid into strain energy by compression of the fluid and stretching of the pipe. To explain the sequence of events the simplest hypothetical case will be considered, when the valve closure is instantaneous and there is no stretching of the pipe; this case gives rise to the highest pressures in the system.

When the valve closes the liquid immediately upstream of the valve is brought to rest instantaneously. This causes its pressure to rise by an amount P. In any consistent set of units

$$P = wav$$

where w is the density of the liquid
   a is the velocity of sound in the liquid
   v is the change in linear velocity of the liquid
      which is its linear flow rate before closure.

The cessation of flow of liquid is propagated back up the pipeline at the speed of sound and as each part of the liquid comes to rest its pressure is increased by the amount P. Therefore a steep pressure front of height P travels up the pipeline at the speed of sound and it is this disturbance that is known as a pressure surge.

Ahead of the surge the liquid is still moving forward and still has the pressure distribution applied to it by the pump. Behind it the liquid is stationary and its pressure has been increased at all points by the constant amount P. There is still a downstream pressure gradient behind the surge but a continuous series of pressure adjustments takes place in this part of the pipeline with the object of reaching the same pressure throughout the stationary liquid. These pressure adjustments also travel through the liquid at the speed of sound.

When the surge reaches the pump the pressure at the pump outlet (leaving aside the atmospheric and hydrostatic components) becomes the sum of the surge pressure P, and the output pressure of the pump at zero throughput, since flow through the pump has ceased. The process of pressure equalisation continues downstream of the pump. Again taking the hypothetical worst case, if the pressure is not relieved in any way the final result of the pressure changes down-stream of the pump is that the pressure throughout the whole length of stationary liquid reaches the pressure at the outlet of the pump, that is the sum of P and the pump outlet pressure at zero throughput. The final pressure adjustment to achieve this condition leaves the pump as soon as the original surge arrives at the pump and travels down to the valve at the speed of sound. The whole process therefore takes a time $2L/a$ from the instant of valve closure, where L is the length of the line and a is the speed of sound in the liquid. This time interval is known as the pipeline period.

In this simplified description, therefore, the liquid at any point in the line experiences an abrupt increase in pressure by an amount P followed by a slower, but still rapid, further increase until the pressure reaches the sum of P and the pump outlet pressure at zero throughput.

In practical circumstances the valve closure is not instantaneous and there is then some relief of the surge pressure through the valve while it is closing. The results are that the height of the pressure surge is less than in the hypothetical case, and the pressure front is less steep.

At the upstream end of the line some pressure relief occurs through the pump and this also serves to lessen the maximum pressure reached. If the effective closure time of the valve is several times greater than the pipeline period pressure relief is extensive and a hazardous situation is unlikely to arise.

Loss of pressure through the pump continues after the elapse of a time equal to the pipeline period until the pressure throughout the line between the pump and the closed valve is reduced to the pump output pressure at zero throughput. This situation would have resulted from the very slow closure of the valve, but the pressure surge would not then have occurred.

Downstream of the valve an analogous process is initiated when the valve closes, except that as the liquid is brought to rest there is a fall of pressure which travels downstream at the velocity of sound. However, the pressure drop is relieved by gas evolution from the liquid so that serious results are unlikely to occur, although the subsequent collapse of the gas bubbles may generate shock waves.

20.3   ASSESSMENT OF PRESSURE SURGES

20.3.1   EFFECTIVE CLOSURE TIME OF THE VALVE

In order to determine whether a serious pressure is likely to occur in a pipeline system the first step is to compare the time taken by the valve to close with the pipeline period.

The effective closure time, that is the period during which the rate of flow is in fact decreasing rapidly, is significantly less than the total time of movement of the valve spindle. It depends upon the design of the valve which determines the relationship between valve port area and spindle position. Another critical factor is the proportion of the total pressure available from the pump which is applied across the valve as it closes. This depends upon such things as the ratio of valve diameter to pipeline diameter and upon the length of the line upstream of the valve. In a long pipeline substantial flow reduction is usually achieved only during the closure of the last quarter or less of the valve port area. A long line therefore increases pressure surge problems not only through its effect upon the pipeline period but also because it tends to decrease the effective closure time of the valve.

If the effective valve closure time is less than, or equal to, the pipeline period, the system is liable to serious pressure surges. Surges of reduced, but still significant strength can be expected when the effective valve closure time is greater than the pipeline period, but they become negligible when it exceeds several times that period.

20.3.2   DERIVATION OF TOTAL PRESSURE IN THE SYSTEM

In the normal type of ship/shore system handling petroleum liquids, where the shore tank communicates to the atmosphere, the maximum pressure applied across the pipe wall at any point during a pressure surge is the sum of the hydrostatic pressure, the output pressure of the pump at zero throughput and the surge pressure. The first two of these pressures are usually known.

If the effective valve closure time is less than or equal to the pipeline period the value of the surge pressure used in determining the total pressure during the surge should be P, derived as indicated in Section 20.2. If it is somewhat greater than the pipeline period a smaller value can be used in place of P and, as already indicated, the surge pressure becomes negligible if the effective valve closure time is several times greater than the pipeline period.

20.3.3   OVERALL SYSTEM DESIGN

In this Chapter the simple case of a single pipeline has been considered. In practical cases the design of a possibly complex system should be taken into account. For example, the combined effects of valves in parallel or in series has to be examined. In some cases the surge effect may be increased; this can occur with two lines in parallel if closure of the valve in one line increases the flow in the other line before this line in its turn is shut down. On the other hand correct operation of valves in series in a line can minimize surge pressure.

20.4   REDUCTION OF PRESSURE SURGE HAZARD

20.4.1   GENERAL PRECAUTIONS

If as a result of the calculations summarized in Section 20.3 it is found that the potential total pressure exceeds or is close to the strength of any part of the pipeline system it is advisable to obtain expert advice.

In the case of manually operated valves good operating procedures should avoid pressure surge problems. It is important that a valve at the end of a long pipeline should not be closed against the flow and all changes in valve settings should be made slowly.

Where motorized valves are installed several steps can be taken to alleviate the problem:

Reduce the linear flow rate, that is the rate of transfer of cargo, to a value which makes the likely surge pressure tolerable.

Increase the effective valve closure time. In very general terms total closure times should be of the order of 30 seconds or preferably more. Valve closure rates should be steady and reproducible, although this may be difficult to achieve if spring return valves or actuators are needed to ensure that valves fail safe to the closed position. A more even rate of flow reduction may be achieved by careful attention to valve port design, or by the use of a valve actuator which gives a very slow rate of closure over, say, the final 15% of the port closure.

Use a pressure relief system, surge tanks or similar devices to absorb the effects of the surge sufficiently quickly.

20.4.2 LIMITATION OF FLOW RATE TO AVOID THE RISK OF A DAMAGING PRESSURE SURGE

In the operational context pipeline length and, very often, valve closure times are fixed and the only practical precaution against the consequences of an inadvertent rapid valve closure, eg. during topping off, is to limit the linear flow rate of the oil to a maximum value V_{max}. This flow rate is related to the maximum acceptable surge pressure, P_{max}, by the equation (see Section 20.2):

$$P_{max} = wav_{max}$$

If the internal diameter of the pipeline is d, the corresponding maximum acceptable volumetric flow rate, Q_{max}, is given by:

$$Q_{max} = \frac{\pi d^2}{4} v_{max}$$

$$= \frac{\pi}{4\,wa} \, d^2 P_{max}$$

With sufficient accuracy,

a, the velocity of sound in petroleum, is 1300 metres/second

w, the density of oils, is 850 kilograms/cubic metre so that, approximately,

$$Q_{max} = 7 \cdot 1 \times 10^{-7} d^2 P_{max}$$

where Q_{max} is in cubic metres/second, d in metres and P_{max} in Newtons/square metre.

In two alternative sets of units,

$$Q_{max} = 0 \cdot 025 d^2 P_{max}$$

where Q_{max} is in cubic metres/hour, d in metres and P_{max} in kilograms force/square metre.

or $Q_{max} = 0 \cdot 16 d^2 P_{max}$

$$= \frac{d^2 P_{max}}{6} \quad \text{approximately}$$

where Q_{max} is in cubic metres/hour, d in inches and P_{max} in kilograms force/square centimetre.

Chapter 21

Fire Fighting – Theory and Equipment

The types of fire that may be encountered are described, together with the means of extinguishing fires. Descriptions are given of fire fighting equipment to be found on tankers and recommendations made for that at terminals.

21.1   THEORY OF FIRE FIGHTING

Fire requires a combination of fuel, oxygen and a source of ignition. Most combustible or flammable substances, some only when heated, give off gas which burns if ignited when mixed with an appropriate quantity of oxygen, as in air.

Fires can be controlled and extinguished by the removal of heat, fuel or air. The main aim when fire fighting must therefore be to reduce the temperature or to remove the fuel or to exclude the supply of air with the greatest possible speed.

21.2   TYPES OF FIRE

21.2.1   COMBUSTIBLE MATERIAL FIRES

Examples of such fires are bedding, clothing, cleaning rags, wood, canvas, ropes and paper fires.

Cooling by large quantities of water, or the use of extinguishing agents containing a large proportion of water, is of primary importance when fighting fires of such ordinary combustible material. Cooling the source and surrounding area should continue long enough to ensure that no re-ignition is possible.

21.2.2   LIQUID PETROLEUM FIRES

Foam is an efficient agent for extinguishing most liquid petroleum fires. It should be applied so as to flow evenly and progressively over the burning surface, avoiding undue agitation. This can best be achieved by directing the foam jet against any vertical surface adjacent to the fire, both in order to break the force of the jet and to build up an unbroken smothering blanket. If there is no vertical surface the jet should be advanced in oscillating sweeps with the wind, taking care to avoid plunging it into the liquid. Foam spray streams, while limited in range, are also effective.

Volatile oil fires of limited size can be extinguished by water fog or water spray. Dry chemical powder or vaporizing halon liquids are also effective in dealing with such fires.

Non-volatile oil fires which have not been burning for too long can be extinguished by water fog or water spray if the whole of the burning surface is accessible. The surface of the liquid transfers its heat rapidly to the water droplets which present a very large cooling surface and the flame can be extinguished with advancing and oscillating sweeps of fog or spray across the whole width of the fire.

Any oil fire which has been burning for some time is more difficult to extinguish with water, since the oil will have been heated to a progressively greater depth and cannot readily be cooled to a point where it ceases to give off gas. Furthermore, the use of a water jet may spread the burning oil by splashing or overflow. This effect can also arise through agitation of the oil caused by violent boiling of the water. Water should only be applied to oil fires as a spray or fog, although jets of water can play a valuable role in cooling hot bulkheads and tank walls.

The best way of dealing with such fires in tanks is by means of a smothering agent, such as foam,

133

carbon dioxide, or in some cases dry chemical, coupled if possible with sealing off the tank and cooling adjacent areas or spaces.

An aspect that must be borne in mind with liquid petroleum is the risk of re-ignition, so that a continuing watch and preparedness should be maintained.

21.2.3   LIQUEFIED PETROLEUM GAS FIRES

Fires involving escaping liquefied petroleum gas should, where possible, be extinguished by stopping the gas flow. If the flow of gas cannot be stopped it may be safer to allow the fire to continue to burn, at the same time using water spray to cool and control the effect of radiant heat.

Extinguishing the flame may result in a wide spread of unignited gas and subsequent wider spread of flame if it is re-ignited.

In order to reach and close the valve controlling the flow of gas it may be necessary to extinguish flames from small leaks in its vicinity. In this case dry powder extinguishers should be used.

Water jets should never be used directly into a liquefied petroleum gas fire. Foam will not extinguish such fires.

21.2.4   ELECTRICAL EQUIPMENT FIRES

These may be caused by short circuit, over heating or the spreading of a fire from elsewhere. The immediate action should be to de-energize the equipment, and a non-conductive agent, such as carbon dioxide, halon or dry chemical, should then be used.

21.3   EXTINGUISHING AGENTS — COOLING

21.3.1   WATER

Water is the most common cooling agent. This is largely because water possesses very good heat absorbing qualities and, at terminals and on ships, is available in ample quantities.

A water jet, although excellent for fighting fires involving combustible materials, should not be used on burning oil, or on burning cooking oil or fat in galleys because of the danger of spreading the fire.

Water spray and water fog may be used effectively against oil fires and for making a screen between the fire fighter and the fire.

Owing to the danger of electrical shock, water should not be directed towards any electrical equipment.

A wetting agent may be added to water when it is to be used on tightly packed combustible materials. This has the effect of lowering its surface tension and thus increasing its effective penetration.

21.3.2   FOAM

Foam has a limited heat absorbing effect and should not normally be used for cooling.

21.4   EXTINGUISHING AGENTS — SMOTHERING

21.4.1   FOAM

Foam is an aggregation of small bubbles, of lower specific gravity than oil or water, which flows across the surface of a burning liquid and forms a coherent smothering blanket. It will also reduce the surface temperature of the liquid by the absorption of some heat.

There are a number of different types of foam concentrates available. These include standard protein foam, fluoro-protein foams and synthetic concentrates. The synthetics are divided into aqueous film forming foam (AFFF) and hydrocarbon surfactant type foam concentrates. Normally the protein, fluoro-protein and AFFF concentrates are used at 3% to 6% by volume concentration in water. The hydrocarbon surfactant type concentrates are available for use at 1% to 6% by volume concentration.

134

High expansion foam has an expansion ratio from about 150:1 to 1500:1. It is made from hydrocarbon surfactant concentrates and is used to fill rapidly an enclosed space and to extinguish a fire by preventing the movement of free air in the compartment. The foam generator, which may be fixed or mobile, sprays the foam solution on to a fine mesh net through which air is driven by a fan. High expansion foam is unsuitable for use in outside locations as it cannot readily be directed on to a hot fire and is quickly dispersed in light winds.

Medium expansion foam has an expansion ratio from about 15:1 up to 150:1. It is made from the same concentrates as high expansion foam, but its aeration does not require a fan. Portable applicators can be used to deliver considerable quantities of foam on to spill fires, but their throw is limited and the foam is liable to be dispersed in moderate winds.

Low expansion foam has an expansion ratio from about 3:1 up to about 15:1. It is made from protein based or synthetic concentrates and can be applied to spill or tank fires from fixed monitors or portable applicators. Good throw is possible and the foam is resistant to wind.

Foam applicators should be directed away from liquid petroleum fires until any water in the system has been flushed clear.

Foam should not come into contact with any electrical equipment.

The various foam concentrates are basically incompatible with each other and should not be mixed in storage. However, some foams separately generated with these concentrates are compatible when applied to a fire in sequence or simultaneously. The majority of foam concentrates can be used in conventional foam making devices suitable for producing protein foams. The systems should be thoroughly flushed out and cleaned before changing agents as the synthetic concentrates may dislodge sediment and plug the proportioning equipment.

Some of the foams produced from the various concentrates are compatible with dry chemical powder and are suitable for combined use. The degree of compatibility between the various foams and between the foams and dry chemical varies and should be established by suitable tests.

The compatibility of foam compounds is a factor to be borne in mind in considering joint operations with other services.

Foam concentrates may deteriorate with time depending on the storage conditions. Storage at high temperatures and in contact with air will cause sludge and sediment to form. This may affect the extinguishing ability of the expanded foam. Samples of the foam concentrate should therefore be returned periodically to the manufacturer for testing and evaluation.

21.4.2   CARBON DIOXIDE

Carbon dioxide is an excellent smothering agent for extinguishing fires, when used in conditions where it will not be widely diffused. Carbon dioxide is therefore effective in enclosed areas such as machinery spaces, pumprooms and electrical switch rooms where it can penetrate into places that cannot be reached by other means. On an open deck or jetty area carbon dioxide is comparatively ineffective.

Carbon dioxide does not damage delicate machinery or instruments and, being a non-conductor, can be used safely on or around electrical equipment.

Due to the possibility of static electricity generation, carbon dioxide should not be injected into any space containing a flammable atmosphere which is not on fire.

Carbon dioxide is asphyxiating and cannot be detected by sight or smell. No one should enter confined or partially confined spaces when carbon dioxide extinguishers have been used unless supervised and protected by suitable breathing apparatus and lifeline. Canister type respirators should not be used. Any compartment which has been flooded with carbon dioxide must be fully ventilated before entry without breathing apparatus.

21.4.3   STEAM

Steam is inefficient as a smothering agent because of the substantial delay that may occur before sufficient air is displaced to render the atmosphere incapable of supporting combustion. Steam should not be injected into any space containing an unignited flammable atmosphere due to the possibility of static electricity generation.

21.4.4 SAND

Sand is relatively ineffective as an extinguishing agent and is only useful on small fires on hard surfaces. Its basic use is to dry up small spills.

21.5 FLAME INHIBITORS

21.5.1 GENERAL

Flame inhibitors are materials which interfere chemically with the combustion process, and thereby extinguish the flames. However cooling or removal of fuel is necessary if re-ignition is to be prevented.

21.5.2 DRY CHEMICAL POWDER

Dry chemical powder is discharged from an extinguisher as a free flowing cloud. It is most effective in dealing initially with a fire resulting from an oil spill on a jetty or on the deck of a tanker and can also be used in confined spaces. It is especially useful on burning liquids escaping from leaking pipelines and joints. It is a non-conductor and is suitable therefore for dealing with electrical fires. It must be directed into the flames.

Dry chemical powder has a negligible cooling effect and affords no protection against re-ignition, arising, for example, from the presence of hot metal surfaces.

Certain types of dry chemical powder can cause a breakdown of a foam blanket and only those labelled 'foam compatible' should be used in conjunction with foam.

Dry chemical powder clogs and becomes useless if it is allowed to become damp when stored or when extinguishers are being filled.

21.5.3 VAPORIZING LIQUIDS (HALONS)

Vaporizing liquids, like dry chemical powder, have a flame inhibiting effect and also have a slight smothering effect. There are a number of different liquids available, all halogenated hydrocarbons, often identified by a system of halon numbers.

The halons are most effective in enclosed spaces such as computer centres, storage rooms, tanker engine or pump rooms, generator enclosures and similar locations.

All halons are considered to be toxic to some degree because contact with hot surfaces and flame causes them to break down yielding toxic substances. All personnel should therefore evacuate the area where halons are to be used, although it is possible to start the discharge of halons before the evacuation is complete as the normal concentrations encountered in extinguishing fires are acceptable for brief periods. After the fire has been extinguished the area should be thoroughly ventilated. If it is necessary to enter the area before ventilating, suitable breathing apparatus should be used.

Carbon tetrachloride should not be used as it is highly toxic.

21.6 TANKER FIRE FIGHTING EQUIPMENT

The requirements for ships' fire fighting equipment are laid down by the regulations of the particular country in which the tanker is registered. These regulations are generally based on the principles of the International Convention for the Safety of Life at Sea.

21.7 TANKER FIXED FIRE FIGHTING INSTALLATION — COOLING

All tankers are provided with a water fire fighting system consisting of pumps, a fire main with hydrant points, fire hoses complete with couplings, and jet nozzles or, preferably, jet/spray nozzles. A sufficient number of hydrants is provided and so located to ensure that two jets of water can reach any part of the ship. Certain bulkheads are sometimes fitted with permanent water spray lines.

An International Shore Fire Connection should be provided on tankers so that an external water supply can be coupled to any hydrant in the ship's fire main. These connections should be available for immediate use (see Appendix E.)

21.8   TANKER FIXED FIRE FIGHTING INSTALLATIONS — SMOTHERING

One or more, or a combination of, the different smothering systems listed below may be installed on board tankers.

21.8.1   CARBON DIOXIDE FLOODING SYSTEM

This is designed to fight fires in the engine room, boiler room and pumproom. The system normally consists of a battery of large carbon dioxide cylinders. The carbon dioxide is piped from the cylinder manifold to suitable points having diffuxing nozzles. An alarm should be activated in the compartment before the carbon dioxide is released to give personnel time to evacuate the compartment.

21.8.2   FOAM SYSTEMS

These are used for fighting fire in the cargo spaces, on the cargo deck, in the pumproom or in the engine spaces. A foam system has storage tanks containing foam concentrate. Water from the fire pumps picks up the correct proportion of foam concentrate from the tank through a proportionator and the foam solution is then conveyed through permanent supply lines to offtake points.

21.8.3   WATER FOG

Water fog is supplied through a system of high pressure water lines and fog nozzles. A ring of nozzles around the inside of the tank opening effectively blankets a cargo tank hatch fire. Some ships are also fitted with fixed pressurized water fog protection for boiler room, machinery spaces, and pumprooms.

21.8.4   WATER WALL

Some ships have a fixed system to give a protective water wall between the cargo decks and the poop front.

21.8.5   INERT GAS SYSTEM

The purpose of an inert gas system is to prevent cargo tank fires or explosions. It is not a fixed fire fighting installation, but in the event of a fire the system may be of assistance in extinguishing it.

21.8.6   STEAM SMOTHERING SYSTEM

Steam smothering systems may be fitted on older tankers. Their use should be discouraged because of their inefficiency and the risk of static electricity generation.

21.9   TERMINAL FIRE FIGHTING EQUIPMENT

The type and quantity of fire fighting equipment should be related to the size, location and frequency of use of the terminal; the layout of the terminal, and the petroleum products handled are also relevant.

In ports with many terminals or in congested industrial locations the local authority or port authority provides the main fire fighting capability. Arrangements may exist between oil terminals or with other industries in the same area for assistance in the event of a fire.

Because of these many variables it is impractical here to make specific recommendations for fire fighting equipment. Each terminal should be studied individually when deciding upon the type, location and use of equipment.

21.10   TERMINAL PORTABLE FIRE FIGHTING EQUIPMENT

21.10.1   GENERAL

Portable fire extinguishers should be made available at each berth to allow terminal personnel to attack an outbreak of fire immediately in order to limit the area of fire, to extinguish the fire and thereafter to prevent re-ignition.

21.10.2 FOAM EXTINGUISHERS

Small foam extinguishers with capacities of about 10 litres are too limited to be effective in most cases in the event of a fire at a terminal.

Sizes in the order of 100 litres capacity pre-mix foam appliances are most effective for use at berths. These produce 1000 litres of foam and it is desirable to have a jet length of about 12 metres (40 feet).

21.10.3 DRY CHEMICAL EXTINGUISHERS

Dry chemical (foam compatible) extinguishers are available in a range of capacities. The length of the application hose may have to be limited, in accordance with the manufacturer's recommendation, to maintain nozzle velocity throughout total discharge.

21.10.4 CARBON DIOXIDE EXTINGUISHERS

Carbon dioxide extinguishers have little value at berths or on jetties except at points where minor electrical fires could occur.

Electrical sub-stations located on jetties should be provided with an adequate number of carbon dioxide extinguishers or may have a fixed carbon dioxide system installed.

21.11 TERMINAL FIXED FIRE FIGHTING EQUIPMENT

21.11.1 FIRE WATER MAINS AND PUMPS

Fire water pipelines, either sea or fresh water, should extend as near to the heads of jetties as possible with a number of accessible water take off (hydrant) points which should be spaced not more than two or three standard hose lengths apart. The take off (hydrant) points generally consist of headers with individually valved outlets fitted with a fire hose connection suitable for the particular type of fire hose coupling in use locally. Isolating valves should be fitted so as to maintain the efficiency of the system in the event of a fracture.

The hydraulics of fire water or foam pipeline systems dictate the characteristics of the fixed pumping capacities required. It may be desirable to consider whether such fixed pumping units should have two independent sources of power or whether mobile pumps should be available for use in the event of a breakdown of the fixed pumping unit; these may also be used for boosting fire water mains pressure.

Terminals should have a suitable connection or adaptor fitted with an International Shore Fire Connection through which water could be supplied to a tanker's fire main if required (see Appendix E.)

The minimum capacities and pressures for fire water mains are dependent upon whether the system is to be used for cooling or for the production of foam, and upon the length of jet required.

At some locations, precautions against the freezing of fire water mains may be necessary.

21.11.2 FOAM MAINS

Where pipelines for foam solution or concentrate are provided the lines should have a number of accessible take off (hydrant) points which should be spaced not more than two or three standard hose lengths apart. The take off (hydrant) points generally consist of a header fitted with two outlets individually valved and fitted with a fire hose connection suitable for the particular type of fire hose coupling in use locally. Isolating valves should be fitted so as to retain the efficiency of the line in the event of fracture. Suitable pipeline drain valves and wash out facilities should be provided. A foam solution pipeline of this type should cater for a design minimum of 115 cubic metres/hour (500 US gallons/minute) of solution.

Foam concentrate can be distributed through a smaller bore pipe system to the tanks supplying the inductors of fixed or mobile foam making appliances.

Fixed pipelines for generated (aerated) foam are of limited value due to pressure losses in the system and lack of projection.

21.11.3   MONITORS AND CANNONS

The terms monitor and cannon may be used interchangeably; in this guide the term monitor is used to mean both.

In general monitors may be used for foam or water, although specific types may be designed solely for foam. Large capacity monitors would normally be on a fixed mounting or on a mobile unit.

The effective height of the liquid stream required from a monitor is dictated by the particular use envisaged; if required to assist in the event of a tanker fire, height of freeboard is important and with large tankers this can be in excess of 17 metres (55 feet). Minimum requirements for monitor operations are a jet length of 37 metres (120 feet) and a jet height of 15 metres (50 feet) in still air.

Monitors may be mounted on fixed towers, remotely controlled either from the tower base or at a distance. Tower base controls may need special protection. Fixed tower installations may have the drawback that with the wind in the wrong direction smoke may obscure vision and sighting.

Foam and water monitors can also be installed on articulated or telescopic booms and be remotely operated. This provides additional flexibility over fixed monitors, for example if the tanker is loaded, the boom can be lowered and extended over the tanker to apply the foam gently with a minimum of disturbance.

Two basic types of booms are available. One has only a monitor at the top while the other has a monitor and a platform or basket to carry personnel. There are advantages for the unit with the basket in that it can be used to place fire fighters on or take them off the vessel if the gangway is involved in the fire. In addition, personnel can be elevated to observe the fire and direct the fire fighting.

Ideally, booms or towers should be installed on tugs. Booms have advantages over stationary elevated towers on tugs for both fire fighting and tug operations. With the boom lowered, the tug can manoeuvre under hawsers or other obstructions and then elevate the boom to the desired position. Fixed monitors on towers or on the deck of a tug do not have this flexibility.

21.11.4   FIXED WATER SPRAY OR DRENCHER SYSTEM

A fixed water spray or drencher system installed for fire protection should incorporate drencher heads having 12 millimetres (0·5 inch) minimum orifice openings, rather than small holes drilled in a pipe header which can become clogged due to corrosion or by painting over the holes.

The design of a fire water system should ensure that drencher systems or similar fixed cooling arrangements do not materially reduce the volume of water available for fire fighting.

21.12   WATER BORNE FIRE FIGHTING EQUIPMENT

Water borne equipment is highly effective in fire fighting at a terminal. Such a capability is normally best provided by working tugs fitted with fire fighting equipment, including foam facilities, which should be capable of tackling a deck fire on the largest tanker likely to use the port. In very special circumstances consideration may be given to the provision of a specifically equipped fire fighting tender.

Fire fighting craft, especially those at terminals with buoy mooring berths should have a connection for an International Shore Fire Connection (see Appendix E) for use in boosting pressure in, or supplies to, a tanker's fire water mains, or a suitable adaptor for this purpose. The craft should also have a connection to enable them to supply water to or boost pressure in the terminal fire main.

21.13   PROTECTIVE CLOTHING

All clothing gives some protection against heat and consequently from burns but, because it is not fire-proof, it will be scorched if exposed to flame.

The most effective fire protective clothing presently available is made of light weight fire resistant fabric incorporating an aluminium covering, and is sometimes referred to as a fire proximity suit. This type of suit is not suitable for direct entry into fire areas. Heavier weight suits, termed fire entry suits, permit personnel actually to enter the fire area wearing breathing apparatus.

Although early suits were made of asbestos, they are not now recommended. When compared with newer types of material, asbestos absorbs and transmits heat much more quickly, and clothing made of asbestos provides protection only for a short period. Asbestos must be kept dry, otherwise there is a danger that the wearer will be scalded when exposed to fire. Personnel wearing gloves should be standing by ready to remove asbestos clothing that has become very hot.

All protective clothing should be kept serviceable and dry, and should be properly fastened while being worn.

On tankers protective clothing should be stowed near lockers that contain breathing apparatus.

Appendices

Appendix A

SHIP/SHORE SAFETY CHECK LIST

VESSEL _____

BERTH _____

INSTRUCTIONS FOR COMPLETION:

The safety of operations requires that all questions should be answered affirmatively after checking by both ship and terminal representatives. If an affirmative answer is not possible, the reason should be given and agreement reached upon appropriate precautions between the ship and the terminal.

	Ship Representative	Terminal Representative	Remarks
1. Is the ship securely moored? —			
2. Are emergency towing wires correctly positioned?			
3. Is there safe access between ship and shore?			
4. Is the ship ready to move under its own power?			
5. Is there an effective deck watch in attendance on board and adequate supervision on the terminal?			
6. Is the agreed ship/shore communication system operative?			
7. Have the procedures for cargo, bunker and ballast handling been agreed?			
8. Has the emergency shut down procedure been agreed?			
9. Are fire hoses and fire fighting equipment on board and ashore ready for immediate use?			
10. Are cargo and bunker hoses and/or arms in good condition and properly rigged?			
11. Are scuppers effectively plugged, and drip trays in position, both on board and ashore?			
12. Are unused cargo and bunker connections, including the stern discharge line, if fitted, blanked?			
13. Are sea and overboard discharge valves, when not in use, closed and lashed?			
14. Are all cargo and bunker tank lids closed?			
15. Is the agreed tank venting system being used?			
16. Are hand torches of an approved type?			
17. Are portable VHF/UHF transceivers of an approved type?			
18. Are the ship's main radio transmitter aerials earthed?			
19. Are electric cables to portable electrical equipment disconnected from power?			
20. Are all external doors and ports in the amidships accommodation closed?			
21. Are all doors and ports in the after accommodation leading into or overlooking the tank deck closed?			
22. Are air conditioning intakes which may permit the entry of petroleum gas closed?			
23. Are window-type air conditioning units disconnected?			
24. Are smoking requirements being observed?			
25. Are the requirements for the use of galley and other cooking appliances being observed?			
26. Are naked light requirements being observed?			

Declaration:

We have checked with each other the items listed on this check list in the course of a joint inspection, and have satisfied ourselves that the entries we have made are correct to the best of our knowledge.

For Ship   Name _____   Rank _____   Signature _____

For terminal   Name _____   Position _____   Signature _____

                Time _____   Date _____

Acknowledgement of repetitive checks	Time and date						
	Initials: For ship						
	For terminal						

143

Specimen letter for issue to masters of tankers at terminals

Company ....

Terminal ....

Date ....

The Master,
s.s./m.v. ....

Port: ....

Dear Sir,

SAFETY REQUIREMENTS

Responsibility for the safe conduct of operations on board your ship while at our terminal rests with you as master. Nevertheless, since our personnel, property and other shipping may also suffer serious damage in the event of accident aboard your ship, we wish, before operations start, to seek your full co-operation and understanding on the safety requirements set out in the Ship/Shore Safety Check List.

These safety requirements are based on safe practices widely accepted by the oil and tanker industries. We therefore expect you and all under your command to adhere strictly to them throughout your stay alongside this terminal. We, for our part, will ensure that our personnel do likewise and co-operate fully with you in the mutual interest of safe and efficient operation.

In order to assure ourselves of your compliance with these safety requirements, we shall, before the start of operations and thereafter from time to time, instruct a member of our staff to visit your ship. After reporting to you or your deputy he will join one of your officers in a routine inspection of cargo decks and accommodation spaces.

If we observe any infringement on board your ship of any of these safety requirements, we shall bring this immediately to the attention of yourself or your deputy for corrective action. If such action is not taken in a reasonable time we shall adopt measures which we consider to be the most appropriate to deal with the situation and we shall notify you accordingly.

If you observe any infringement of these requirements by terminal staff, whether on the jetty or on board your ship, please bring this immediately to the notice of our representative who is nominated as your contact during your stay in port. Should you feel that any immediate threat to the safety of your ship arises from any action on our part, or from equipment under our control, you are fully entitled to demand an immediate cessation of operations.

The senior terminal representative on duty is ....

Telephone number ....

UHF/VHF communication channel ....

IN THE EVENT OF CONTINUED OR FLAGRANT DISREGARD OF THESE SAFETY REQUIRE-MENTS BY ANY SHIP, WE RESERVE THE RIGHT TO STOP ALL OPERATIONS AND TO ORDER THAT SHIP OFF THE BERTH FOR APPROPRIATE ACTION TO BE TAKEN BY THE CHARTERERS AND OWNERS CONCERNED.

Please acknowledge receipt of this letter by countersigning and returning the attached copy.

Signed:

....

Terminal representative

Receipt of this letter is acknowledged

Signed:

....

Master

s.s./m.v. ....

Date .... Time ....

Appendix B

FIRE NOTICE

FIRE
INSTRUCTIONS IN CASE OF FIRE
DO NOT HESITATE TO RAISE THE ALARM

TERMINAL FIRE ALARM

At this terminal the fire alarm signal is:

....

....

IN CASE OF FIRE

1. Sound one or more blasts of the ship's whistle each blast of not less than ten seconds duration supplemented by a continuous sounding of the general alarm system.
2. Contact the terminal.
   Telephone number ....
   UHF/VHF communication channel ....

ACTION — SHIP

Fire on your ship
— Raise alarm
— Fight fire and prevent fire spreading
— Inform terminal
— Cease all cargo operations and then close all valves
— Stand by to disconnect hoses or arms
— Bring engines to standby
Fire on other ship or ashore
Stand by, and when instructed:
— Cease all cargo operations and then close all valves
— Disconnect hoses or arms
— Bring engines and crew to standby, ready to unberth

ACTION — TERMINAL

Fire on a Ship
— Raise alarm
— Contact ship
— Cease all cargo operations and then close all valves
— Stand by to disconnect hoses or arms
— Stand by to assist fire fighting
— Inform all ships
— Implement terminal emergency plan
Fire Ashore
— Raise alarm
— Cease all cargo operations and then close all valves
— Fight fire and prevent fire spreading
— If required stand by to disconnect hoses or arms
— Inform all ships
— Implement terminal emergency plan

IN THE CASE OF FIRE THE TERMINAL PERSONNEL WILL DIRECT THE MOVEMENT OF VEHICULAR TRAFFIC ASHORE

Note: Wording in capitals may be printed in red for greater emphasis.

Appendix C

OIL CARGO HOSE

C.1.   **GENERAL**

Oil cargo hose (sometimes called oil suction and discharge hose) should conform to recognized standard specifications as laid down by a National Authority such as the British Standards Institution (BS.1435) or as recommended by the Oil Companies International Marine Forum (OCIMF) and confirmed by established hose manufacturers. Hose should be of a grade and type suitable for the service and operating conditions in which it is to be used.

Special hose is required for use at high temperatures, such as with hot asphalt, and low temperatures.

As a general indication of hose which may be supplied for normal cargo handling duty, the information given in Sections C.2 to C.6 of this Appendix is condensed from the British Standard BS.1435. Reference may also be made to the OCIMF Buoy Mooring Forum Hose Standard — 'Specification for Rubber, Wire-reinforced Oil Suction and Discharge Hoses for Offshore Moorings'.

C.2.   **TYPES AND APPLICATIONS**

C.2.1.   TYPES

For normal duty there are three basic types of hose: R — rough bore; S — smooth bore; L — lightweight.

There are also a number of special hose types having the same basic construction but modified for particular purposes, such as for submarine pipelines and floating hose strings. These can be made for sinking or floating and can have individual floats or integral floatation.

C.2.2.   APPLICATIONS

Rough bore hose (type R) is heavy and robust with an internal lining supported by a steel wire helix. It is used for cargo handling at terminal jetties. A similar hose is made for submarine and floating use (type R × M).

Smooth bore hose (type S) is also used for cargo handling at terminal jetties but is of lighter construction than the rough bore type and the lining is not supported by a wire helix. A similar hose is made for submarine and floating use (type S × M).

Lightweight hose (type L) is for discharge duty or bunkering only and can be used where flexibility and light weight are important considerations.

All of these types of hose may be supplied in electrically continuous or electrically discontinuous construction.

C.3.   **PERFORMANCE**

Hose is classified according to its rated pressure and that stipulated by the manufacturer should not be exceeded. The manufacturer applies a vacuum test to hoses used for suction and discharge service.

Hose of normal standards is usually manufactured for products having a minimum temperature of −20°C (−4°F) to a maximum of 82°C (180°F) and an aromatic hydrocarbon content not greater than 25%. Hose is normally suitable for sunlight and ambient temperatures ranging from −29°C (−20°F) to 52°C (125°F).

C.4. MARKING

Each length of hose manufactured to the British Standard or the OCIMF Hose Standard is marked by the manufacturers with:

The manufacturer's name or trademark.

Identification with the standard specification for manufacture.

Factory test pressure.

Month and year of manufacture.

Manufacturer's serial number.

Whether electrically continuous or electrically discontinuous.

C.5. FLOW VELOCITIES

Peak flow rates are limited by the construction of the hose and the following are indicative of hose supplied under the British Standard or the OCIMF specifications:

a) Light and medium duty hoses — 12 metres/second (40 feet/second)

b) Heavy duty hoses — 15 metres/second (50 feet/second)

For Multi-buoy and SPM facilities, the OCIMF Hose Standards should be applied — for dock facilities, the BS.1435 standards are applicable.

For guidance, the corresponding throughputs are as follows:

Velocity 12 metres/second			
Nominal Inside Diameter of Hose		Throughput	
Inches	Millimetres	Cubic Metres Per Hour	Barrels Per Hour
6	152	788	4,950
8	203	1,400	8,810
10	254	2,180	13,700
12	305	3,150	19,800
16	406	5,600	35,200
20	508	8,750	55,000
24	610	12,600	79,300
30	762	19,700	123,000

Velocity 15 metres/second			
Nominal Inside Diameter of Hose		Throughput	
Inches	Millimetres	Cubic Metres per Hour	Barrels per Hour
6	152	985	6,190
8	203	1,750	11,000
10	254	2,730	17,200
12	305	3,940	24,700
16	406	7,000	44,000
20	508	10,900	68,000
24	610	15,700	99,100
30	762	24,600	154,000

C.6.   TESTING OF HOSES

Periodic testing of hoses should be in accordance with the requirements of the specification to which the hose was manufactured and/or as detailed in the OCIMF Buoy Mooring Forum Hose Guide — 'Guide for the Handling, Storage, Inspection and Testing of Hoses in Field'.

C.7.   HOSE FLANGE STANDARDS

Flange dimensions and drilling should conform to the common standard of ANSI B16.5, BS.1560 Series 150, or equivalent as recommended for flanges on shore pipeline and ship manifold connections.

C.8.   OPERATING CONDITIONS

For oil cargo hose to be used in normal duties:

Oil temperatures in excess of that stipulated by the manufacturer, generally 82°C (180°F), should be avoided.

A flow rate in excess of the manufacturer's recommendation will shorten the life of the hose and should be avoided.

The maximum working pressure stipulated by the manufacturer should be adhered to and surge pressures should be avoided.

The hose life will be shorter in white oil service than with black oils.

The life of a hose can be extended by transferring it from white oil to black oil duties during its service, but hose so transferred should be clearly marked.

C.9.   EXTENDED STORAGE

New hoses in storage before use, or hoses removed from service for a period of 2 months or more, should, as far as practicable, be kept in a cool, dark, dry store in which air can circulate freely. They should be drained and washed out with fresh water and laid out horizontally on solid supports spaced to keep the hose straight. No oil should be allowed to come into contact with the outside of the hose.

If the hose is stored outside it should be well protected from the sun.

Recommendations upon hose storage are given in the OCIMF Buoy Mooring Forum Hose Guide — 'Guide for the Handling, Storage, Inspection and Testing of Hoses in Field'.

C.10. HOSE WEIGHTS

C.10.1. WEIGHT OF HOSE STRINGS FOR MULTI-BUOY MOORINGS

The following tables gives the approximate weights of hose strings in tonnes (including fittings, floats and pick-up buoy) with all hoses full of crude oil S.G. 0·850. The assumed total lift is 7·5 metres (25 feet) above deck level, with the tanker on light draught.

Size of Tanker	Water Depth in Berth										
Feet Metres	180 54	150 46	120 37	100 30	90 27	80 24	70 21	60 18	50 15	40 12	30 9
20 inches I.D. Hoses											
500,000 DWT	19.5	18.7	18.0	17.5	17.3						
330,000 "	16.9	16.2	15.4	14.9	14.7	14.5					
270,000 "	16.4	15.7	14.9	14.4	14.2	13.9	13.7				
200,000 "	15.9	15.1	14.4	13.9	13.7	13.4	13.2	12.9			
100,000 "	14.3	13.6	12.9	12.4	12.1	11.9	11.6	11.4	11.2		
70,000 "	13.8	13.1	12.4	11.9	11.6	11.4	11.1	10.9	10.6	10.4	
50,000 "	13.4	12.7	12.0	11.5	11.2	11.0	10.7	10.5	10.3	10.0	9.8
35,000 "	13.1	12.3	11.6	11.1	10.8	10.6	10.4	10.1	9.9	9.6	9.4
18,000 "	12.4	11.7	11.0	10.5	10.2	10.0	9.7	9.5	9.2	9.0	8.7
16 inches I.D. Hoses											
500,000 DWT	13.5	13.0	12.4	12.0	11.8						
330,000 "	11.8	11.2	10.7	10.3	10.1	9.9					
270,000 "	11.4	10.9	10.3	10.0	9.8	9.6	9.4				
200,000 "	11.1	10.5	10.0	9.6	9.4	9.2	9.1	8.9			
100,000 "	10.1	9.5	8.9	8.6	8.4	8.2	8.0	7.8	7.7		
70,000 "	9.7	9.2	8.6	8.2	8.1	7.9	7.7	7.5	7.3	7.1	
50,000 "	9.4	8.9	8.3	8.0	7.8	7.6	7.4	7.2	7.1	6.9	6.7
35,000 "	9.2	8.6	8.1	7.7	7.5	7.3	7.2	7.0	6.7	6.6	6.4
18,000 "	8.7	8.2	7.6	7.3	7.1	6.9	6.7	6.5	6.4	6.2	6.0
12 inches I.D. Hoses											
500,000 DWT	8.9	8.6	8.2	8.0	7.8						
330,000 "	7.8	7.4	7.0	6.8	6.7	6.6					
270,000 "	7.6	7.2	6.8	6.6	6.5	6.4	6.2				
200,000 "	7.3	7.0	6.6	6.4	6.2	6.1	6.0	5.9			
100,000 "	6.6	6.3	5.9	5.7	5.6	5.4	5.3	5.2	5.1		
70,000 "	6.4	6.1	5.7	5.5	5.3	5.2	5.1	5.0	4.9	4.7	
50,000 "	6.3	5.9	5.5	5.3	5.2	5.1	4.9	4.8	4.7	4.6	4.4
35,000 "	6.1	5.7	5.4	5.1	5.0	4.9	4.8	4.6	4.5	4.4	4.3
18,000 "	5.8	5.4	5.1	4.8	4.7	4.6	4.5	4.4	4.2	4.1	4.0
10 inches I.D. Hoses											
500,000 DWT	6.2	5.9	5.7	5.5	5.4						
330,000 "	5.4	5.1	4.9	4.7	4.6	4.5					
270,000 "	5.2	5.0	4.7	4.6	4.5	4.4	4.3				
200,000 "	5.1	4.8	4.6	4.4	4.3	4.2	4.1	4.0			
100,000 "	4.6	4.3	4.1	3.9	3.8	3.7	3.6	3.5	3.4		
70,000 "	4.4	4.2	3.9	3.8	3.7	3.6	3.5	3.4	3.3	3.2	
50,000 "	4.3	4.1	3.8	3.7	3.6	3.5	3.4	3.3	3.2	3.1	3.0
35,000 "	4.2	3.9	3.7	3.5	3.4	3.3	3.2	3.1	3.0	2.9	2.8
18,000 "	4.0	3.7	3.5	3.3	3.2	3.1	3.0	2.9	2.8	2.7	2.6
8 inches I.D. Hoses											
500,000 DWT	4.4	4.2	4.1	4.0	3.9						
330,000 "	3.9	3.7	3.5	3.4	3.3	3.2					
270,000 "	3.7	3.6	3.4	3.3	3.2	3.1	3.0				
200,000 "	3.6	3.5	3.3	3.2	3.1	3.0	2.9	2.8			
100,000 "	3.3	3.1	2.9	2.8	2.7	2.6	2.5	2.4	2.3		
70,000 "	3.2	3.0	2.8	2.7	2.6	2.5	2.4	2.3	2.2	2.1	
50,000 "	3.1	2.9	2.8	2.6	2.5	2.4	2.3	2.2	2.1	2.0	1.9
35,000 "	3.0	2.9	2.7	2.5	2.4	2.3	2.2	2.1	2.0	1.9	1.8
18,000 "	2.9	2.7	2.5	2.4	2.3	2.2	2.1	2.0	1.9	1.8	1.7

WEIGHT OF HOSE STRINGS FOR SINGLE BUOY MOORINGS

The following table gives the approximate weights of hose strings in tonnes (including fittings, floats and pick-up buoy) with all hoses full of crude oil of S.G. 0.850. The assumed total lift is 7·5 metres (25 feet) above deck level, with the tanker on light draught.

Size of Tanker	Inside Diameter of Hose in Inches				
	20	16	12	10	8
500,000 DWT	16.4	11.4	8.2	6.6	4.7
330,000 "	13.6	9.4	6.8	5.4	3.9
270,000 "	13.0	9.1	6.5	5.2	3.7
200,000 "	12.5	8.7	6.2	5.0	3.6
100,000 "	10.8	7.5	5.4	4.3	3.1
70,000 "	10.0	7.1	5.1	4.1	2.9
50,000 "	9.8	6.8	4.9	3.9	2.8
35,000 "	9.4	6.5	4.7	3.7	2.7
18,000 "	8.7	6.0	4.3	3.5	2.5

Appendix D

TYPICAL INSULATING FLANGE JOINT

TYPICAL INSULATING FLANGE JOINT.

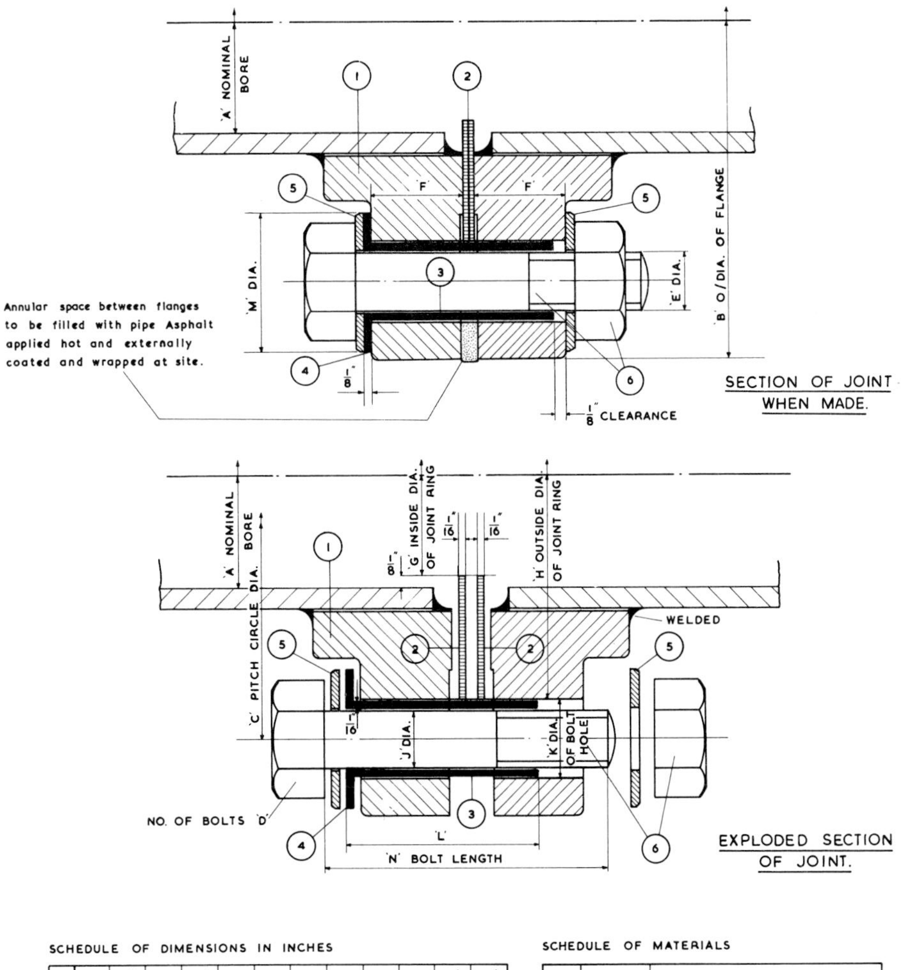

'A' NOMINAL BORE
'F'
'F'
'B' O/DIA. OF FLANGE
'M' DIA.
'E' DIA.
Annular space between flanges to be filled with pipe Asphalt applied hot and externally coated and wrapped at site.
$\frac{1}{8}''$
$\frac{1}{8}''$ CLEARANCE
SECTION OF JOINT WHEN MADE.
'G' INSIDE DIA. OF JOINT RING
'H' OUTSIDE DIA. OF JOINT RING
$\frac{1}{16}''$
$\frac{1}{16}''$
'C' PITCH CIRCLE DIA.
WELDED
'J' DIA.
'K' DIA. OF BOLT HOLE
NO. OF BOLTS 'D'
'L'
'N' BOLT LENGTH
EXPLODED SECTION OF JOINT.

SCHEDULE OF DIMENSIONS IN INCHES

A	1	$1\frac{1}{2}$	2	$2\frac{1}{2}$	3	4	6	8	10	12	$13\frac{1}{4}$	$15\frac{1}{4}$
B	$4\frac{1}{4}$	5	6	7	$7\frac{1}{2}$	9	11	$13\frac{1}{2}$	16	19	21	$23\frac{1}{2}$
C	$3\frac{1}{8}$	$3\frac{7}{8}$	$4\frac{3}{4}$	$5\frac{1}{2}$	6	$7\frac{1}{2}$	$9\frac{1}{2}$	$11\frac{3}{4}$	$14\frac{1}{4}$	17	$18\frac{3}{4}$	$21\frac{1}{4}$
D	4	4	4	4	4	8	8	8	12	12	12	16
E	$\frac{1}{2}$	$\frac{1}{2}$	$\frac{5}{8}$	$\frac{5}{8}$	$\frac{5}{8}$	$\frac{5}{8}$	$\frac{3}{4}$	$\frac{3}{4}$	$\frac{7}{8}$	$\frac{7}{8}$	1	1
F	$\frac{9}{16}$	$\frac{11}{16}$	$\frac{3}{4}$	$\frac{7}{8}$	$\frac{15}{16}$	$\frac{15}{16}$	1	$1\frac{1}{8}$	$1\frac{3}{16}$	$1\frac{1}{4}$	$1\frac{3}{8}$	$1\frac{7}{16}$
G	$\frac{3}{4}$	$1\frac{1}{4}$	$1\frac{3}{4}$	$2\frac{1}{4}$	$2\frac{3}{4}$	$3\frac{3}{4}$	$5\frac{3}{4}$	$7\frac{3}{4}$	$9\frac{3}{4}$	$11\frac{3}{4}$	13	15
H	$2\frac{3}{8}$	$3\frac{1}{8}$	$3\frac{7}{8}$	$4\frac{5}{8}$	$5\frac{1}{8}$	$6\frac{5}{8}$	$8\frac{1}{2}$	$10\frac{3}{4}$	$13\frac{1}{8}$	$15\frac{7}{8}$	$17\frac{1}{2}$	20
J	$\frac{9}{16}$	$\frac{9}{16}$	$\frac{11}{16}$	$\frac{11}{16}$	$\frac{11}{16}$	$\frac{11}{16}$	$\frac{13}{16}$	$\frac{13}{16}$	$\frac{15}{16}$	$\frac{15}{16}$	$1\frac{1}{16}$	$1\frac{1}{16}$
K	$\frac{3}{4}$	$\frac{3}{4}$	$\frac{7}{8}$	$\frac{7}{8}$	$\frac{7}{8}$	$\frac{7}{8}$	1	1	$1\frac{1}{8}$	$1\frac{1}{8}$	$1\frac{1}{4}$	$1\frac{1}{4}$
L	$1\frac{1}{4}$	$1\frac{1}{2}$	$1\frac{5}{8}$	$1\frac{7}{8}$	2	2	$2\frac{1}{8}$	$2\frac{3}{8}$	$2\frac{1}{2}$	$2\frac{5}{8}$	$2\frac{7}{8}$	3
M	$1\frac{5}{16}$	$1\frac{5}{16}$	$1\frac{1}{2}$	$1\frac{1}{2}$	$1\frac{1}{2}$	$1\frac{1}{2}$	$1\frac{3}{4}$	$1\frac{3}{4}$	$1\frac{15}{16}$	$1\frac{15}{16}$	$2\frac{1}{8}$	$2\frac{1}{8}$
N	$2\frac{1}{4}$	$2\frac{1}{2}$	$2\frac{3}{4}$	3	$3\frac{1}{4}$	$3\frac{1}{4}$	$3\frac{1}{2}$	$3\frac{3}{4}$	4	4	$4\frac{1}{2}$	$4\frac{1}{2}$

SCHEDULE OF MATERIALS

ITEM	MATERIAL	DESCRIPTION
1	Steel	Flange to ANSI B 16·5 — Bolt holes drilled to suit dimensions scheduled opposite. Can be screw-on, slip on, or weld neck type.
2	'Klingerite'	Joint rings $\frac{1}{16}''$ thick. See note.
3	'Tufnol'	Bolt insulating sleeves. — Crow Grade.
4	'Tufnol'	Bolt washer $\frac{1}{8}''$ thick. Crow Grade.
5	Steel	Plain round washer B.S.
6	Steel	B.S.W. Bright bolts and nuts.

Appendix E

INTERNATIONAL SHORE FIRE CONNECTION

The purpose of the International Shore Fire Connection is to connect the fire water supply from shore to a ship's fire main or to interconnect the fire mains of two ships. The shore fire connection provides a standardized joint between two systems where each otherwise have couplings or connections that do not match.

All ships, jetties and apparatus ever likely to require an emergency source of fire water or to provide it should have at least one shore fire connection.

The flange on the connection has the dimensions shown on the drawing. The bolt holes may be either slotted or drilled as shown. The flat flange face must match with all other connection flanges. Bolts and gaskets should be readily available.

The connection should have a nipple or boss threaded or shaped to connect with the usual coupling on the hose or fire hydrant of the owner of the connection.

Fire hose having a shore fire connection on the end is led to its counterpart and the flange joints are bolted together. If the shore fire connection is permanently fixed to a hydrant or pipe then a portable connection for use on a hose must be available in case the opposite fire main has only a fixed connection.

If fixed on a vessel the connection should be accessible from either side of the vessel and should be plainly marked. The shore fire connection should be ready for use when a ship is in port.

International Shore Fire Connection (See overleaf for diagram).
Extracted from the International Convention for the Safety of Life at Sea, 1960.

INTERNATIONAL SHORE FIRE CONNECTION

FLANGE PROVIDED BY THE SHIP
DIMENSIONS IN MILLIMETRES

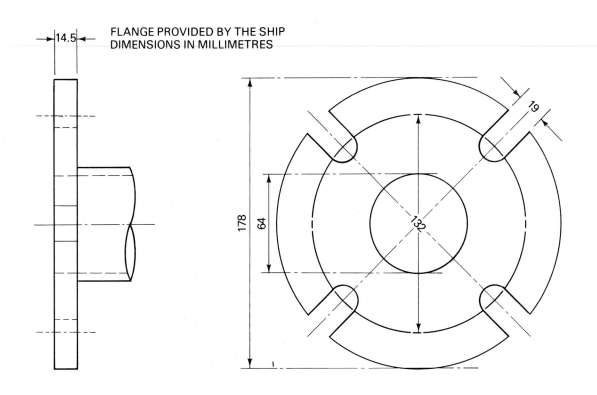

FLANGE PROVIDED BY THE SHORE
DIMENSIONS IN MILLIMETRES

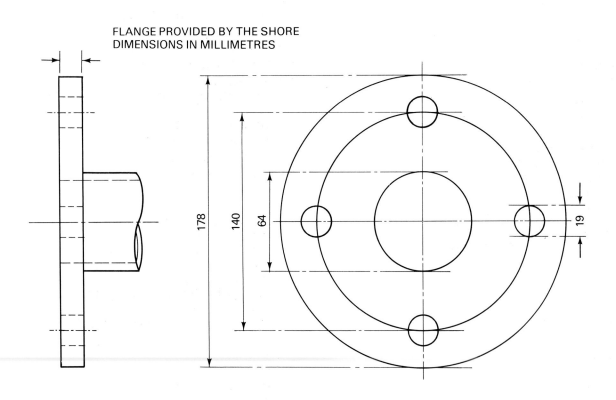

Index

in emergency   13.2.3, 13.2.4, 13.2.12, 13.2.16, 13.2.17

TVP, *see* True vapour pressure

UFL, *see* Upper flammable limit

UHF/VHF transceivers, portable   2.4.4, 4.3

Ullaging
  equipment   19.5.2
  high vapour pressure oils   7.4.2, Table 7-1
  inerted tanks   9.2.6, 9.3.2, 19.5.5
  manual, inhalation of gas   7.2.1, 7.2.2
  static accumulator oils   7.4.2, 7.4.3, Table 1, 19.5.3
  synthetic fibre ropes   7.2.3

Upper flammable limit (UFL)   *Definitions*, 1.1, 8.2.1, 14.2.2, 14.2.3

Vapour pressure   14.1
  bubble point   14.1.1
  Reid (RVP)   14.1.2
  true (TVP)   14.1.1

Valves
  butterfly and non-return   7.3.4, 20.1
  high velocity venting   6.2.3, 11.3.1
  pressure/vacuum relief   *Definitions*, 2.13, 6.2.3
  sea and overboard discharge   6.9.2

Ventilation
  accommodation   6.1.3, 6.1.4, 6.1.5
  pump room   2.15.1
  tanks   8.3.1, 8.3.2, 8.3.3, 10.4.1, 10.4.4

Venting, gases
  ballasting   16.2.3

gas freeing   16.2.4
inert gas purging   16.2.5
loading   16.2.2

Vent outlets, cargo tanks   6.2.3
  combination carriers   11.3.1, 11.3.2

Very high vapour pressure cargoes, loading   7.5.5, 16.(

Volatile petroleum   *Definitions*, 7.4.2, Table 7.1, 14.2.

Walkie-talkies   2.4.4, 4.3

Wandering leads   2.4.2, 4.8.2

Washing machines
  fixed, crude oil washing   8.4.3
  fixed, electrostatic probes   19.3.2
  static electricity   8.2.2, 8.2.3, 19.2, 19.3.2, 19.4.2

Water
  fog   *Definitions*, 13.6, 21.2.2, 21.3.1, 21.8.3
  slugs   19.4.2
  spray   *Definitions*, 12.2.7, 13.6, 21.2.2
  wall   21.8.4

Weights
  multibuoy moorings   6.6.3, C.10.1
  single buoy moorings   6.6.3, C.10.2

Winch
  self stowing mooring   *Definitions*, 3.3.5
  tension   *Definitions*, 3.3.4

Work permit   *Definitions*, 4.1.2, 4.10.2, 4.10.4, 10.5.6

Work permit, hot   *Definitions*, 2.7.3, 4.1.2, 4.10.4, 10.5

Zinc anodes   2.9

Zones, hazardous   4.8, 18.1.2, 18.1.3, 18.3.4